D1084960

WILLY LOMAN

Major Literary Characters

THE ANCIENT WORLD THROUGH THE SEVENTEENTH CENTURY

ACHILLES
Homer, *Iliad*

CALIBAN
William Shakespeare, *The Tempest*
Robert Browning, *Caliban upon Setebos*

CLEOPATRA
William Shakespeare, *Antony and Cleopatra*
John Dryden, *All for Love*
George Bernard Shaw, *Caesar and Cleopatra*

DON QUIXOTE
Miguel de Cervantes, *Don Quixote*
Franz Kafka, *Parables*

FALSTAFF
William Shakespeare, *Henry IV, Part I, Henry IV, Part II, The Merry Wives of Windsor*

FAUST
Christopher Marlowe, *Doctor Faustus*
Johann Wolfgang von Goethe, *Faust*
Thomas Mann, *Doctor Faustus*

HAMLET
William Shakespeare, *Hamlet*

IAGO
William Shakespeare, *Othello*

JULIUS CAESAR
William Shakespeare, *Julius Caesar*
George Bernard Shaw, *Caesar and Cleopatra*

KING LEAR
William Shakespeare, *King Lear*

MACBETH
William Shakespeare, *Macbeth*

ODYSSEUS/ULYSSES
Homer, *Odyssey*
James Joyce, *Ulysses*

OEDIPUS
Sophocles, *Oedipus Rex, Oedipus at Colonus*

OTHELLO
William Shakespeare, *Othello*

ROSALIND
William Shakespeare, *As You Like It*

SANCHO PANZA
Miguel de Cervantes, *Don Quixote*
Franz Kafka, *Parables*

SATAN
The Book of Job
John Milton, *Paradise Lost*

SHYLOCK
William Shakespeare, *The Merchant of Venice*

THE WIFE OF BATH
Geoffrey Chaucer, *The Canterbury Tales*

THE EIGHTEENTH AND NINETEENTH CENTURIES

AHAB
Herman Melville, *Moby-Dick*

ISABEL ARCHER
Henry James, *Portrait of a Lady*

EMMA BOVARY
Gustave Flaubert, *Madame Bovary*

DOROTHEA BROOKE
George Eliot, *Middlemarch*

CHELSEA HOUSE PUBLISHERS

Major Literary Characters

DAVID COPPERFIELD
Charles Dickens, *David Copperfield*

ROBINSON CRUSOE
Daniel Defoe, *Robinson Crusoe*

DON JUAN
Molière, *Don Juan*
Lord Byron, *Don Juan*

HUCK FINN
Mark Twain, *The Adventures of Tom Sawyer, Adventures of Huckleberry Finn*

CLARISSA HARLOWE
Samuel Richardson, *Clarissa*

HEATHCLIFF
Emily Brontë, *Wuthering Heights*

ANNA KARENINA
Leo Tolstoy, *Anna Karenina*

MR. PICKWICK
Charles Dickens, *The Pickwick Papers*

HESTER PRYNNE
Nathaniel Hawthorne, *The Scarlet Letter*

BECKY SHARP
William Makepeace Thackeray, *Vanity Fair*

LAMBERT STRETHER
Henry James, *The Ambassadors*

EUSTACIA VYE
Thomas Hardy, *The Return of the Native*

TWENTIETH CENTURY

ÁNTONIA
Willa Cather, *My Ántonia*

BRETT ASHLEY
Ernest Hemingway, *The Sun Also Rises*

HANS CASTORP
Thomas Mann, *The Magic Mountain*

HOLDEN CAULFIELD
J. D. Salinger, *The Catcher in the Rye*

CADDY COMPSON
William Faulkner, *The Sound and the Fury*

JANIE CRAWFORD
Zora Neale Hurston, *Their Eyes Were Watching God*

CLARISSA DALLOWAY
Virginia Woolf, *Mrs. Dalloway*

DILSEY
William Faulkner, *The Sound and the Fury*

GATSBY
F. Scott Fitzgerald, *The Great Gatsby*

HERZOG
Saul Bellow, *Herzog*

JOAN OF ARC
William Shakespeare, *Henry VI*
George Bernard Shaw, *Saint Joan*

LOLITA
Vladimir Nabokov, *Lolita*

WILLY LOMAN
Arthur Miller, *Death of a Salesman*

MARLOW
Joseph Conrad, *Lord Jim, Heart of Darkness, Youth, Chance*

PORTNOY
Philip Roth, *Portnoy's Complaint*

BIGGER THOMAS
Richard Wright, *Native Son*

CHELSEA HOUSE PUBLISHERS

Major Literary Characters

WILLY LOMAN

Edited and with an introduction by
HAROLD BLOOM

CHELSEA HOUSE PUBLISHERS
New York ◇ Philadelphia

Jacket illustration: Lee J. Cobb as Willy Loman in the
original Broadway production of *Death of a Salesman* (1949)
(The Bettmann Archive). *Inset:* Title page of the first edition
of *Death of a Salesman* (New York: Viking Press, 1949)
(Beinecke Rare Book and Manuscript Library, Yale University).

Chelsea House Publishers

Editor-in-Chief   Remmel T. Nunn
Managing Editor   Karyn Gullen Browne
Picture Editor   Adrian G. Allen
Art Director   Maria Epes
Manufacturing Manager   Gerald Levine

Major Literary Characters

Managing Editor   S. T. Joshi
Copy Chief   Richard Fumosa
Designer   Maria Epes

Staff for WILLY LOMAN

Picture Researcher   Vicky Haluska
Assistant Art Director   Barbara Niemczyc
Production Manager   Joseph Romano
Production Coordinator   Marie Claire Cebrian

© 1991 by Chelsea House Publishers, a division
of Main Line Book Co.

Introduction © 1991 by Harold Bloom

Printed and bound in the United States of America

5 7 9 8 6 4

Library of Congress Cataloging-in-Publication Data

Willy Loman / edited and with an introduction by Harold Bloom.
p.   cm.—(Major literary characters)
Includes bibliographical references and index.
ISBN 0-7910-0962-9.—ISBN 0-7910-1017-1 (pbk.)
1. Miller, Arthur, 1915–   Death of a salesman.   2. Miller, Arthur,
1915–   —Characters—Willy Loman.   3. Loman, Willy
(Fictitious character)   I. Bloom, Harold.   II. Series.
PS3525.I5156D4387   1990
812'.52—dc20
90-35864
CIP

CONTENTS

CONTENTS

THE ANALYSIS OF CHARACTER

Harold Bloom

"Character," according to our dictionaries, still has as a primary meaning a graphic symbol, such as a letter of the alphabet. This meaning reflects the word's apparent origin in the ancient Greek *charactēr*, a sharp stylus. *Charactēr* also meant the mark of the stylus' incisions. Recent fashions in literary criticism have reduced "character" in literature to a matter of marks upon a page. But our word "character" also has a very different meaning, matching that of the ancient Greek *ēthos*, "habitual way of life." Shall we say then that literary character is an imitation of human character, or is it just a grouping of marks? The issue is between a critic like Dr. Samuel Johnson, for whom words were as much like people as like things, and a critic like the late Roland Barthes, who told us that "the fact can only exist linguistically, as a term of discourse." Who is closer to our experience of reading literature, Johnson or Barthes? What difference does it make, if we side with one critic rather than the other?

Barthes is famous, like Foucault and other recent French theorists, for having added to Nietzsche's proclamation of the death of God a subsidiary demise, that of the literary author. If there are no authors, then there are no fictional personages, presumably because literature does not refer to a world outside language. Words indeed necessarily refer to other words in the first place, but the impact of words ultimately is drawn from a universe of fact. Stories, poems, and plays are recognizable as such because they are human utterances within traditions of utterances, and traditions, by achieving authority, become a kind of fact, or at least the sense of a fact. Our sense that literary characters, within the context of a fictive cosmos, indeed are fictional personages is also a kind of fact. The meaning and value of every character in a successful work of literary representation depend upon our ideas of persons in the factual reality of our lives.

Literary character is always an invention, and inventions generally are indebted to prior inventions. Shakespeare is the inventor of literary character as we know it; he reformed the universal human expectations for the verbal imitation of personality, and the reformation appears now to be permanent and uncannily inevitable. Remarkable as the Bible and Homer are at representing personages, their characters are relatively unchanging. They age within their stories, but their habitual modes of being do not develop. Jacob and Achilles unfold before us, but without metamorphoses. Lear and Macbeth, Hamlet and Othello severely modify themselves not only by their actions, but by their utterances, and most of all through *overhearing themselves,* whether they speak to themselves or to others. Pondering what they themselves have said, they will to change, and actually do change, sometimes extravagantly yet always persuasively. Or else they suffer change, without willing it, but in reaction not so much to their language as to their relation to that language.

I do not think it useful to say that Shakespeare successfully imitated elements in our characters. Rather, it could be argued that he compelled aspects of character to appear that previously were concealed, or not available to representation. This is not to say that Shakespeare is God, but to remind us that language is not God either. The mimesis of character in Shakespeare's dramas now seems to us normative, and indeed became the accepted mode almost immediately, as Ben Jonson shrewdly and somewhat grudgingly implied. And yet, Shakespearean representation has surprisingly little in common with the imitation of reality in Jonson or in Christopher Marlowe. The origins of Shakespeare's originality in the portrayal of men and women are to be found in the *Canterbury Tales* of Geoffrey Chaucer, insofar as they can be located anywhere before Shakespeare himself. Chaucer's savage and superb Pardoner overhears his own tale-telling, as well as his mocking rehearsal of his own spiel, and through this overhearing he is emboldened to forget himself, and enthusiastically urges all his fellow-pilgrims to come forward to be fleeced by him. His self-awareness, and apocalyptically rancid sense of spiritual fall, are preludes to the even grander abysses of the perverted will in Iago and in Edmund. What might be called the character trait of a negative charisma may be Chaucer's invention, but came to its perfection in Shakespearean mimesis.

The analysis of character is as much Shakespeare's invention as the representation of character is, since Iago and Edmund are adepts at analyzing both themselves and their victims. Hamlet, whose overwhelming charisma has many negative components, is certainly the most comprehensive of all literary characters, and so necessarily prophesies the labyrinthine complexities of the will in Iago and Edmund. Charisma, according to Max Weber, its first codifier, is primarily a natural endowment, and implies a primordial and idiosyncratic power over nature, and so finally over death. Hamlet's uncanniness is at its most suggestive in the scene of his long dying, where the audience, through the mediation of Horatio, itself is compelled to meditate upon suicide, if only because outliving the prince of Denmark scarcely seems an option.

Shakespearean representation has usurped not only our sense of literary character, but our sense of ourselves as characters, with Hamlet playing the part of the largest of these usurpations. Insofar as we have an idea of human disinterestedness, we tend to derive it from the Hamlet of Act V, whose quietism has about it a ghostly authority. Oscar Wilde, in his profound and profoundly witty dialogue, "The Decay of Lying," expressed a permanent insight when he insisted that art shaped every era, far more than any age formed art. Life imitates art, we imitate Shakespeare, because without Shakespeare we would perish for lack of images. Wilde's grandest audacity demystifies Shakespearean mimesis with a Shakespearean vivaciousness: "This unfortunate aphorism about art holding the mirror up to Nature is deliberately said by Hamlet in order to convince the bystanders of his absolute insanity in all art-matters." Of *Hamlet*'s influence upon the ages Wilde remarked that: "The world has grown sad because a puppet was once melancholy." "Puppet" is Wilde's own deconstruction, a brilliant reminder that Shakespeare's artistry of illusion has so mastered reality as to have changed reality, evidently forever.

The analysis of character, as a critical pursuit, seems to me as much a Shakespearean invention as literary character was, since much of what we know about how to analyze character necessarily follows Shakespearean procedures. His hero-villains, from Richard III through Iago, Edmund, and Macbeth, are shrewd and endless questers into their own self-motivations. If we could bear to see Hamlet, in his unwearied negations, as another hero-villain, then we would judge him the supreme analyst of the darker recalcitrances in the selfhood. Freud followed the pre-Socratic Empedocles, in arguing that character is fate, a frightening doctrine that maintains the fear that there are no accidents, that overdetermination rules us all of our lives. Hamlet assumes the same, yet adds to this argument the terrible passivity he manifests in Act V. Throughout Shakespeare's tragedies, the most interesting personages seem doom-eager, reminding us again that a Shakespearean reading of Freud would be more illuminating than a Freudian exegesis of Shakespeare. We learn more when we discover Hamlet in the Freudian Death Drive, than when we read *Beyond the Pleasure Principle* into *Hamlet.*

In Shakespearean comedy, character achieves its true literary apotheosis, which is the representation of the inner freedom that can be created by great wit alone. Rosalind and Falstaff, perhaps alone among Shakespeare's personages, match Hamlet in wit, though hardly in the metaphysics of consciousness. Whether in the comic or the modern mode, Shakespeare has set the standard of measurement in the balance between character and passion.

In Shakespeare the self is more dramatized than theatricalized, which is why a Shakespearean reading of Freud works out so well. Character-formation after the passing of the Oedipal stage takes the place of fetishistic fragmentings of the self. Critics who now call literary character into question, and who proclaim also the death of the author, invariably also regard all notions, literary and human, of a stable character as being mere reductions of deeper pre-Oedipal desires. It becomes clear that the fortunes of literary character rise and fall with the prestige of nor-mative conceptions of the ego. Shakespeare's Iago, who wars against being, may be the first deconstructionist of the self, with his proclamation of "I am not what I am." This constitutes the necessary prologue to any view that would regard a fixed ego as a virtual abnormality. But deconstructions of the self are no more modern than Modernism is. Like literary modernism, the decentered ego came out of the Hellenistic culture of ancient Alexandria. The Gnostic heretics believed that the psyche, like the body, was a fallen entity, mechanically fashioned by the Demiurge or false creator. They held however that each of us possessed also a spark or pneuma, which was a fragment of the original Abyss or true, alien God. The soul or psyche within every one of us was thus at war with the self or pneuma, and only that sparklike self could be saved.

Shakespeare, following after Chaucer in this respect, was the first and remains still the greatest master of representing character both as a stable soul and a wavering self. There is a substance that endures in Shakespeare's figures, and there is also a quicksilver rendition of the unsettling sparks. Racine and Tolstoy, Balzac and Dickens, follow in Shakespeare's wake by giving us some sense of pre-Oedipal sparks or drives, and considerably more sense of post-Oedipal character and personality, stabilizations or sublimations of the fetish-seeking drives. Critics like Leo Bersani and René Girard argue eloquently against our taking this mimesis as the only proper work of literature. I would suggest that strong fictions of the self, from the Bible through Samuel Beckett, necessarily participate in both modes, the sublima-tion of desire, and the persistence of a primordial desire. The mystery of Hamlet or of Lear is intimately invested in the tangled mixture of the two modes of representation.

Psychic mobility is proposed by Bersani as the ideal to which deconstructions of the literary self may yet guide us. The ideal has its pathos, but the realities of literary representation seem to me very different, perhaps destructively so. When a novelist like D. H. Lawrence sought to reduce his characters to Eros and the Death Drive, he still had to persuade us of his authority at mimesis by lavishing upon the figures of *The Rainbow* and *Women in Love* all of the vivid stigmata of normative personality. Birkin and Ursula may represent antithetical and uncanny drives, but they develop and change as characters pondering their own pronounce-ments and reactions to self and others. The cost of a non-Shakespearean repre-sentation is enormous. Pynchon, in *The Crying of Lot 49* and *Gravity's Rainbow,* evades the burden of the normative by resorting to something like Christopher Marlowe's art of caricature in *The Jew of Malta.* Marlowe's Barabas is a marvelous rhetorician, yet he is a cartoon alongside the troublingly equivocal Shylock. Pyn-chon's personages are deliberate cartoons also, as flat as comic strips. Marlowe's achievement, and Pynchon's, are beyond dispute, yet they are like the prelude and the postlude to Shakespearean reality. They do not wish to engage with our hunger for the empirical world and so they enter the problematic cosmos of literary fantasy.

No writer, not even Shakespeare or Proust, alters the available stock that we agree to call reality, but Shakespeare, more than any other, does show us how much of reality we could encounter if only we retained adequate desire. The strong literary representation of character is already an analysis of character, and is part of the healing work of a literary culture, which implicitly seeks to cure violence through a normative mimesis of ego, *as if it were stable,* whether in actuality it is or is not. I do not believe that this is a social quest taken on by literary culture, but rather that we confront here the aesthetic essence of what makes a culture *literary,* rather than metaphysical or ethical or religious. A culture becomes literary when its conceptual modes have failed it, which means when religion, philosophy, and science have begun to lose their authority. If they cannot heal violence, then literature attempts to do so, which may be only a turning inside out of the critical arguments of Girard and Bersani.

I conclude by offering a particular instance or special case as a paradigm for the healing enterprise that is at once the representation and the analysis of literary character. Let us call it the aesthetics of being outraged, or rather of successfully representing the state of being outraged. W. C. Fields was one modern master of such representation, and Nathanael West was another, as was Faulkner before him. Here also the greatest master remains Shakespeare, whose Macbeth, himself a bloody outrage, yet retains our imaginative sympathy precisely because he grows increasingly outraged as he experiences the equivocation of the fiend that lies like truth. The double-natured promises and the prophecies of the weird sisters finally induce in Macbeth an apocalyptic version of the stage actor's anxiety at missing cues, the horror of a phantasmagoric stage fright of missing one's time, of always reacting too late. Macbeth, a veritable monster of solipsistic inwardness but no intellectual, counters his dilemma by fresh murders, that prolong him in time yet provoke him only to a perpetually freshened sense of being outraged, as all his expectations become still worse confounded. We are moved by Macbeth, however estrangedly, because his terrible inwardness is a paradigm for our own solipsism, but also because none of us can resist a strong and successful representation of the human in a state of being outraged.

The ultimate outrage is the necessity of dying, an outrage concealed in a multitude of masks, including the tyrannical ambitions of Macbeth. I suspect that our outrage at being outraged is the most difficult of all our affects for us to represent to ourselves, which is why we are so inclined to imaginative sympathy for a character who strongly conveys that affect to us. The Shrike of West's *Miss Lonelyhearts* or Faulkner's Joe Christmas of *Light in August* are crucial modern instances, but such figures can be located in many other works, since the ability to represent this extreme emotion is one of the tests that strong writers are driven to set for themselves.

However a reader seeks to reduce literary character to a question of marks on a page, she will come at last to the impasse constituted by the thought of death, her death, and before that to all the stations of being outraged that memorialize her own drive towards death. In reading, she quests for evidences that are strong representations, whether of her desire or her despair. Such questings constitute the necessary basis for the analysis of literary character, an enterprise that always will survive every vagary of critical fashion.

EDITOR'S NOTE

This volume brings together a representative selection of the best criticism so far available that has been devoted to Willy Loman, the protagonist of Arthur Miller's drama, *Death of a Salesman*. I am grateful to Richard Fumosa for his assistance in editing this book.

My introduction considers the central problem of Willy Loman's status as a stage representation: is he a tragic figure, or merely pathetic? A selection of critical excerpts follows, beginning with Herbert J. Muller's judgment that Loman's effect upon us was social, not tragic, and continuing through such diverse reactions as those of the playwright Lorraine Hansberry, the Marxist scholar Raymond Williams, and Miller himself, until we conclude with Louis Harap commenting upon the Jewish element in Loman's nature.

Full-scale critiques begin with Miller's own crucial ruminations on Loman, and continue with a symposium in which the dramatist himself participates. Ruby Cohn's discussion centers upon Willy's language, which establishes him as one of Miller's "articulate victims," after which Dan Vogel defends Loman's tragic status as an Oedipal searcher for truth.

In A. D. Choudhuri's interpretation, the salesman's illusion is seen as dignified by the supposedly affirmative gesture of his suicide, while Robert N. Wilson sees all of us as psychologically implicated in Willy's defeat.

Jeremy Hawthorn traces the social-psychic roots of Loman's disintegration, after which C. W. E. Bigsby broadly contextualizes Willy both in Miller's work and in modern American drama. The dramatic rhythm of Loman's fate is established by Leah Hadomi as a dialectic of fantasy and reality, after which Kay Stanton concludes this volume with a fiercely feminist reading, one in which Willy's self-destruction is attributed to the pernicious aspects of the masculine American dream.

INTRODUCTION

Willy Loman most certainly is a major *dramatic* character, and so he necessarily needs to be considered when we estimate who merits inclusion in the vital company of major American literary characters. If there is a legitimate tragic drama by an American author, then it must be *Death of a Salesman.* Arthur Miller's grand insight into Willy Loman is that his protagonist is slain by his need for love, for familial love. Insofar as Loman possesses tragic dignity, that eminence derives from his relation to fatherhood. Linda's comment upon her husband—"a small man can be just as exhausted as a great man"—would be an aesthetic disaster if Loman's exhaustion were his salient quality. The exhaustion of Willy Loman simply lacks the cognitive and spiritual qualities that mark the exhaustion of King Lear. Lear and Loman scarcely can be compared without destroying Miller's creation, which makes all the more unfortunate that curious passage in Miller's introduction to his *Collected Plays* in which we are meant to accept the juxtaposition:

> An aged king—a pious man—moves toward life's end. Instead of reaping the benefits of his piety, he finds himself caught in bewildering circumstances. Because of a mistake—an error in judgment—a tragic reversal has taken place in his life. Where he has been priest, knower of secrets, wielder of power, and symbol of life, he now finds himself adjudged defiler, usurper, destroyer, and necessary sacrifice. Like the traditional hero, Loman begins his long season of agony. In his descent, however, there is the familiar tragic paradox; for as he moves toward inevitable destruction, he acquires that knowledge, that sense of reconciliation, which allows him to conceive a redemptive plan for his house.

All that Loman actually shares with Lear or Oedipus is agony; there is no other likeness whatsoever. Miller has little understanding of Classical or Shakespearean tragedy; he stems entirely from Ibsen. Yet Loman is hardly Ibsenite either. A tragedy of familial love is not primarily a social drama, one concerned with the illusions of society, and Ibsen was careful to keep the two modes unconfused. Miller is richly confused, and never more so than in his depiction of Loman. That confusion, aptly castigated by the critic Eric Bentley, nevertheless does not destroy Loman as a dramatic character, perhaps because in Miller's (and Loman's) true tradition, family tragedy and social realities are inextricably linked by a tragic social history. The history of the Jewish people is marked by an inward turn in family romance, precisely resulting from the terrors, or at least the discomforts, of societal persecution. Willy Loman is not Jewish, if we are to follow Miller's intentions, but Loman makes little sense as a character unless we see him as a kind of internal exile.

Miller remarks of *Salesman* that it "was written in a mood of friendly partnership with the audience." In reply to an interviewer's question as to whether he was influenced by Jewish tradition, the playwright stressed the Jewish refusal of nihilism:

> Jews can't afford to revel too much in the tragic because it might overwhelm them. Consequently, in most Jewish writing there's always the caution, "Don't push it too far toward the abyss, because you're liable to fall in."

Loman falls in, but is that abyss tragic or pathetic? The answer partly depends upon whether the issue is one of aesthetic dignity, or whether Miller's social sense of tragedy can prevail against traditional canons. Does Loman have enough individuality to sustain the context of tragedy? Again Miller insists upon a social answer:

> . . . to me the tragedy of Willy Loman is that he gave his life, or sold it, in order to justify the waste of it. It is the tragedy of a man who did believe that he alone was not meeting the qualifications laid down for mankind by those clean-shaven frontiersmen who inhabit the peaks of broadcasting and advertising offices. From those forests of canned goods high up near the sky, he heard the thundering command to succeed as it ricocheted down the newspaper-lined canyons of his city, heard not a human voice, but a wind of a voice to which no human can reply in kind, except to stare into the mirror at a failure.

Are we then surrounded by millions of tragic falls in our country, and in our time? Is every American suicide a tragedy? Miller rejects pathos as his mode, and insists upon the aesthetic dignity of tragedy. As readers and as playgoers do we find a quality in Loman that transcends pathos? Let us again be guided by Miller's own formulations:

> The possibility of victory must be there in tragedy. Where pathos rules, where pathos is finally derived, a character has fought a battle he could not possibly have won. The pathetic is achieved when the protagonist is, by virtue of his witlessness, his insensitivity or the very air he gives off, incapable of grappling with a much superior force.
>
> Pathos truly is the mode for the pessimist. But tragedy requires a nicer balance between what is possible and what is impossible. And it is curious,

although edifying, that the plays we revere, century after century, are the tragedies. In them, and in them alone, lies the belief—optimistic, if you will, in the perfectibility of man.

What victory could Loman have won? And what authentic tragic dramas possess a belief in human perfectibility? I cannot answer either question, and I sadly doubt that Miller could answer them either. But pathos has a possible aesthetic dignity also, and need not be witless, insensitive, or incapable. Miller himself had later doubts about his representation of pathos in Loman:

> There is great danger in pathos, which can destroy any tragedy if you let it go far enough. My weakness is that I can create pathos at will. I feel that Willy Loman lacks sufficient insight into this situation which would have made him a greater, more significant figure.

One can doubt that Loman, stronger in understanding, would still be Loman. Insight need not be a precondition for the tragic hero. Coriolanus lives and dies without insight, yet is always tragic. As is perhaps inevitable, Miller both overestimates and underestimates his protagonist's stature. The aesthetic dignity of Loman is substantial, yet essentially is one of pathos rather than of ethos, of personality rather than of character. Loman needs the love of his family, and needs to love them. It is a terrible pathos that Loman has confused himself into the belief that without success he does not deserve to be loved. But this is a generous pathos, and moves us profoundly. In exile from himself, Loman fails to see that familial love never can be deserved, or undeserved, but only is, or is not.

The crucial question might be: what sent Loman into his internalized exile? The form of that exile is unappeasable yearning, since no success and no popularity could gratify so ceaseless a need. It is Loman's psychic poverty that appeals to us, that nearly overwhelms us. Poor Loman essentially wants to sell himself, and so nothing could suffice for him to buy himself back. Essentially a dreamer, Willy is fated to dream only dreams of guilt, the guilt of a bad father and a bad husband who wanted only to be the best of fathers and the best of husbands. The dreadful sadness is that love kills Loman—Linda's love, and Biff's love. Linda's love for her husband contains very little understanding of him, and Biff's love is so marked by ambivalence that Willy is doomed to interpret it wrongly. Excessive love, love without understanding, his own love, and his family's love, have combined to send Willy into the desert of himself, to wander there as an exile from the only affections that could sustain and save him. Miller, whatever his own confusions about the nature of tragedy, has an immense capacity for the dramatic representation of the destructive sorrows of familial love.

Jewish tradition indeed refuses all nihilism, and insists that God's love and familial love possess the same ethos, even if that identity is by no means always obvious. The paradigm for Jewish family love is the long exile of Joseph from his father Jacob, and the eventual triumph of their reunion. Miller's achievement is that

Loman's pathos is noble, precisely because Loman dies the death of a father, rather than the death of a salesman. It is not the dream of success, or of popularity, that destroys Loman, but the dream of a more perfect family love. The final pathos of Loman is a normative pathos, and takes his suffering to the borders of ethos, to where moral character could be forged. Something deeply in exile within Miller returns from repression in Willy Loman, and that something appears to be an element in the moral history of the Jews. Loman is universal, and could be the everyman of every tradition. Miller, however, is in a particular tradition of moral prophecy, one that urges the hearts of the parents to turn towards the hearts of the children, and those of the children towards the parents, lest the earth be smitten with a curse.

—H. B.

CRITICAL EXTRACTS

HERBERT J. MULLER

As the study of a little man succumbing to his environment, rather than a great man destroyed through his greatness, ⟨*Death of a Salesman*⟩ is characteristically modern. There is no question of grandeur in such a tragedy; the "hero" may excite pity, but nothing like awe. There is a question of dignity and human significance. While the dramatic reviewers were generally enthusiastic about the play as a heart-warming one, or even an "epic drama," the fastidious critics of the quarterlies generally dismissed it as a "very dull business," without illumination or pity, or a string of clichés of "unrelieved vulgarity." It strikes me as a basically humane, honest work. It gives some dignity to the tragedy of Willy by an at once unsparing and sympathetic treatment of his easy good nature, his passion to be well liked, his want of any mind or soul of his own. The pathetic Willy may even symbolize Everyman in the wider sense felt by John Mason Brown: "what he would like to be, what he is, what he is not, and yet what he must live and die with."

But Miller, too, strains for a "big" play. His supra-realistic effects—such as the expressionistic setting, the musical themes for the various characters, and the portentous apparitions of Brother Ben—are too fancy for little Willy, and seem more pretentious because of the flat colloquial dialogue. So do the occasional efforts to sound a deep note. "I search and search and I search, and I can't understand it, Willy," his wife laments over his grave; but throughout the play she has not been searching and has understood Willy well enough. Miller's own understanding of him, however, is unclear. Sometimes it appears that the main cause of his tragedy is capitalism; sometimes it is Babbittry, his own weaknesses; sometimes it is the universal plight of the Little Man. The uncertain intention has led to curiously divergent judgments of simple Willy. In England, Ivor Brown remarked, he was taken as "a poor, flashy, self-deceiving little man," whose passion for popularity was more contemptible than natural; the play was coolly received. In America, Brooks Atkinson described him as "a good man who represents the homely, decent, kindly virtues of a middle-class society"; Broadway audiences wept over him. Marxists might explain the tears shed by New Yorkers over his kind of failure, whom in real life they would despise, as a sentimental evasion of their responsibility for such failures. In any case, the excitement over Willy would seem to be more a social than a literary portent.

—HERBERT J. MULLER, "Modern Tragedy," *The Spirit of Tragedy*
(New York: Knopf, 1957), pp. 316–17

GERALD WEALES

Willy Loman is Miller's most completely realized character, so alive that he steps out of the thematic frame of the play. In his introduction, Miller insists at length that the play is a growth from a random collection of images, all centering around the salesman figure, all expressing in some sense the futility of Willy's life. But the play is more than a chronicle of a beaten man, even one who went down fighting. For Miller, Willy's tragedy lies in the fact that he had an alternative that he did not take, that having chosen the wrong star he reached for it until he died of stretching. According to the introduction Biff represents "a system of love which is the opposite of the law of success." The conflict of these opposites—which may not really be opposites—is confused in the play by an idea that runs throughout, one that can be summed up in Biff's words at the grave, "He had the wrong dreams." If this phrase means simply that Willy wanted power and prestige when he should have wanted love, then what is the meaning of the often repeated indications that Willy was good with his hands, the suggestion that had he been an artisan his life would have been less futile? Willy is so carefully conceived as a victim of self-delusion—the flashbacks indicate that from the beginning he lied to himself and to others about his present as well as his future—that it is impossible to conceive of him as ever having a right dream. The theme of the play is swallowed by the excellence of the character who should embody it.

—GERALD WEALES, "Plays and Analysis," *Commonweal*, July 12, 1957, p. 382

JOHN GASSNER

Without incorporating the unadmirable qualities of men and their times, indeed, tragic literature would be literature in a void. We tend to see the heroic element without the antiheroic in the old masterpieces. We ennoble the "tragic flaw" and play down that which is shameful about it or about the milieu that produced it. I like, therefore, Cedric Whitman's reference to "the self-slain greatness" of the tragic character and William McCollom's statement in his recent book, *Tragedy*, that "the hero's shame is the corollary of his genius." But the role of the "unnoble" element in drama has yet to be explored. We have to pick up the clue that Nietzsche left us in juxtaposing Dionysian and Apollonian aspects in *The Birth of Tragedy*.

The heroic element or the "genius" of the tragic character should, of course, also receive due weight. But we must come to understand it a little better than we usually do in the case of contemporary characters such as Willy Loman, the salesman-hero of *Death of a Salesman*. Arthur Miller has insisted upon the tragic worth of this greatly flawed character, and anybody familiar with the struggles of the little man and not too sheltered or snobbish to be capable of sympathy should know what heroism is required of the Willy Lomans of the world. Or if this appeal is too "common" for some members of the literary and academic world perhaps they will respond to the monitions of the poem by Goethe in which admission to the Moslem paradise of heroes is claimed on the grounds that it was heroic enough to be a human being. Willy Loman indeed makes himself a tragic hero of sorts by his abundant capacity for suffering in the present action; by his fine resentment of slights, by his battle for self-respect, and by his refusal to surrender all expectations of triumph for, and through, his son. Willy is passionately unwilling to resign himself to failure and the cheat of days. His very agony gives him tragic stature within the recognizable world of middle-class realities, and it is surely true that the tragic hero is not tragic by status prior to his action in a play. Tragedy is no one's prerogative; it is, rather, *earned* damnation and redemption. The tragic hero *makes himself* tragic—by his struggle and suffering.

Moreover, he makes himself tragic *differently* in different societies. Even awareness on the hero's part, the "tragic awareness" upon which so much stress has been placed of late, is bound to be different in the case of different characters differently conditioned by the social situation. Miller would be justified in insisting that, within limits that are themselves valid dramatic factors in *Death of a Salesman*, Willy does arrive at self-realization—that is, at a degree of self-realization that can be convincingly Willy's. And I, for one, fail to perceive any virtue in recognitions that are conspicuously out of character and have been imposed upon the play from without—that is, from the author's philosophy of tragedy or from "literature," as in the case of *Winterset*.

The most convincing and, to my mind, also the most significant characters make themselves tragic in collaboration with their world. In tragedy, as William McCollom has rightly observed, there is both "self-determination" and "social determination." In various scenes set in the present and the past, Willy seeks the truth about himself and his situation. The search is his, for we must not ignore the fact that all the flashbacks and hallucinations in *Death of a Salesman* are in Willy's own anguished consciousness. Willy pursues the "truth" and struggles against it within his personal and social limits no less arduously and catastrophically than Oedipus. It is possible to say, then, that Miller's protagonist brings both personal and social meanness into his play, but that he also brings personal stature and heroism into it.

The one thing Miller could not do—that Miller's scrupulousness indeed would not have allowed him to do—is to give Willy *an interesting mind*. And it is chiefly this limitation, along with a limitation of language (because the character is an urban commoner while the author is rarely a poet), that has made me contemplate the use of such a term as "low tragedy," my intention being to distinguish modern democratic drama from the aristocratic "high tragedy" of earlier ages. Perhaps indeed the genius of our century resides precisely in "low tragedy," if we are to allow ourselves a generalization concerning the taste and aptitude of the age. For there is a difference in the degree of tragic exaltation and exhilaration, of tragic realization and liberation or catharsis, as well as a difference in tone such as appears when we contrast the relative informality of discourse by a Giraudoux or Cocteau with tragic dialogue by Marlowe, Shakespeare, and Racine. "Low tragedy" is the only term that seems sufficiently descriptive of *The Lower Depths* and *The Iceman Cometh, The Tragedy of Nan* and *Desire under the Elms, The Three Sisters* and *The House of Bernarda Alba, The Weavers* and *The Plough and the Stars*, Drayman *Henschel* and *Death of a Salesman, Rosmersholm* and *John Gabriel Borkman*, and even Giraudoux' *Electra* and Cocteau's *The Infernal Machine.*

If "low tragedy" were employed descriptively rather than pejoratively, it could become useful in calling attention to a modern type of tragedy different from the typical forms of classic and Elizabethan tragic writing. And surely the term does not have to be derogatory; powerful dramatic impressions have been created, for instance, by O'Casey's colloquial passionateness and O'Neill's prosaic masonry. When I use the terms "low comedy" and "high comedy" to describe the work of Plautus and Terence respectively, I certainly do not intend a slur on Plautine comedy. It is possible to describe differences without establishing hierarchies. And when I nevertheless, accept the superiority of *Hamlet* to, let us say, *Death of a Salesman*, it is not because I think of Shakespeare's tragedy as "more tragic," but because I consider it more expressive, *and more beautiful.*

—JOHN GASSNER, "Tragic Perspectives: A Sequence of Queries,"
Tulane Drama Review 2, No. 3 (May 1958): 20–22

LORRAINE HANSBERRY

We knew who Willy Loman was instantaneously; we recognized his milieu. We also knew at once that he represented that curious paradox in what the *English* character in that *English* play could call, though dismally, "The American Age." Willy Loman was a product of a nation of great military strength, indescribable material wealth, and incredible mastery of the physical realm, which nonetheless was unable, in 1946, to produce a *typical* hero who was capable of an affirmative view of life.

I believe it is a testament to Miller's brilliance that it is hardly a misstatement of the case, as some preferred to believe. Something has indeed gone wrong with at least part of the American dream, and Willy Loman is the victim of the detour. Willy had to be overwhelmed on the stage as, in fact, his prototypes are in everyday life. Coming out of his section of our great sprawling middle class, preoccupied with its own restlessness and displaying its obsession for the possession of trivia, Willy was indeed trapped. His predicament in a New World where there just aren't anymore forests to clear or virgin railroads to lay or native American empires to first steal and then build upon left him with nothing but some left-over values which had forgotten how to prize industriousness over cunning, usefulness over mere acquisition, and, above all, humanism over "success." The potency of the great tale of a salesman's death was in our familiar recognition of his entrapment which, suicide or no, is *deathly.*

—LORRAINE HANSBERRY, "An Author's Reflections: Willy Loman,
Walter Younger, and He Who Must Live," *Village Voice,*
August 12, 1959, p. 7

TOM F. DRIVER

The following passage occurs in a discussion of Willy Loman's stature as a tragic figure:

> How can we respect a man who goes to such extremities over something he could in no way help or prevent? The answer, I think, is not that we respect the man, but that we respect the Law he has so completely broken, wittingly or not, for it is that Law which, we believe, defines us as men. The confusion of some critics viewing *Death of a Salesman* in this regard is that they do not see that Willy Loman has broken a law without whose protection life is insupportable if not incomprehensible to him and to many others; it is the law which says that a failure in society and in business has no right to live. Unlike the law against incest, the law of success is not administered by statute or church, but it is very nearly as powerful in its grip upon men. The confusion increases because, while it is a law, it is by no means a wholly agreeable one even as it is slavishly obeyed, for to fail is no longer to belong to society, in his estimate.

The confusion, I am afraid, lies not with the critics but with the playwright, and it is a very illustrative one. There is, in fact, no "law which says that a failure in society and in business has no right to live." It would, indeed, suit Miller's polemic better if there were. There is a *delusion* that a failure in society and in business has no right to live. To some people, such as Willy Loman, it may indeed seem like a law. But it is one thing for a character in a play to act as if something were a law, and quite another thing for the playwright to believe it. Miller's subsequent remarks in this same section of his essay make it perfectly clear that he himself, the audience, and also Willy Loman, do as a matter of fact have criteria according to which they suspect that this "law" is a hoax. It is in fact not a law but a false *credo,* which Willy shares with many persons, and the result of the attempt to make a false *credo* into a law results only in pathetic irony.

What is it, one wonders, that prevents Miller from probing Willy's consciousness and ours to the point of finding the truly objective world in which we still, in fact, believe and according to which Willy's "law" strikes us as so pathetic? If we ask where in the play one touches bed-rock, the answer is nowhere. Is the law of success *really* a law? No. Miller tells us that "the system of love," which is "embodied in Biff Loman" was meant to counter Willy's "law." But if that is true, it was unfortunately not dramatized. That is, the way in which Biff's "law" of love judges and invalidates Willy's "law" of success is not revealed, and so the one is not actually a truth which is being brought to bear dramatically on the other.

The same ambiguity is seen in the question of society versus the individual. John Gassner said long ago that Arthur Miller had "split his play between *social causation* and *individual responsibility* for Willy's fate." Is Willy's "law" the result of some defect in himself? If so, what is the nature of this defect, and what genuine law does it confound? Or is his "law" imposed upon him by a white-collar industrial society? If so, what is wrong with such a society and what truth does it prevent Willy Loman from seeing? Miller would probably resist making a decision in favor of either the individual or the social causation, and rightly so. But in that case, if he is interested in theatre worth the name of art, he has an obligation to examine his complex situation until the roots of Willy's anxiety are exposed, an exposure which would cause us to know something about the reality in which we are, if only unconsciously, living. It is in the lack of penetration into the objective philosophical situation that Miller fails us, with the result that we must settle for no more enlightenment upon our situation than pathetic Willy had upon his.

—TOM F. DRIVER, "Strength and Weakness in Arthur Miller,"
Tulane Drama Review 4, No. 4 (May 1960): 49–50

HENRY POPKIN

Miller's ideas and his technique are best illustrated in his most successful play, *Death of a Salesman*. This play exhibits all the most characteristic traits, in their plainest, most emphatic form. Plainness is achieved because Miller makes a principle out of his usual vagueness. The principle is Expressionism. The vague, typical hero becomes the embodiment of typicality, Willy the low man, who carries his status in his name. His friends Charley and Bernard—the only other family we see—have no last name at all, and neither does Willy's employer. Furthermore, the salesman is, as we have observed, the most representative member of our commercial society; in a sense, when the salesman dies, this society dies. Every strand of evidence, in and out of the play, points to the symbolic reading of the salesman's role. Replying to the many salesmen who thought they saw their own story writ large in the play, Miller has insisted: "I have and had not the slightest interest in the selling profession." The mystery of the salesman's product is preserved for symbolic reasons. Miller tantalizes us with references to stores in Boston and to Willy's eye for color, but, in response to questions, he invariably answered that the product Willy was selling was himself. Preserving the mystery keeps Willy the archetypal salesman of our time.

The details of Willy's origin are equally vague—or universal. Even if we recognize some of the stresses of Jewish family life, what is more highly visible is Miller's determined effort to iron out these specific elements, to make the family Everyfamily or Anyfamily. The Anyfamily quality is reflected in Miller's delight with Thomas Mitchell's Irish Willy Loman, and it is manifest also in his obvious intention of making the Loman family history recapitulate the history of the nation. Willy's father used to set out across the continent from Boston; Willy remembers sitting under a covered wagon in South Dakota while his brother Ben went on to look for their father in Alaska. Somehow, this sounds like an improbable origin for Willy Loman, salesman, of Brooklyn. The point is, I think, that Willy is not the product just of this family but of the adventurous American past. The colorful background helps to make Brooklyn's hapless Willy as commonplace as he is required to be. The shabbiness of Willy's life is made abundantly clear when his colorful brother stops off on his way to the gold fields and asks, "chuckling," "So this is Brooklyn, eh?" The very presence of the daring entrepreneur is enough to show up the salesman who has been playing it safe all his life.

Willy is much more emphatically a representative figure, an American Everyman, than any of Miller's other characters; accordingly, his problems are much less personal dilemmas than they are public issues. Willy is a useful instrument for Miller's social criticism. This quality of his is the first trait by which we identify this play as an example of Expressionism. Certainly this concern with large social issues is the key to Miller's definition of Expressionism in his Harvard lecture ("The Family in Modern Drama," *Atlantic Monthly,* April 1956): "It is a form . . . which manifestly seeks to dramatize the conflict of either social, religious, or moral forces *per se.*" In his most recent article, Miller finds that the Greeks and the Expressionists are alike in their effort "to present the hidden forces."

The hallmarks of Expressionism are its employment of symbolic characters— The Man, the Woman, the Nameless One (all three in Ernst Toller's *Man and the Masses*), Elmer Rice's Mr. Zero, Miller's Loman—and its presentation of dream states in which hidden forces of every variety become plainly visible. It was against the pioneer Expressionist, August Strindberg, that Zola lodged the complaint that he did not know the last names of the characters in *The Father;* the characters of this play are like Miller's Charley and Bernard in this respect, but no one complained about Miller's rootless figures. Perhaps the audience took it for granted that their name was Everyman. Certainly the acquired taste for Expressionism has made headway since the first American experiments in the 1920's. This dramatic *genre* had been in vogue among *avant garde* audiences for half a century before Miller adopted it. What is new is its presence in a popular success of fabulous proportions. If Strindberg won the connoisseur's attention with *The Dream Play,* O'Neill with *The Hairy Ape,* and Elmer Rice with *The Adding Machine,* what popular fame these writers earned rested on other plays. But with *Death of a Salesman,* Expressionism descended, in a slightly watered-down form, to the mass audience.

The Everyman element is obvious enough. To locate the dream-elements of the play also requires no great effort. Willy Loman's dreams occupy half the play; they are the dreams of all the world, the dreams of a happy, hopeful past and the inescapable dream of past guilt. The recollections are not straight flashbacks in the manner of the films, but they are distorted, speeded up, heightened by repetition and selection. The accompanying music and the distinctive lighting of the original production compelled us to set these remembrances apart from objective reality. Further testimony of unreality is to be found in one figure who appears in them but seems to have no existence in the real world—Uncle Ben, the embodiment of the American will to succeed. He is the fantastically rich relative who shuttles between the outposts of imperialism, Alaska and Africa. Long ago, he set out for Alaska to dig gold; he found himself on the way to Africa instead, and so he made his fortune in diamonds. When Willy last sees him, he is heading for Alaska. During the dream sequences, Willy seems unable to tell truth from fantasy, the present from the past. He loses himself in his recollections, interrupting a conversation with his neighbor Charley to address the absent Ben, losing all sense of the present in a men's room while he recalls his past exposure by his son. Willy is sick; his mental breakdown is certified by the hold his recollections have on him and by the great amount of obvious distortion in them. He has symptoms of schizophrenia, but his sickness is not his alone. His identification with Everyman assures us that, as in other Expressionist plays, we are examining the malady not of an individual but of society.

Willy is drab and average; the surest guarantee of his drabness is in his commitment to the standard ideals, the standard commercial products, and even the standard language. His fidelity to the great American dream of success is at the very heart of the play. He believes in this dream in its simplest, its final form. Years ago, Horatio Alger preached that success was the reward of virtue, while Herbert Spencer and his American disciples preached that it was the reward of strength; Willy's brother Ben would seem to belong to the Spencerian or Social Darwinist school of success through strength. But Willy himself subscribes to a different and later form of the dream; he believes, with Dale Carnegie, that success is the reward of making friends and influencing people—being impressive, being persuasive, being well liked. One becomes successful by being confident, by thinking of success, and therefore success is all Willy knows, all he believes. The cultural heroes whose names are heard in Willy's household are without exception figures from the world of well publicized triumphs. Where Odets dots his dialogue with references to exponents of high art, low art, mass culture, the world of wealth, the world of politics, Miller has only these comparable references—B. F. Goodrich, Edison, Red Grange, and J. P. Morgan (the last of them cited to Willy by his neighbor). Like certain characters in Saul Bellow's recent fiction, Willy feels that successful men possess a secret which could be passed on to him; in vain he asks his brother Ben and his friend Charley to tell him the secret. Ben replies: "William, when I walked into the jungle, I was seventeen. When I walked out I was twenty-one. And, by God, I was rich!" That is to say, the riddle remains a riddle.

Willy Loman's catastrophe is one of the poignant and inevitable misfortunes of our society and our time. The various formulations of the idea of success, whether created by Horatio Alger or Herbert Spencer or Dale Carnegie, have contributed to the state of mind that makes failure a crime. Success is a requirement that Americans make of life. Because it seems magical and inexplicable, as it is to Willy, it can be considered the due of every free citizen, even those with no notable or measurable talents. One citizen is as good as any other, and he cannot be proved to be a natural-born failure any more than he can be stripped of his civil rights. The citizen may justly and perhaps even logically ask—If Edison, Goodrich, and Red Grange can make it, why not me, why not Willy Loman? In effect, this is the question Willy asks his brother Ben. It is unanswerable; the consequent disappointment that Willy feels is one of the great American exasperations. He postpones his anguish by transferring his ambitions to his sons, and so the play's free use of time permits us to observe aspiration and failure in both generations. The problems, the exasperation, and the pathos of this family were sufficiently serious and important to make *Death of a Salesman* a moving play and a spectacular success. As a resourceful and understanding treatment of a critical human problem, this play makes an unmistakable claim upon us. But to examine it as closely as it deserves is to discover that Willy transfers his qualities and his characteristic confusions to the play itself. This is a very subjective play; it seldom takes us outside the ideas, the aspirations, even the vocabulary of the doomed salesman.

Willy's language reflects his resoluteness in the pursuit of success. It is devoid of words for anything but the necessities of life and the ingredients or symbols of success. This world is full of aspirin, arch supports, saccharin (all the wrong cures for what ails Willy), Studebakers, Chevrolets, shaving lotion, refrigerators, silk stockings, washing machines. It is the only play I know that could stock a mail-order catalog. Everything but these commonplace objects is washed out of the characters' speech. In moments of excitement, they do not rise above "Knock him dead, boy," or "I'm gonna knock Howard for a loop," or "Knock 'em dead." In a context like this, phrases like "twist of mockery" or "masterful man" sound poetic, but the true fabric of language here is woven of the most ordinary stuff. Some dubious rhetoric is permitted on the few occasions when it is necessary to point a moral. This function is usually Linda's, but, at Willy's funeral, it comes to be shared by Charley, who speaks a eulogy not for Willy but, with striking appropriateness, for his calling: "A salesman is got to dream, boy. It comes with the territory." Buried under platitudes, Willy is allowed no more individuality in death than he has exhibited in life.

—HENRY POPKIN, "Arthur Miller: The Strange Encounter,"
Sewanee Review 68, No. 1 (Winter 1960): 48–54

LEONARD MOSS

Willy Loman characterizes himself by the manner in which he speaks. "Well, bottoms up!...And keep your pores open!" he crudely reminds his extracurricular girlfriend, in tasteless cant of the thirties. When he gropes for metaphoric originality he cannot escape staleness: "Because you got a greatness in you, Biff, remember that . . . Like a young God. Hercules—something like that. And the sun, the sun all around him." His most pathetic laments are stock phrases: "Where are you guys, where are you?" he calls to his sons, "The woods are burning!"

Willy indicates his superficiality through hackneyed catchwords that advertise a business ethic based on "personal attractiveness." "Because the man who makes an appearance in the business world, the man who creates personal interest, is the man who gets ahead," he pontificates, in an aphoristic rhythm; "Be liked and you will never want." Childlike, he gains assurance by repeating his facile success formulas: "It's not what you do, Ben. It's who you know and the smile on your face! It's contacts, Ben, contacts! The whole wealth of Alaska passes over the lunch table at the Commodore Hotel, and that's the wonder, the wonder of this country, that a man can end with diamonds here on the basis of being liked!" (His wife and younger son echo the favorite magical cliché; Hap's compliment to Biff is "you're well liked," and Linda asks, "Why must everybody conquer the world? You're well liked.") Stressing the potent terms, Willy explains, "I realized that selling was the greatest career a man could want...there was personality in it, Howard. There was respect, and comradeship, and gratitude in it." Even his sons' names—Happy and Biff—reflect his naive euphoria.

The Salesman suggests his moral immaturity and confusion in another way through his many self-contradictions when offering advice to Biff. Though he warns that " 'Gee' is a boy's word," he uses the term frequently. He shouts at his son, "Not finding yourself at the age of thirty-four is a disgrace!" but later adds, "Greatest thing in the world for him to bum around." "Biff is a lazy bum," he grumbles; then, "And such a hard worker. There's one thing about Biff—he's not lazy." He gives this advice before the interview with Oliver: "Walk in very serious. You are not applying for a boy's job. Money is to pass. Be quiet, fine, and serious. Everybody likes a kidder, but nobody lends him money." A few lines after he cautions, "Walk in with a big laugh. Don't look worried. Start off with a couple of your good stories to lighten things up. It's not what you say, it's how you say it—because personality always wins the day." Memories of past conversations reproduce similar inconsistencies. He excused Biff's stealing a football from the school locker room: "Sure, he's gotta practice with a regulation ball, doesn't he? Coach'll probably congratulate you on your initiative!" Yet he soon forgot this excuse: "He's giving it back, isn't he? Why is he stealing? What did I tell him? I never in my life told him anything but decent things." ("Why am I always being contradicted?" he wonders.)

Still other techniques could be cited, particularly the associations operative in Willy's nightmarish recollections, but enough has been said to make the point that

Miller's dialogue is most telling when it works by implication rather than by expli-
cation.

—LEONARD MOSS, "Arthur Miller and the Common Man's Language,"
Modern Drama 7, No. I (Summer 1964): 55–56

RAYMOND WILLIAMS

Th(e) sense of the victim is very deep in Miller. *The Crucible* may remind us,
dramatically, of *Enemy of the People,* but there is a wholly new sense of the terrible
power of collective persecution. Individuals suffer for what they are and naturally
desire, rather than for what they try to do, and the innocent are swept up with the
guilty, with epidemic force. The social consciousness has now changed, decisively.
Society is not merely a false system, which the liberator can challenge. It is actively
destructive and evil, claiming its victims merely because they are alive. It is still seen
as a false and alterable society, but merely to live in it, now, is enough to become
its victim. In *Death of a Salesman* the victim is not the nonconformist, the heroic but
defeated liberator; he is, rather, the conformist, the type of the society itself. Willy
Loman is a man who from selling things has passed to selling himself, and has
become, in effect, a commodity which like other commodities will at a certain point
be discarded by the laws of the economy. He brings tragedy down on himself, not
by opposing the lie, but by living it. Ironically, the form of his aspiration is again the
form of his defeat, but now for no liberating end; simply to get by, to see himself
and his sons all right. The connection between parents and children, seen as
necessarily contradictory, is again tragically decisive. A new consciousness is then
shaped: that of the victim who has no living way out, but who can try, in death, to
affirm his lost identity and his lost will.

—RAYMOND WILLIAMS, "Modern Tragic Literature: From Hero to Victim,"
Modern Tragedy (Stanford: Stanford University Press, 1966), pp. 103–4

JOHN VON SZELISKI

Reality says there are no heroes. Our politics says all men are created equal. Politics
and expedient theology say that nobody ought to be far more important, far richer,
or far more gifted than anyone else. We reject the superman as we reject Naziism's
superrace. Democracy, unionism, socialism, and even Christianity have often made
the "common" man the central character of contemporary education, religion,
government and culture. The contemporary hero would be a freak. These are
today's realities, but they don't do away with continuing concerns about the size or
importance of a protagonist.

Our epoch's classic case of the rank-stature problem as a facet of tragic character is of course *Death of a Salesman.* I will review some of Miller's theory on the tragedy of the common man. Miller requests that we not confuse rank and stature, or pay more attention to a character because he assumes greater social rank. "So long as the hero may be said to have had alternatives of a magnitude to have materially changed the course of his life, it seems to me that in this respect at least, he cannot be debarred from the heroic role." To Miller it doesn't matter if the hero falls from a great or a small height, whether he is highly conscious or only dimly aware of what is going on, as long as there is intensity: "human passions to surpass his given bonds" and "the fanatic insistence upon his self-conceived role" (which defines Hitler and Nero as well as one possible Hamlet). Any play of character, says Miller, must show characters who are somewhat self-deluded or less than fully self-aware. Only in a play of "forces" like *Prometheus* can characters be fully aware. Then he contends that brave death makes his man more human; to Miller, Willy dies in joy. "In terms of his character, he has achieved a very powerful piece of knowledge," namely, that he is loved by his son and is forgiven. But is mere joy via delusion, in the manner of Robert Mayo, enough? Miller's answer: "It goes without saying that in a society where there is basic disagreement as to the right way to live, there can hardly be agreement as to the right way to die, and both life and death must be heavily weighted with meaningless futility." This logic is hard to follow. Moreover, why accept this common-denominator approach? Aren't there men of stature who *know* something about best values of death—or life? Miller seems to dislike the stature concept as much as rank: "Our society—and I am speaking of every industrialized society in the world—is so complex, each person being so specialized an integer, that the moment any individual is dramatically characterized and set forth as a hero, our common sense reduces him to the size of a complainer, a misfit." But nonhero Willy is also a complainer and misfit. The audience still must decide whether or not it cares about a "little man."

In the Brooklyn democracy of *Death of a Salesman,* the man of high stature is not only absent from the stage, he is not to be admired when he does exert his indirect force. It is the shadowy presence of the successful and rich man that incites Willy Loman to foolish quests for a false social stature. This call to Babbittry in the jungle of capitalism (and the seeming disgust with capitalism) is what allowed occasional Marxist interpretations of the play. It appears that the rich and powerful—the Bill Olivers and even the Brother Bens of the world—have avarice to thank for their stature. Their veneer of glamor and power serves as a false paragon to the millions of little men in the world. It has the same pernicious effect that the false ideal of movie stardom has upon the young and impressionable. The key in either case is immaturity. It takes maturity to recognize the fact that the ideal "big man"—as the little man wants to see him—does not really exist. In *Death of a Salesman,* except for the medium-successful Charley, the only such idol allowed on the stage is, significantly, an apparition.

In business, according to Willy's failure to charm his way to the top, the big man survives because he is the fittest, and his fitness is in his ruthless aggression. The little man is incapable of ruthlessness, because he is too sensitive. (Being "down" so long "sensitizes" him?) His bruised nature is what is needed to move the audience, and Willy's weakness has the same air about it as George Barnwell's whining impotence in *The London Merchant,* the latter having been so unmanly as to let a woman coax him into crime. Willy's Linda seems another vestige of the sentimental tragedy. She is like the long-suffering and incredibly patient women of the lachrymose eighteenth-century dramas who brought tears to the audience's eyes with their ability to forgive in the face of their husbands' infidelity.

I think we still look in vain for the equation between Willy's common rank *or* stature and tragic heroism. Miller's big intent, of course, is that the society in the theatre will pay Willy some attention because society in the play has abandoned him. Because capitalism ran him into the ground? Or because he represents the universal misery of the Little Man? Linda's famous "attention" speech only reflects the new heroic values Miller would like to develop, or those of a society unable to conceive of a big and noble man. Since the playwright makes no suggestions about man aspiring to spiritual worths, Willy's worth will have to be equated with having his name in the paper and making a lot of money—the indexes which Linda uses. Not having achieved these things, he is less than great. But Linda does not define his worth. She says, "such a person." This phrase only refers back to "human being" and she does not add anything to show why he, more than any other human being, should receive the attention. Literally, this means that no matter what a human being does, he is worthy of the attention Miller hopes we give Willy.

Linda also concludes that "a small man can be just as exhausted as a great man." But the significant point is determining what exhausts him. In sentimental social drama, a "hero" may be exhausted by simply staying out of trouble or existing. Any human being can be exhausted on the greatest variety of quests from the ridiculous to the sublime. He may also make a quest that is for himself only. The tragic hero's goal is an affirmative one and affects far more people than himself. What he does is something not everyone works for every day. Willy's industry, on the other hand, is not tragic exhaustion because he works for his family, his company, and his creditors with certainly no greater results than thousands of breadwinners like him. His benefactors include a "philandering bum," an understandably ungrateful vagrant, and a wife who, however sweetly and patiently, only does the wash "as of old." The too-long held pessimistic attitude results in this notion of Miller's that heroic stature consists in simply managing to exist without becoming a criminal or complete savage.

The pessimist apparently doesn't believe in greatness in any measure. Miller's defense of the tragedy of the common man in no way proves that we don't still want to get involved with heroes of significant strength—and stature. Concluding his criticisms of our writers' "insignificance neurosis," Colin Wilson ends on an even more urgent note: "The responsibility of literature in the twentieth century becomes appallingly clear: to illuminate man's freedom." ⟨. . .⟩

Willy Loman is an excessively material creature. His externals-minded set of values is in league with the Loman theory of the excusable immorality. Stealing is all right for Biff because he's going to charm people and go places. Cultivating an athletic personality is better than studying, because "appearances" are what count. Willy's love for his boys stresses their exterior attractions: their builds, looks, physical ability. It dislocates them because it is a denial of natural order. Instead one must *act* one's way into being noticed, through sham. Biff is characterized as "carrying a football which he keeps squeezing as though to locate himself in the world." Biff and Happy know you build a future by getting ahead of the next guy—but without understanding the process or the necessity. Happy's name is an irony, for he does not know pleasure even in his repeated sexual conquests. Without clear good, evil pales as well.

Part of the atmosphere of perennial defeat in this household comes from the impersonality of the automated, mechanized society that has substituted mass mediocrity for slowly cultured quality. The Lomans know intimately the seemingly petty defeats of broken-down refrigerators, carburetor trouble, and the like. At the same time, they respond, with all "common" men ("common" by the advertising industry's definition of mass attraction) to the mass-production values. Willy himself, as a salesman, must represent those values to the consumer. Willy and Linda can leak out their earnings for a mountain of minor repairs, and then justify their decision to purchase a particular brand by saying: "They had the biggest ads of any of them!" Miller's comment in another interview points to another aspect of such adopted values; "Willy is a victim; he didn't originate this thing. He believes that selling is the greatest thing anybody can do."

Miller says he was careful not to inject a personal statement of his philosophy into the play. Yet Willy is so obviously wrong in all he does, all the while "meaning well" and loving his family, that a statement of values seems especially needed. We only see a world which is mutually infected by Willy's helplessly perverted dreams and codes. If the characters are deliberately and pessimistically drawn as limited intelligences, there can be little perspective on values from within the play. Could Linda be a source? She seems most sensible and most objective, but she has a policy of single-minded support of Willy. Her love is then impressive but her values routine.

Willy's self-building only develops the ground for his later paranoia, when he decides the world has treated him badly in the light of his greatness *as he imagined it:*

> And they know me, boys, they know me up and down New England. The finest people. And when I bring you fellas up, there'll be open sesame for all of us, 'cause one thing, boys: I have friends. I can park my car in any street in New England, and the cops protect it like their own.

Thus the Loman men feed on each other's empty values, resulting in their eventual cynicism about modern life in the city: eat, sleep, work, and then more of the same. Lack of values means lack of ethic plus lack of knowledge. The result: pessimism and cynicism. Eventually Biff vaguely wants to marry "somebody with character, with resistance:" that is, both Happy and Biff agree they must seek someone to challenge them as Linda and Willy have not.

The object of Willy's code is understandable. He's got a poignant dream and we can sympathize with it. We all desire recognition, and we want him to have it, wrong and false though he may be. He will share it with his family, too. But his means to this object remain at least amoral if not immoral. While Miller naturally criticizes Willy, it is nonetheless clear that Willy is Miller's (and our) pathos-object. It is sad what was expedient to the Lomans, but this is not a moral statement, even though Miller is normally one of our more moral playwrights.

Willy's dangerous thinking, forced on him by society, is also somewhat inherited, and Willy in turn will pass this on to Biff, and Biff would pass it on to his children. Willy's brother Ben says to Biff what is probably the same thing Willy heard from his father years ago: "Never fight fair with a stranger, boy. You'll never get out of the jungle that way." There are two interesting suppositions here: that they *are* in a jungle, and that one must force one's way out. They are keystones of the Loman pessimism, and ironically Willy is not aware enough to be a fighter. These only explain and do not justify Willy's perennial defensiveness. The main conclusion is that those who get out of the jungle are the treacherous battlers and connivers and thus the earth is inherited by some cross between rats and apes. Accordingly, Ben's repeated boast that he was rich at seventeen is Willy's favorite piece of literature: "That's just the spirit I want to imbue them with! To walk into a jungle! I was right! I was right! I was right!"

So Willy is destroyed by his values, and they are not moral or ethical values, but situational and material codes. They alienate Biff even as Biff learns of no alternative to this type of value. That is Willy's greatest loss and the final impetus for suicide. Simply put, Willy is a professional failure. His values wouldn't matter to the company if only he could maintain his quota and not act so strangely.

Death of a Salesman, for all its excellence as a drama, then shares the typical weaknesses of the other pessimistic plays when it comes to moral statement. Nothing has been said distinctly or strongly in any of the areas that might pass for such statement—not on sin, or error, or moral belief, or mere common-sense values. But even this is not the ultimate problem with the pessimistic would-be tragedy. It is finally a matter of enlightenment.

—JOHN VON SZELISKI, *Tragedy and Fear: Why Modern Tragic Drama Fails* (Chapel Hill: University of North Carolina Press, 1971), pp. 106–9, 162–65

STANLEY KAUFFMANN

Death of a Salesman contains the idea for a great play, and I would maintain that its immense international success comes from the force of that idea prevailing over the defects in execution. The force takes hold with the very title, which is highly evocative, and is amplified by the opening sight of Willy Loman coming in the door. That sight is a superb theater image of our time, as unforgettable an icon as Mother Courage and her wagon (another traveling salesman!): the salesman home, "tired to death," lugging his two heavy sample cases, rejected by the big milk-filled bosom of the country from which he had expected so much nourishment.

The force of the play's idea continues fitfully to grasp at us: the idea of a man who has sold things without making them, who has paid for things without really owning them; an insulted extrusion of commercial society battling for some sliver of authenticity before he slips into the dark.

But to see the play again is to see how Arthur Miller lacked the control and vision to fulfill his own idea. First consider the diction of the play, because a play is its language, first and finally. *Salesman* falters badly in this regard. At its best, its true and telling best, the diction is first-generation Brooklyn Jewish. ("Attention, attention must be finally paid to such a person.") But often the dialogue slips into a fanciness that is slightly ludicrous. To hear Biff say, "I've been remiss," to hear Linda say, "He was crestfallen, Willy" is like watching a car run off the road momentarily onto the shoulder. (I've never heard anyone use the word "crestfallen" in my life.) Then there is the language of Willy's brother Ben, the apparition of piratical success. He speaks like nothing but a symbol, and not a symbol connected with Willy in any perceptible way. Miller *says* he's Willy's brother, that's all. The very use of diamonds as the source of Ben's wealth has an almost childishly symbolic quality about it. When Miller's language is close to the stenographic, the remembered, it's good; otherwise, it tends to literary juvenility, a pretended return from pretended experience.

Thematically, too, the play is cloudy. It's hard to believe that, centrally, Miller had anything more than muzzy anti-business, anti-technology impulses in his head. Is Willy a man shattered by business failure and by disappointment in his sons? Then why, when he is younger and at least making a living, when he is proud of his sons and they of him, does he lie about his earnings to Linda and then have to correct himself? Why, at the peak of his life, does he undercut his own four-flushing to tell her that people don't take to him, that they laugh at him? The figure that comes through the play is not of a man brought down by various failures but of a mentally unstable man in whom the fissures have increased. Willy is shown to be at least as much a victim of psychopathy as of the bitch goddess. When was he ever rational or dependable? Is this a tragedy of belief in the American romance or the end of a clinical case?

But assume, for argument, that Willy is not a psychopath, that he was a relatively whole man now crushed by the American juggernaut. What is the play's attitude toward that juggernaut, toward business ideals? There is no anagnorisis for Willy, no moment of recognition: he dies believing in money—in fact, he kills himself for it, to give his son Biff the insurance benefit as a stake for more business. His son Happy is wedded to money values and says over his father's coffin that he's going to stick to them for his father's sake. Biff was so aggrandized by his father that he became kleptomaniacal as a boy and even now, after his father-as-idol has collapsed, can't resist stealing a successful man's fountain pen as a niggling vindictiveness against that man's success and his own non-success. The only alternatives to the business ethos ever produced in the play are Willy's love of tools and seeds, building and planting, and Biff's love of outdoor life. As between romances, I'll take business.

Miller confuses matters even further by the success of young Bernard next door as a lawyer in the Establishment world, a success for which Willy feels envy. What we are left with is neither a critique of the business world nor an adult vision of something different and better, but the story of a man (granting he was sane) who failed, as salesman and father, and who made things worse by refusing to the end to admit those failures, which he knew were true. That is one play, and possibly a good one if it were realized; but it is quite a different one from a play that, in its atmosphere and mannerisms, implies radical perception about deep American ills.

Some other points. When I saw the film in 1952, which made the environment more vivid, I couldn't help wondering why Willy had money worries: he had almost paid off the mortgage on his house, which was a piece of real estate in an increasingly valuable and desirable section, to judge by the building going on all around it. I don't think this is a petty literal point in a realistic play whose lexicon is bill-paying. Further, all the dialogue about Willy's father, with his wagon-travels through the West and his flutes, seems falser than ever, Miller's imposition on this Brooklyn play to give it historical base and continental sweep. As with the character of Ben, there is a schism in tenor between this material and the rest of the play. Last, a point that is strangely more apparent now than it was in 1949 when *Salesman* first appeared: the play is set in the late 1940s and reaches back some fifteen years, yet there is scarcely a mention of World War II. How did Biff and Happy escape it? If they didn't, wouldn't the reunited brothers have had something to say about it? And wouldn't the war have had some effect on Willy's past-cum-present view of promise-crammed America?

Some of the play is touching still: Willy when he is at his most salesman-like, the Requiem over his coffin, and much of the material on Miller's favorite theme, the love-hate of father and son. But these are sound moments in a flabby, occasionally false work. Miller had gift enough to get the idea, but then settled for the dynamics of the idea itself, supported by a vague high-mindedness, to write his play for him. As the world knows, many viewers and readers have taken the intent for the deed. Some have not. And for one viewer this new production only emphasizes the gap between intent and accomplishment.

—STANLEY KAUFFMANN, *"Death of a Salesman"* [1975], *Persons of the Drama* (New York: Harper & Row, 1976), pp. 142–45

A R T H U R   G A N Z

We commonly expect the conflicting forces that have set a play in motion to clash decisively in its climactic scene and there to reveal its central motive. In *Death of a Salesman,* however, this scene is strangely inconclusive. The nearest thing to it is that in which Biff's faith in his father and his father's ideals, and thus in himself, is shattered. The scene has been held back out of chronological sequence till just before the end of the play and is obviously meant to reveal the hollowness of Willy's philosophy as the source of Biff's degeneration. But it does nothing of the sort. When Biff finds Willy with a woman in his hotel room, he at once concludes that his father's total view of life is erroneous, that his character is worthless, and that he, Biff, is irretrievably lost. But why should he? In extenuation Willy says truthfully that he was lonely and that the woman meant nothing to him. Biff himself, we are told, has cut a considerable swath among the high school girls. Sons less devoted have forgiven their fathers more. At this point in the play, Miller clearly wishes to show through Biff the nature of Willy's error. Yet, strangely unable to do so, he is forced to invent irrelevant, psychologically untenable emotional entanglements that hardly conceal his failure.

If we set aside the play's structure and attempt to examine Willy's philosophy directly, similar problems arise. Willy is a man so foolish as to believe that success in the business world can be achieved not by work and ability but by being "well liked," by a kind of hearty popularity that will open all doors and provide favors and preferential treatment. So convinced is Willy of the rightness of his doctrine that he raises his sons by it and, without intending to, subtly undermines their moral character, turning one into a lecher and the other into a thief. If the death of Willy Loman is to be any more significant than the death of many another pathetic incompetent, and Miller clearly wishes it to be so, then Willy's doctrine, the ultimate cause of his downfall, must be both dangerous and widespread. When pushed to Willy's extreme, it is no doubt dangerous, but that it is widespread is doubtful. That many Americans are obsessed by the idea of commercial success is surely a truth, though hardly an original one; that large numbers of such persons intend to achieve their goals primarily by cultivating the art of camaraderie is most unlikely. We are, in other words, being elaborately warned against a danger that is not dangerous. Indeed, Willy's touching desire to be liked often strikes us as one of his most endearing characteristics. For all his bluster and his terrible incomprehension, we do like him. His death moves us, perhaps because he so obviously wanted us to be moved. The desire to be liked functions in the play emotionally, but intellectually it is meaningless. It is not at the root of the socioeconomic ills of modern American society, and a critique of that society based upon it would be entirely without validity. Yet a critique of some pretensions seems to be present in the play: if it is not based on Willy's doctrine, we may reasonably ask what it is based on.

Unfortunately, the question is more easily asked than answered, for the play, when closely examined, yields not one critique but at least three, each distinct and each negating the other. From one point of view, Miller's dissatisfaction with the society that Willy Loman exemplifies stems from an implicit comparison between it and a previous one that was stronger, simpler, and more noble. So considered, Willy's society is no more than the corruption of the pioneer vision of a pastoral edenic world peopled by a dignified race finding fulfillment in its labors. Willy, then, represents the degeneration of an older, stronger stock, described by his brother Ben:

> Father was a very great and a very wild-hearted man. We would start in Boston, and he'd toss the whole family into the wagon, and then he'd drive the team right across the country; through Ohio, and Indiana, Michigan, Illinois, and all the Western states. And we'd stop in the towns and sell the flutes that he'd made on the way. Great inventor, Father. With one gadget he made more in a week than a man like you could make in a lifetime.

Willy's father, too, was a salesman, but he was also a pioneer and sold the artistic products of his own hands. The end of this speech is colored by Ben's character, but even that character is ambiguous, for Ben's business in Alaska and his offer to Willy suggest the pioneer developer as much as the capitalist exploiter. It is this character of the hardy, simple man, happy in a rural environment (as the cowboys of *The Misfits* might have been happy) that Willy's dreams seem to have corrupted. Biff says that he and his brother should work outdoors; Willy is never happier than when doing manual work about the house. But this life is not possible. Brooklyn is no longer a place where one can hunt rabbits (again, a hint of the lost Eden) but a place where the few anachronistic houses like Willy's are ringed by the characterless apartment buildings of an industrial-commercial civilization. Dave Singleman, the eighty-four-year-old salesman upon whom Willy had modeled himself, derived respect and friendship from his work, but Willy is alone in a world that ignores him.

If the central motive of this play is a critique of American society as the corrupted remnant of a great pioneer vision, then Willy has much to answer for. If the thousands of Willys whom Miller evidently finds in our society have through their stupidity and vulgarity destroyed the rustic happiness that Miller appears to see in the American past, then they are guilty of a great crime and deserve their fates. But Miller does not seem to condemn Willy, at least not very forcefully, for there is a strong suggestion that his fate has been thrust upon him by forces beyond his control or indeed his comprehension. The pathetic picture of the tired old salesman, helpless in an overwhelming environment, does not suggest the righteous destruction of the wicked. There are other men in the play far worse than Willy. The speech about Willy's pioneer-flutist father is delivered by Ben (no one else is available to give it), but he is a very different sort of person. Ben presents his philosophy when he says, "Why, boys, when I was seventeen I walked into the jungle, and when I was twenty-one I walked out . . . And by God I was rich." When sparring with Biff, Ben trips him, threatens him with the point of an umbrella, and then advises, "Never fight fair with a stranger, boy. You'll never get out of the jungle that way." The jungle is clearly the brutal, competitive modern world in which the strong and ruthless like Ben will triumph and the weak like Willy will go under.

Here, then, is no image of Willy as destroyer but rather of Willy as victim, coldly fired by the firm he has served for thirty-four years. "Business is business," says the young employer whom Willy has known as a child. Willy agrees that business is business, but he does not really believe it. When he tries to explain why he chose to remain a salesman, he says, " 'Cause what could be more satisfying than to be able to go, at the age of eighty-four, into twenty or thirty different cities, and pick up a phone, and be remembered and loved and helped by so many different people?" Willy's error, as we see him here, is a failure to understand the harshness of the world he has attempted so ineptly to conquer. He has tried to find a world of private affections where there was only a jungle.

The critique suggested here is not so much of Willy as of Willy's world. Since it implies that Willy is essentially innocent and has been destroyed by the competitive system, we may call it the socialist critique (though the author's personal politics are not made explicit). Such an attitude would seem to underlie the requiem spoken by Willy's friend, Charley: "You don't understand: Willy was a salesman . . . He's a man way out there in the blue, riding on a smile and a shoeshine. And when they start not smiling back—that's an earthquake. And then you get yourself a couple of spots on your hat, and you're finished. Nobody dast blame this man. A salesman is got to dream, boy. It comes with the territory." If this speech means anything very specific, it means that Willy was, in essence, not at fault. His foolish and dangerous dreams came with the territory; that is, they were the inevitable product of an evil system for which he was not responsible.

Yet there is still another critical point of view in the play, and Charley is its spokesman as well. In fact, he and his son, Bernard, offer a continuing contrast with Willy and his sons. Because Miller so clearly extends to Charley and Bernard a degree of approval which he withholds from the Lomans, he has, intentionally or not, made Willy's neighbors a symbolic commentary on Willy himself. They have self-understanding where Willy does not; they are at ease in a world where Willy is tormented. When, in desperation, Willy comes to his friend after he has been fired, Charley tries to show him his error: "The only thing you got in this world is what you can sell. And the funny thing is that you're a salesman, and you don't know that." "I've always tried to think otherwise, I guess," Willy answers. "I always felt that if a man was impressive, and well liked, that nothing—"; "Why must everybody like you?" Charley cries. "Who liked J. P. Morgan? Was he impressive? In a Turkish bath he'd look like a butcher. But with his pockets on he was very well liked." Charley does not say that the commercial world of salesmanship is inherently wrong but that Willy has confused it with something else. Because the world of J. P. Morgan is hard, one cannot get ahead in it by means of a false impressiveness but by work and ability. The exemplar of this doctrine is his son, Bernard. While Biff was playing football and being taught by his father that he could get what he wanted simply by being liked, Bernard was working at his studies. When we see them later, Bernard is a successful young lawyer on his way to argue a case before the Supreme Court, and Biff is a failure and a near kleptomaniac. Bernard and his father, then, represent reliance on the bourgeois virtues of honesty and hard work rather than a socialist rejection of competitive society.

That in some way Miller intends to criticize our society through Willy Loman is unquestionable; that he clearly understands the nature of his own criticism, however, is doubtful. After all, he has suggested, with a kind of naive romanticism, that the Loman ethic has corrupted a simple and noble pioneer dream; he has seemed to portray Willy as the pathetic victim of a ruthless competitive system; he has also managed to imply that Willy's error has been his attempt to substitute an empty creed for the solid qualities of honesty and work. That Miller has held these incompatible views and embodied them in his finest play suggests that he has written out of a deep dissatisfaction with the social world and an almost equally severe confusion about one's role in it.

Moreover, just as he has been unable to present a coherent attitude toward the external world, so Miller has offered a view of the self too simplified to convince us that his work is an adequate representation of reality. Miller's central characters, each the living embodiment of his point of view, have been engaged in an action their creator clearly considers the most significant one a man can undertake, the personal search for dignity and identity in a hostile world. In this search Willy Loman resembles the cowboys of *The Misfits* as well as Miller's other significant characters, for each of them, though he lives most explicitly amid the problems of the modern social world (Miller's one historical play is a thinly disguised presentation of the McCarthy era, and his biblical fable derives from personal material), is on a private quest for a self in which above all he will find an ultimate core of virtue. When he has achieved this aim—and a Miller hero of the early plays almost inevitably does so—he has, in the mind of his author, reached the point of rest at the end of his journey. This faith in the efficacy of self-recognition as a mode of achieving virtue is far more central to his view of life than any of his ideas, however serious, concerning the immediate problems of society. But as with many a faith the difficulties of acquiring and retaining it are great.

—ARTHUR GANZ, "Arthur Miller: Eden and After," *Realms of the Self: Variations on a Theme in Modern Drama* (New York: New York University Press, 1980), pp. 125–30

MICHAEL SPINDLER

In selling, the presentation of personality is all-important, since the salesman can best sell his product by impressing the buyer, by winning his confidence and trust, by making himself likeable, by selling himself. (When asked what Willy was selling, Miller writes that he could only reply 'Himself'.) This emphasis gives rise to a character orientation which Erich Fromm, writing at the same time as *Salesman,* called the 'marketing orientation'. A salesman, like Willy, is not concerned with the attainment of some objective achievement but with the creation of a pleasing personality that will be saleable, and since he is trying to sell himself, he experiences his qualities and abilities as commodities estranged from him. This self-alienation has serious consequences, as David Riesman, following Fromm, points out. It diminishes the individual's sense of a hard core of self and, consequently, the externalised values of prestige and public image become substitutes for a genuine feeling of identity. For it is not the genuine self that is put in the market for economic success but the cosmetic self that is free from any nonsaleable idiosyncrasies. When this artificial self succeeds, Riesman suggests, doubts about the loss of identity may be quieted, but since self-evaluation has been surrendered to the market, failure in the market will be translated by the individual into self-contempt. Miller indicates through Willy's frequent self-contradiction that he has no personal centre, a fact which Biff confirms when he says that Willy has no character. Willy has seized upon the notion of commercial success as a substitute for genuine identity, and when he begins to fail in the market he translates this failure into self-contempt and insecurity:

> WILLY: Oh, I'll knock 'em dead next week. I'll go to Hartford. I'm very well liked in Hartford. You know, the trouble is, Linda, people don't seem to take to me.
> LINDA: Oh, don't be foolish.
> WILLY: I know it when I walk in. They seem to laugh at me.

Since the salesman experiences himself as a commodity, he will inevitably experience others in the same way and assess their worth according to their success in the market. Thus Biff is a 'lazy bum' on this basis because his farm jobs lack status and he has yet to bring home thirty-five dollars a week. ⟨. . .⟩

⟨. . .⟩ Miller is by no means a complete determinist. He does not allow Willy to be just a passive victim, a human atom driven by forces much larger than himself. He shows him making choices—selling, not Alaska—so that he must share some of the blame for his condition. Willy's crisis, then, is a personal one, but through the realm of values, through its ideological aspect, emphasized by Miller, it connects with the crisis of values in the society at large. Willy's problem, in a similar way to Clyde Griffiths's, is due not to a lack of values but rather to the plurality of value-systems operating in a society undergoing rapid change. That society was losing contact with a residual set of production-oriented values as it committed itself wholeheartedly to mass consumerism, and the resultant ideological conflict led to anxiety and disorientation among individuals living through that social change. Miller indicts the commercial ethos of success for its lack of any nourishing values, but the only solution he offers his characters is escape—death for Willy, and back to the land for Biff, back to an agrarian, productive life. In *Salesman* he does not really face the vexing question of how one is to live and work and retain integrity—attain 'autonomy', to adopt Riesman's term—in an urban society where all the pressures are towards false consciousness and the loss of selfhood.

—MICHAEL SPINDLER, "Consumer Man in Crisis: Arthur Miller's *Death of a Salesman,*" *American Literature and Social Change: William Dean Howells to Arthur Miller* (Bloomington: Indiana University Press, 1983), pp. 206, 212

ARTHUR MILLER

I have been catching a certain tone of condescension toward Willy's character coming from Linda and Willy—from him, especially—from time to time. Perhaps it is unconscious; or possibly I misunderstand. It came at me yesterday and again two or three times today, an indefinable but dangerous attitude that could lead to a satiric interpretation, which would leave Ying Ruocheng unable to sustain the role the whole length of the play. (I am not sure he has yet caught on to how physically difficult this part is going to be.) But most important, I cannot let the play become a satire.

"I want to say a few things about the play and Willy now," I announce. They become silent quickly. It is now clear, incidentally, that they normally discuss a play for days and sometimes weeks before trying to do scenes and, like all actors, would—up to a certain point—much prefer interesting general discussions to hard work. But I am coming to realize that in this type of theatre there is no rush to do anything. "You are all aware, I'm sure, that Willy is foolish and even ridiculous sometimes. He tells the most transparent lies, exaggerates mercilessly, and so on. But I want you to see that the impulses behind him are not foolish at all. He cannot bear reality, and since he can't do much to change it, he keeps changing his ideas of it." I am veering close to ideology; I note some agreement here, but it is uneasy. Charley is especially rapt and unable, I believe, to come down on the side of my argument. "But the one thing he is not, is passive. Something in him knows that if he stands still he will be overwhelmed. These lies and evasions of his are his little swords with which he wards off the devils around him. But his activist nature is what leads mankind to progress, doesn't it. It can create disaster, to be sure, but progress also. People who are able to accept their frustrated lives do not change conditions, do they. So my point is that you must look behind his ludicrousness to what he is actually confronting, and that is as serious a business as anyone can imagine. There is a nobility, in fact, in Willy's struggle. Maybe it comes from his refusal ever to relent, to give up."

—ARTHUR MILLER, *Salesman in Beijing* (New York: Viking Press, 1984), pp. 26–27

GEORGE E. WELLWARTH

A good example of an unintentionally synthetic drama in a "free" society is Arthur Miller's *Death of a Salesman.* Miller's intention was clearly twofold: to write an analytic drama posing the problem of the ordinary worker in a conscienceless, capitalistic society and implicitly condemning the system; and to write a modern tragedy adapting Aristotelian theory to allow for a common man as tragic protagonist. Miller's success in achieving his stated aims has been the subject of considerable debate, principally among those critics who feel that an adherence to Aristotelian guidelines for the writing of tragedy is still important. Miller himself has argued that tragedy consists of "the underlying fear of being displaced, the disaster inherent in being torn away from our chosen image of what and who we are in the world." As a definition of tragedy this is perhaps as valid as any, but it does not apply to Miller's protagonist. Willy Loman is indeed torn away from his image of what and who he is in the world, but that image was never chosen by him. Willy is under the delusion that he has chosen his self-image, but it has in fact been chosen for him, as it has been for the millions who make up the common horde that Miller intends Willy to represent. It is here that the feedback mechanism of the sociohuman machine becomes evident. The common man has not chosen his self-image, nor has it been deliberately devised by some powerful individual Machiavellian mind and artfully insinuated to him as his own. The common man's relation to the social machine is a symbiotic one, and the creation of his image of himself is accomplished reciprocally between himself and the multiplication of himself that constitutes the major part of society. It is based simultaneously on the need of the mass to cohere and form the mortar that holds itself together and the individual's need to belong to something other than himself—in short, to bow down to something greater than himself. Willy Loman and those he represents are the victims of a delusion collectively created by themselves and believed in and worshiped as fervently as any deity ever was. Willy's mind is incapable of independent thought and therefore of self-realization. It is a befuddled mess of slogans derived from the flimflam of advertising jargon and the cant of popularized palliative psychology. And he uses these stock phrases as verbal talismans to ward off reality and self-realization, much as the invocation of imagined creatures in another world was once believed effective in warding off the imagined evil of this one.

Willy Loman is the compleat synthetic man as well as the prototypical common man Miller intends him to be. Willy *believes*. He believes in the myths of the capitalistic society in which he is subsumed. He believes in the myth of log cabin to president, which he transforms into a myth of seedy drudge to big business executive. He believes in the pot of gold at the end of the rainbow, realized in his mind by his brother Ben who walked into the jungle and came out rich. He believes in appearance, in phoniness, in acceptance ("not just liked, but well liked") by those he regards as the gods of the machine. Above all, he believes in advertising slogans: "Chevrolet, Linda, is the greatest car ever built." But somehow his faith does not sustain him ("That goddam Chevrolet, they ought to prohibit the manufacture of that car"), and he has to work harder and harder, bolster his self-delusion more and more to sustain his feeling of integration. At the end he is spewed out by the machine as a useless part and desperately immolates himself in his faith by dying so his son can collect the insurance money and thus pay his entrance fee at the portals of the machine he had left to seek the hard reality of self-realization.

—GEORGE E. WELLWARTH, *Modern Drama and the Death of God* (Madison: University of Wisconsin Press, 1986), pp. 144–45

LOUIS HARAP

Distortion of sense of family is also one of the implications derivable from the multi-meaninged *Death of a Salesman*. Willy Loman pursues the false, spurious values of a commercialized society by which he believes he can advance the position of his family's well-being as he conceives it. And when Willy is confronted by indubitable failure in his vocation and with rejection by his son Biff, who cannot forgive either Willy's night with a woman or the false values that Willy inculcated in him, Willy believes he can recover family solidarity by endowing it with his insurance money through his suicide. The Jewish elements in *Salesman* are more specific as well. We know that the character of Willy was suggested by a salesman Miller had actually known, and the dramatist's attempt to avoid ethnic identification was not altogether successful. To be sure, the American shibboleths of the salesman are only too well known—"It's contacts, . . . I got important contacts!" as Willy says. "It's not what you do, Ben. It's who you know and the smile on your face! It's contacts." But Miller's outlook on this question was specifically framed in the course of his experience with the business environment of his father's garment shop, and he even knew a salesman who had committed suicide. When I saw the play, one scene struck me as typically Jewish and might have been transposed from the Yiddish theater. Bernard, boyhood friend of Biff and now a successful lawyer, comes in to say goodbye to Willy before leaving for Washington to argue a case before the Supreme Court. The Jewish overtones of this scene struck me forcibly as I witnessed it.

More explicitly Jewish, however, was the use of Yiddishized English expressions. The most famous phrase in the play is one such—"Attention must be paid" (*gib achtung*), as Linda admonishes her sons. Most telling of all was the underlying saturation in his Jewish milieu in the first decade or so of his creativity. When *Salesman* was reenacted in Yiddish translation in 1951, George Ross, an actor and director, was struck by the ease with which the play fitted into the Jewish scene. In fact, Ross asserted that "this Yiddish play is really the original, and the Broadway production was merely—Arthur Miller's translation into English." Ross further maintained that the Yiddish Willy was a better realized character than he was in the English version, in which Willy was supposed to be the "American Everyman" and hence lacking in concreteness. Miller seemed to have lost this concreteness in "censoring out the Jewish part" of the milieu he was treating. In the process, wrote Ross, the focus was shifted from a play about an unsuccessful salesman to "a play about a Jewish *family*." If that is indeed the case, then the English version is closer to Miller's intention. It was not lack of success that was central to Miller's aim. If so, Willy would have been accounted merely pathetic. But Miller intended him as a "tragic" figure because, Miller wrote, Willy "was agonized by his awareness of being in a false position, so constantly haunted by the hollowness of all he had placed his faith in." At the stage of development at which he wrote the play, however, the Jewish figurations of Miller's mentality remained sharp, and it would seem true, as Mary McCarthy remarked, that "Willy seemed to be Jewish, to judge by his speech-cadences."

—LOUIS HARAP, Dramatic Encounters: The Jewish Presence in Twentieth-Century American Drama, Poetry, and Humor and the Black-Jewish Literary Relationship (Westport, CT: Greenwood Press, 1987), pp. 124–25

PRISCILLA S. McKINNEY

From the play's beginning, we learn how closely Linda, always supportive of Willy, complements him psychically as well. If she lacks Willy's temperament, she counters his discontent by being all that is protective and loving, in the way that Willy is not. She parries his insults "with infinite patience," and Willy himself acknowledges that she is his "foundation and . . . support." She denies to him that he is unlikable, tells him that to her he is the handsomest man in the world, shares in and helps to create his optimism, and even rejects Biff because of his disrespect for him—an attitude which would be difficult to understand, given Linda's problems with Willy and her natural love for her son, unless we see her as the voice for Willy's inner needs. "You can't just come to see me, because I love him. . . . He's the dearest man in the world to me, and I won't have anyone making him feel unwanted and low and blue. . . . Either he's your father and you pay him that respect, or else you're not to come here."

In contrast to Linda's loyalty is Willy's cruel treatment of his wife, which is the most flagrant evidence of his self-destructive bent. In Biff's words, "he always wiped the floor" with her. Nor can he face the fact that he himself creates the arguments between them, saying at one point that is it the fault of Linda's fatigue since "she keels over" from waxing the floor. Linda, ironically, excuses Willy's behavior by saying, "the man is exhausted." This theme of fatigue, which is prominent in *Salesman,* supports Thomas E. Porter's view of the play as an "anti-myth," a "rags to riches formula in reverse. . . . The events of the play are a mirror image of the hero's progress. Willy Loman's history begins at the end of the line." Clearly, both Willy and his alter ego have spent themselves in the struggle, but neither is capable of seeing the error of their materialistic goals. Benjamin Nelson, in fact, sees Linda as a "root figure in the catastrophe of her husband and sons" because of her own need for security:

... for all her knowledge of Willy as a struggling and weary provider, she can never totally abrogate her faith in him as the Great Salesman.... She knows the truth about her husband but will not wholly face it with him or with herself. Instead she continually helps to inflate Willy's overblown image despite her suspicions of its falsity.

Jung would see Willy's problem as overidentification with his professional persona at the expense of the needs of the self, a stifling shortsightedness which Linda naively encourages.

One of the most trying aspects of Willy's struggle has been his failure to remain faithful to his psychic mate. Linda, for all her apparent goodness, has at times had to give way to The Woman, who operates not only outside the home "as part of the impersonal forces that corrupt," as Porter notes, but outside Willy's better nature as well. Through Willy's self-deception and internal arguments (evidenced by those with Linda), he has managed to separate the good and corrupt aspects of his nature, never allowing the good to recognize the bad, and never reconciling the two. In Jungian terms, the conflicting claims of wife/mother and sexual companion exemplify the positive and negative potential of all archetypes. Willy has a "split anima," which is itself a duality of Western culture, according to Demaris Wehr. Even on a superficial level, Ronald Hayman sees Willy's affairs as an expression of his shaky self-image. Always at risk at home of having his "bluff called," he can temporarily win feminine approval through "wisecracks and gifts of silk stockings." All of these views are compatible, each suggesting the deep rift in Willy's psyche.

To the end, Willy's lack of self-knowledge is mirrored in Linda's. Although Linda realizes that Willy is giving up the struggle—"He's dying, Biff"—and even cooperates with him by leaving the rubber hose attached to the gas pipe, she never knows the reason for Willy's insecurity, or what it is that has come between Willy and Biff. Her avoidance of the knowledge of his promiscuity, even when Biff almost gives it away, is similar to Willy's tendency to escape to his dream world with Ben. According to C. W. E. Bigsby, "there is a clear connection between her refusal to challenge those illusions and his death." To face reality, especially the consequences of his sinfulness, is too painful to Willy, who would rather have "good news" to tell the woman who has suffered with him. He would prefer to bury the truth than to face it. Although Miller intended to develop Willy's self-awareness enough to provoke his suicide, Willy's death lacks the recognition required to make it tragedy in the dramatic sense; thus life becomes pathetic in a real sense for the psychic partner he leaves behind. To the degree that she continues to live in the world and mind of Willy, Linda is doomed to insecurity and ignorance. At Willy's grave, "Linda cannot understand the mystery as Willy could not understand it" ((Harold) Clurman). Just as Willy "never knew who he was," so, too, Linda is left in an agony of self-doubt and uncertainty.

—PRISCILLA S. MCKINNEY, "Jung's 'Anima' in Arthur Miller's Plays," *Studies in American Drama, 1945–Present* 3 (1988): 48–50

CRITICAL ESSAYS

Arthur Miller

INTRODUCTION TO
COLLECTED PLAYS

The first image that occurred to me which was to result in *Death of a Salesman* was of an enormous face the height of the proscenium arch which would appear and then open up, and we would see the inside of a man's head. In fact, *The Inside of His Head* was the first title. It was conceived half in laughter, for the inside of his head was a mass of contradictions. The image was in direct opposition to the method of *All My Sons*—a method one might call linear or eventual in that one fact or incident creates the necessity for the next. The *Salesman* image was from the beginning absorbed with the concept that nothing in life comes "next" but that everything exists together and at the same time within us; that there is no past to be "brought forward" in a human being, but that he is his past at every moment and that the present is merely that which his past is capable of noticing and smelling and reacting to.

I wished to create a form which, in itself as a form, would literally be the process of Willy Loman's way of mind. But to say "wished" is not accurate. Any dramatic form is an artifice, a way of transforming a subjective feeling into something that can be comprehended through public symbols. Its efficiency as a form is to be judged—at least by the writer—by how much of the original vision and feeling is lost or distorted by this transformation. I wished to speak of the salesman most precisely as I felt about him, to give no part of that feeling away for the sake of any effect or any dramatic necessity. What was wanted now was not a mounting line of tension, nor a gradually narrowing cone of intensifying suspense, but a bloc, a single chord presented as such at the outset, within which all the strains and melodies would already be contained. The strategy, as with *All My Sons*, was to appear entirely unstrategic but with a difference. This time, if I could, I would have told the whole story and set forth all the characters in one unbroken speech or even one sentence or a single flash of light. As I look at the play now its form seems the form of a confession, for that is how it is told, now speaking of what happened

From *Collected Plays* (New York: Viking Press, 1957), pp. 23–36.

yesterday, then suddenly following some connection to a time twenty years ago, then leaping even further back and then returning to the present and even speculating about the future.

Where in *All My Sons* it had seemed necessary to prove the connections between the present and the past, between events and moral consequences, between the manifest and the hidden, in this play all was assumed as proven to begin with. All I was doing was bringing things to mind. The assumption, also, was that everyone knew Willy Loman. I can realize this only now, it is true, but it is equally apparent to me that I took it somehow for granted then. There was still the attitude of the unveiler, but no bringing together of hitherto unrelated things; only pre-existing images, events, confrontations, moods, and pieces of knowledge. So there was a kind of confidence underlying this play which the form itself expresses, even a naïveté, a self-disarming quality that was in part born of my belief in the audience as being essentially the same as myself. If I had wanted, then, to put the audience reaction into words, it would not have been "What happens next and why?" so much as "Oh, God, of course!"

In one sense a play is a species of jurisprudence, and some part of it must take the advocate's role, something else must act in defense, and the entirety must engage the Law. Against my will, *All My Sons* states, and even proclaims, that it is a form and that a writer wrote it and organized it. In *Death of a Salesman* the original impulse was to make that same proclamation in an immeasurably more violent, abrupt, and openly conscious way. Willy Loman does not merely suggest or hint that he is at the end of his strength and of his justifications, he is hardly on the stage for five minutes when he says so; he does not gradually imply a deadly conflict with his son, an implication dropped into the midst of serenity and surface calm, he is avowedly grappling with that conflict at the outset. The ultimate matter with which the play will close is announced at the outset and is the matter of its every moment from the first. There is enough revealed in the first scene of *Death of a Salesman* to fill another kind of play which, in service to another dramatic form, would hold back and only gradually release it. I wanted to proclaim that an artist had made this play, but the nature of the proclamation was to be entirely "inartistic" and avowedly unstrategic; it was to hold back nothing, at any moment, which life would have revealed, even at the cost of suspense and climax. It was to forego the usual preparations for scenes and to permit—and even seek—whatever in each character contradicted his position in the advocate-defense scheme of its jurisprudence. The play was begun with only one firm piece of knowledge and this was that Loman was to destroy himself. How it would wander before it got to that point I did not know and resolved not to care. I was convinced only that if I could make him remember enough he would kill himself, and the structure of the play was determined by what was needed to draw up his memories like a mass of tangled roots without end or beginning.

As I have said, the structure of events and the nature of its form are also the direct reflection of Willy Loman's way of thinking at this moment of his life. He was the kind of man you see muttering to himself on a subway, decently dressed, on his way home or to the office, perfectly integrated with his surroundings excepting that unlike other people he can no longer restrain the power of his experience from disrupting the superficial sociality of his behavior. Consequently he is working on two logics which often collide. For instance, if he meets his son Happy while in the midst of some memory in which Happy disappointed him, he is instantly furious at Happy, despite the fact that Happy at this particular moment deeply desires to be of use to him. He is literally at that terrible moment when the voice of the past is no longer distant but quite as loud as the voice of the present. In dramatic terms the form, therefore, *is* this process, instead of being a once-removed summation or indication of it.

The way of telling the tale, in this sense, is as mad as Willy and as abrupt and as suddenly lyrical. And it is difficult not to add that the subsequent imitations of the form had to collapse for this particular reason. It is not possible, in my opinion, to graft it onto a character whose psychology it does not reflect, and I have not used it since because it would be false to a more integrated—or less disintegrating—personality to pretend that the past and the present are so openly and vocally intertwined in his mind. The ability of people to down their past is normal, and without it we could have no comprehensible communication among men. In the hands of writers who see it as an easy way to elicit anterior information in a play it becomes merely a flashback. There are no flashbacks in this play but only a mobile concurrency of past and present, and this, again, because in his desperation to justify his life Willy Loman has destroyed the boundaries between now and then, just as anyone would do who, on picking up his telephone, discovered that this perfectly harmless act had somehow set off an explosion in his basement. The previously assumed and believed-in results of ordinary and accepted actions, and their abrupt and unforeseen—but apparently logical—effects, form the basic collision in this play, and, I suppose, its ultimate irony.

It may be in place to remark, in this connection, that while the play was sometimes called cinematographic in its structure, it failed as a motion picture. I believe that the basic reason—aside from the gross insensitivity permeating its film production—was that the dramatic tension of Willy's memories was destroyed by transferring him, literally, to the locales he had only imagined in the play. There is an inevitable horror in the spectacle of a man losing consciousness of his immediate surroundings to the point where he engages in conversations with unseen persons. The horror is lost—and drama becomes narrative—when the context actually becomes his imagined world. And the drama evaporates because psychological truth has been amended, a truth which depends not only on what images we recall but in what connections and contexts we recall them. The setting on the stage was never shifted, despite the many changes in locale, for the precise reason that, quite simply, the mere fact that a man forgets where he is does not mean that he has really moved. Indeed, his terror springs from his never-lost awareness of time and place. It did not need this play to teach me that the screen is time-bound and earth-bound compared to the stage, if only because its preponderant emphasis is on the visual image, which, however rapidly it may be changed before our eyes, still displaces its predecessor, while scene-changing with words is instantaneous; and because of the flexibility of language, especially of English, a preceding image can be kept alive through the image that succeeds it. The movie's tendency is always to wipe out what has gone before, and it is thus in constant danger of transforming the dramatic into narrative. There is no swifter method of telling a "story" but neither is there a more difficult medium in which to keep a pattern of relationships constantly in being. Even in those sequences which retained the real backgrounds for Willy's imaginary confrontations the tension between now and then was lost. I suspect this loss was due to the necessity of shooting the actors close-up—effectively eliminating awareness of their surroundings. The basic failure of the picture was a formal one. It did not solve, nor really attempt to find, a resolution for the problem of keeping the past constantly alive, and that friction, collision, and tension between past and present was the heart of the play's particular construction.

A great deal has been said and written about what *Death of a Salesman* is supposed to signify, both psychologically and from the socio-political viewpoints. For instance, in one periodical of the far Right it was called a "time bomb expertly placed under the edifice of Americanism," while the *Daily Worker* reviewer thought it entirely decadent. In Catholic Spain it ran longer than any modern play and it has been refused production in Russia but not, from time to time, in certain satellite countries, depending on the direction and velocity of the wind. The Spanish press, thoroughly controlled by Catholic orthodoxy, regarded the play as commendable proof of the spirit's death where there is no God. In America, even as it was being cannonaded as a piece of Communist propaganda, two of the largest manufacturing corporations in the country invited me to address their sales organizations in conventions assembled, while the road company was here and there picketed by the Catholic War Veterans and the American Legion. It made only a fair impression in London, but in the area of the Norwegian Arctic Circle fishermen whose only contact with civilization was the radio and the occasional visit of the government boat insisted on seeing it night after night—the same few people—believing it to be some kind of religious rite. One organization of salesmen raised me up nearly to patron-sainthood, and another, a national sales managers' group, complained that the difficulty of recruiting salesmen was directly traceable to the play. When the movie was made, the producing company got so frightened it produced a sort of trailer to be shown before the picture, a documentary short film which demonstrated how exceptional Willy Loman was; how necessary selling is to the economy; how secure the salesman's life really is; how idiotic, in short, was the feature film they had just spent more than a million dollars to produce. Fright does odd things to people.

On the psychological front the play spawned a small hill of doctoral theses explaining its Freudian symbolism, and there were innumerable letters asking if I was aware that the fountain pen which Biff steals is a phallic symbol. Some, on the other hand, felt it was merely a fountain pen and dismissed the whole play. I received visits from men over sixty from as far away as California who had come across the country to have me write the stories of their lives, because the story of Willy Loman was exactly like theirs. The letters from women made it clear that the central character of the play was Linda; sons saw the entire action revolving around Biff or Happy, and fathers wanted advice, in effect, on how to avoid parricide. Probably the most succinct reaction to the play was voiced by a man who, on leaving the theater, said, "I always said that New England territory was no damned good." This, at least, was a fact.

That I have and had not the slightest interest in the selling profession is probably unbelievable to most people, and I very early gave up trying even to say so. And when asked what Willy was selling, what was in his bags, I could only reply, "Himself." I was trying neither to condemn a profession nor particularly to improve it, and, I will admit, I was little better than ignorant of Freud's teachings when I wrote it. There was no attempt to bring down the American edifice nor to raise it higher, to show up family relations or to cure the ills afflicting that inevitable institution. The truth, at least of my aim—which is all I can speak of authoritatively—is much simpler and more complex.

The play grew from simple images. From a little frame house on a street of little frame houses, which had once been loud with the noise of growing boys, and then was empty and silent and finally occupied by strangers. Strangers who could not know with what conquistadorial joy Willy and his boys had once re-shingled the roof. Now it was quiet in the house, and the wrong people in the beds.

It grew from images of futility—the cavernous Sunday afternoons polishing the car. Where is that car now? And the chamois cloths carefully washed and put up to dry, where are the chamois cloths?

And the endless, convoluted discussions, wonderments, arguments, belittle-ments, encouragements, fiery resolutions, abdications, returns, partings, voyages out and voyages back, tremendous opportunities and small, squeaking denoue-ments—and all in the kitchen now occupied by strangers who cannot hear what the walls are saying.

The image of aging and so many of your friends already gone and strangers in the seats of the mighty who do not know you or your triumphs or your incredible value.

The image of the son's hard, public eye upon you, no longer swept by your myth, no longer rousable from his separateness, no longer knowing you have lived for him and have wept for him.

The image of ferocity when love has turned to something else and yet is there, is somewhere in the room if one could only find it.

The image of people turning into strangers who only evaluate one another.

Above all, perhaps, the image of a need greater than hunger or sex or thirst, a need to leave a thumbprint somewhere on the world. A need for immortality, and by admitting it, the knowing that one has carefully inscribed one's name on a cake of ice on a hot July day.

I sought the relatedness of all things by isolating their unrelatedness, a man superbly alone with his sense of not having touched, and finally knowing in his extremity that the love which had always been in the room unlocated was now found.

The image of a suicide so mixed in motive as to be unfathomable and yet demanding statement. Revenge was in it and a power of love, a victory in that it would bequeath a fortune to the living and a flight from emptiness. With it an image of peace at the final curtain, the peace that is between wars, the peace leaving the issues above ground and viable yet.

And always, throughout, the image of private man in a world full of strangers, a world that is not home nor even an open battleground but only galaxies of high promise over a fear of falling.

And the image of a man making something with his hands being a rock to touch and return to. "He was always so wonderful with his hands," says his wife over his grave, and I laughed when the line came, laughed with the artist-devil's laugh, for it had all come together in this line, she having been made by him though he did not know it or believe in it or receive it into himself. Only rank, height of power, the sense of having won he believed was real—the galaxy thrust up into the sky by projectors on the rooftops of the city he believed were real stars.

It came from structural images. The play's eye was to revolve from within Willy's head, sweeping endlessly in all directions like a light on the sea, and nothing that formed in the distant mist was to be left uninvestigated. It was thought of as having the density of the novel form in its interchange of viewpoints, so that while all roads led to Willy the other characters were to feel it was their play, a story about them and not him.

There were two undulating lines in mind, one above the other, the past webbed to the present moving on together in him and sometimes openly joined and once, finally, colliding in the showdown which defined him in his eyes at least—and so to sleep.

Above all, in the structural sense, I aimed to make a play with the veritable countenance of life. To make one the many, as in life, so that "society" is a power and a mystery of custom and inside the man and surrounding him, as the fish is in the sea and the sea inside the fish, his birthplace and burial ground, promise and threat. To speak commonsensically of social facts which every businessman knows and talks about but which are too prosaic to mention or are usually fancied up on the stage as philosophical problems. When a man gets old you fire him, you have to, he can't do the work. To speak and even to celebrate the common sense of businessmen, who love the personality that wins the day but know that you've got to have the right goods at the right price, handsome and well-spoken as you are. (To some, these were scandalous and infamous arraignments of society when uttered in the context of art. But not the businessmen themselves; they knew it was all true and I cherished their clear-eyed talk.)

The image of a play without transitional scenes was there in the beginning. There was too much to say to waste precious stage time with feints and preparations, in themselves agonizing "structural" bridges for a writer to work out since they are not why he is writing. There was a resolution, as in *All My Sons,* not to waste motion or moments, but in this case to shear through everything up to the meat of a scene; a resolution not to write an unmeant word for the sake of the form but to make the form give and stretch and contract for the sake of the thing to be said. To cling to the process of Willy's mind as the form the story would take.

The play was always heroic to me, and in later years the academy's charge that Willy lacked the "stature" for the tragic hero seemed incredible to me. I had not understood that these matters are measured by Greco-Elizabethan paragraphs which hold no mention of insurance payments, front porches, refrigerator fan belts, steering knuckles, Chevrolets, and visions seen not through the portals of Delphi but in the blue flame of the hot-water heater. How could "Tragedy" make people weep, of all things?

I set out not to "write a tragedy" in this play, but to show the truth as I saw it. However, some of the attacks upon it as a pseudo-tragedy contain ideas so misleading, and in some cases so laughable, that it might be in place here to deal with a few of them.

Aristotle having spoken of a fall from the heights, it goes without saying that someone of the common mold cannot be a fit tragic hero. It is now many centuries since Aristotle lived. There is no more reason for falling down in a faint before his *Poetics* than before Euclid's geometry, which has been amended numerous times by men with new insights; nor, for that matter, would I choose to have my illnesses diagnosed by Hippocrates rather than the most ordinary graduate of an American medical school, despite the Greek's genius. Things do change, and even a genius is limited by his time and the nature of his society.

I would deny, on grounds of simple logic, this one of Aristotle's contentions if only because he lived in a slave society. When a vast number of people are divested of alternatives, as slaves are, it is rather inevitable that one will not be able to imagine drama, let alone tragedy, as being possible for any but the higher ranks of society. There is a legitimate question of stature here, but none of rank, which is so often confused with it. So long as the hero may be said to have had alternatives of a magnitude to have materially changed the course of his life, it seems to me that in this respect at least, he cannot be debarred from the heroic role.

The question of rank is significant to me only as it reflects the question of the social application of the hero's career. There is no doubt that if a character is shown on the stage who goes through the most ordinary actions, and is suddenly revealed to be the President of the United States, his actions immediately assume a much greater magnitude, and pose the possibilities of much greater meaning, than if he is the corner grocer. But at the same time, his stature as a hero is not so utterly dependent upon his rank that the corner grocer cannot outdistance him as a tragic figure—providing, of course, that the grocer's career engages the issues of, for instance, the survival of the race, the relationships of man to God—the questions, in short, whose answers define humanity and the right way to live so that the world is a home, instead of a battleground or a fog in which disembodied spirits pass each other in an endless twilight.

In this respect *Death of a Salesman* is a slippery play to categorize because nobody in it stops to make a speech objectively stating the great issues which I believe it embodies. If it were a worse play, less closely articulating its meanings with its actions, I think it would have more quickly satisfied a certain kind of criticism. But it was meant to be less a play than a fact; it refused admission to its author's opinions and opened itself to a revelation of process and the operations of an ethic, of social laws of action no less powerful in their effects upon individuals than any tribal law administered by gods with names. I need not claim that this play is a genuine solid gold tragedy for my opinions on tragedy to be held valid. My purpose here is simply to point out a historical fact which must be taken into account in any consideration of tragedy, and it is the sharp alteration in the meaning of rank in society between the present time and the distant past. More important to me is the fact that this particular kind of argument obscures much more relevant considerations.

One of these is the question of intensity. It matters not at all whether a modern play concerns itself with a grocer or a president if the intensity of the hero's commitment to his course is less than the maximum possible. It matters not at all whether the hero falls from a great height or a small one, whether he is highly conscious or only dimly aware of what is happening, whether his pride brings the fall or an unseen pattern written behind the clouds; if the intensity, the human passion to surpass his given bounds, the fanatic insistence upon his self-conceived role—if these are not present there can only be an outline of tragedy but no living thing. I believe, for myself, that the lasting appeal of tragedy is due to our need to face the fact of death in order to strengthen ourselves for life, and that over and above this function of the tragic viewpoint there are and will be a great number of formal variations which no single definition will ever embrace.

Another issue worth considering is the so-called tragic victory, a question closely related to the consciousness of the hero. One makes nonsense of this if a "victory" means that the hero makes us feel some certain joy when, for instance, he sacrifices himself for "cause," and unhappy and morose because he dies without one. To begin at the bottom, a man's death is and ought to be an essentially terrifying thing and ought to make nobody happy. But in a great variety of ways even death, the ultimate negative, can be, and appear to be, an assertion of bravery, and can serve to separate the death of man from the death of animals; and I think it is this distinction which underlies any conception of a victory in death. For a society of faith, the nature of the death can prove the existence of the spirit, and posit its immortality. For a secular society it is perhaps more difficult for such a victory to document itself and to make itself felt, but, conversely, the need to offer greater proofs of the humanity of man can make that victory more real. It goes without saying that in a society where there is basic disagreement as to the right way to live, there can hardly be agreement as to the right way to die, and both life and death must be heavily weighted with meaningless futility.

It was not out of any deference to a tragic definition that Willy Loman is filled with a joy, however broken-hearted, as he approaches his end, but simply that my sense of his character dictated his joy, and even what I felt was an exultation. In terms of his character, he has achieved a very powerful piece of knowledge, which is that he is loved by his son and has been embraced by him and forgiven. In this he is given his existence, so to speak—his fatherhood, for which he has always striven and which until now he could not achieve. That he is unable to take this victory thoroughly to his heart, that it closes the circle for him and propels him to his death, is the wage of his sin, which was to have committed himself so completely to the counterfeits of dignity and the false coinage embodied in his idea of success that he can prove his existence only by bestowing "power" on his posterity, a power deriving from the sale of his last asset, himself, for the price of his insurance policy.

I must confess here to a miscalculation, however. I did not realize while writing the play that so many people in the world do not see as clearly, or would not admit, as I thought they must, how futile most lives are; so there could be no hope of consoling the audience for the death of this man. I did not realize either how few would be impressed by the fact that this man is actually a very brave spirit who cannot settle for half but must pursue his dream of himself to the end. Finally, I thought it must be clear, even obvious, that this was no dumb brute heading mindlessly to his catastrophe.

I have no need to be Willy's advocate before the jury which decides who is and who is not a tragic hero. I am merely noting that the lingering ponderousness of so many ancient definitions has blinded students and critics to the facts before them, and not only in regard to this play. Had Willy been unaware of his separation from values that endure he would have died contentedly while polishing his car, probably on a Sunday afternoon with the ball game coming over the radio. But he was agonized by his awareness of being in a false position, so constantly haunted by the hollowness of all he had placed his faith in, so aware, in short, that he must somehow be filled in his spirit or fly apart, that he staked his very life on the ultimate assertion. That he had not the intellectual fluency to verbalize his situation is not the same thing as saying that he lacked awareness, even an overly intensified consciousness that the life he had made was without form and inner meaning.

To be sure, had he been able to know that he was as much the victim of his beliefs as their defeated exemplar, had he known how much of guilt he ought to bear and how much to shed from his soul, he would be more conscious. But it seems to me that there is of necessity a severe limitation of self-awareness in any character, even the most knowing, which serves to define him as a character, and more, that this very limit serves to complete the tragedy and, indeed, to make it all possible. Complete consciousness is possible only in a play about forces, like *Prometheus*, but not in a play about people. I think that the point is whether there is a sufficient awareness in the hero's career to make the audience supply the rest. Had Oedipus, for instance, been more conscious and more aware of the forces at work upon him he must surely have said that he was not really to blame for having cohabited with his mother since neither he nor anyone else knew she was his mother. He must surely decide to divorce her, provide for their children, firmly resolve to investigate the family background of his next wife, and thus deprive us of a very fine play and the name for a famous neurosis. But he is conscious only up to a point, the point at which guilt begins. Now he is inconsolable and must tear out his eyes. What is tragic about this? Why is it not even ridiculous? How can we respect a man who goes to such extremities over something he could in no way help or prevent? The answer, I think, is not that we respect the man, but that we respect the Law he has so completely broken, wittingly or not, for it is that Law which, we believe, defines us as men. The confusion of some critics viewing *Death of a Salesman* in this regard is that they do not see that Willy Loman has broken a law without whose protection life is insupportable if not incomprehensible to him and to many others; it is the law which says that a failure in society and in business has no right to live. Unlike the law against incest, the law of success is not administered by statute or church, but it is very nearly as powerful in its grip upon men. The confusion increases because, while it is a law, it is by no means a wholly agreeable one even as it is slavishly obeyed, for to fail is no longer to belong to society, in his estimate. Therefore, the path is opened for those who wish to call Willy merely a foolish man even as they themselves are living in obedience to the same law that killed him. Equally, the fact that Willy's law—the belief, in other words, which administers guilt to him—is not a civilizing statute whose destruction menaces us all: it is, rather, a deeply believed and deeply suspect "good" which, when questioned as to its value, as it is in this play, serves more to raise our anxieties than to reassure us of the existence of an unseen but humane metaphysical system in the world. My attempt in the play was to counter this anxiety with an opposing system which, so to speak, is in a race for Willy's faith, and it is the system of love which is the opposite of the law of success. It is embodied in Biff Loman, but by the time Willy can perceive his love it can serve only as an ironic comment upon the life he sacrificed for power and for success and its tokens.

DEATH OF A SALESMAN:
A SYMPOSIUM

PHILLIP GELB: This series is concerned with "Ideas and the Theatre," and we feel Arthur Miller is qualified both as a thinker and as a dramatist. Actually, I think he also qualifies as a kind of prophet. He is a prophet in the sense that he warns us of the possible bitter harvest that may be reaped from our present limited ways; he calls attention to the moral and ethical decisions that must be made; and he dramatizes the problem and the need for individuality and will. These may well prove to be the ultimate meanings of hope. But why hope? *Death of a Salesman* is generally thought to be Mr. Miller's most important play; is it an affirming one? Let's refresh our memories.

RICHARD WATTS: The title, *Death of a Salesman,* has the virtues not only of being striking and provocative, but also of telling forthrightly what the drama is about. Mr. Miller is describing the last days of a man who is forced to face the terrible fact that he is a failure; that his vague ideal of success has crumbled; that his sons, on whose respect and success he has counted, have only contempt for him. With the utter collapse of Willy Loman's world, there is nothing for him to do but die. The story is as simple as that, and there is such truth in it that it is hard to see how any sensitive playgoer can fail to find something of himself in the mirror that it holds up to life. Only the fatuous observer could think of *Death of a Salesman* as a propaganda play, and yet it manages to go so deeply into contemporary values that it becomes a valid and frightening social criticism. Mr. Miller looks upon the salesman ideal of success with an angry but discerning eye, and he sees its hollowness and treachery. Poor Willy Loman, who thought that for a successful salesman popularity and good fellowship were all and tried to teach his sons what he believed was his wisdom, is a completely credible victim of a prevailing code as the encroachment of old age destroys its shabby plausibility. Set down with frank emotions (this) play is, I suspect, something to make strong men weep and think.

From *Tulane Drama Review* 2, No. 3 (May 1958): 63–69.

GELB: Mr. Watts, that was an excerpt from your review of the play when it first opened in 1949; do you think the play still stands up?

WATTS: Oh yes, I think so. The curious thing about this play is that it really was a tragedy for extroverts. The more extroverted people were that went to it, the more they seemed to be moved by it. Usually with a tragedy here, the wives drag their protesting husbands along and the husbands have an awful time and the wives cry. But I saw again and again that it would be the husband who would be moved by *Death of a Salesman*. He would see something of himself in it. He would get far more out of it usually than his wife did.

GELB: If *Death of a Salesman* is so starkly pessimistic, what is so special about it?

MARTIN DWORKIN: The play is special and Miller's most meaningful work, because he really hit something deep in America when he made that play. The great American idea of the salesman goes back to the old Yankee trader of the Sam Slick type and exists today in the modern huckster who doesn't carry a suitcase or a sample-kit but sells, and in selling he has to take a part of what is human and make it marketable and put a price on it. I consider this Miller's greatest play because his own great skill, his dramatic sense, his artistry, gets beyond his argument so successfully. He has some severe criticisms to make of our society, and yet *Death of a Salesman* criticizes without being propaganda because the characters are so real. The play is an illustration of that paradoxical problem, that so often emerges when discussing works of art, in which the more valid the particularity gets, the more universal it is an exemplification. Willy Loman comes to represent a certain danger, a certain menace, a certain integral nature in salesmanship in general, because he is so much a particular Willy Loman and not simply a slogan out of the 1930's. He represents a condition where a man necessarily has to go out into space with nothing but a smile and a shoe shine and that packet of samples he is selling and get that order! This strange man, out in space, completely divorced from the fundamental productive processes which manufacture the merchandise that he is selling, not quite the friend and not quite the enemy and not quite the instrument of the people to whom he is selling, somehow, this strange intermediary must sell himself in order to sell things.

GORE VIDAL: I disagree! I don't think the play is about salesmanship and money. Rather I think it is more concerned with a human being who tries to live by a certain set of standards to which he cannot measure up and what happens to him as he fails. I think money is a part of it, but it is much more simply keeping up with the Joneses, and bit by bit failing, and what happens. And Mr. Miller is quite beautifully saying that attention must be paid to this sort of failure in our society. I think Miller in a sense sentimentalizes it because I don't think the problem is all that great. I think people adjust to failure quite beautifully, since that is the lot of nearly all of us. It is not as tragic as that, even in this society at the level of a salesman on the Boston route. But except for a certain sentimentality in the handling of it, I think it showed a situation which nobody else had showed on the stage.

JOHN BEAUFORT: I am not sure I agree here. I do not believe Willy Loman is a tragic character. I think that he is a sad character. I think he is a vicious character. The trouble with Willy Loman, as a figure in dramatic tragedy, is that he never starts with any ideals to begin with. He is a man who, from the very beginning of the play, says it is a question of whether you're liked or whether you're well-liked. He encourages his sons to steal and cheat. He has no moral values at all.

GELB: But what if one asks, isn't this Americana? Isn't this the common man?

BEAUFORT: It's one phase of Americana; but if Willy Loman truly represented the whole mass of American civilization of today, I think that the country would be in a terrible state. I just can't accept Willy Loman as the average American citizen. I can accept him as a specimen of a certain aspect of society. We all know that people like Willy Loman exist, and Miller has every right to write about him. I'm perfectly willing to accept him as a dramatic character on the stage; but I will not for a minute accept Willy Loman as the American "Everyman." I think that is nonsense.

GELB: What reasons are there for people doing things in our mid-twentieth century other than to be liked or well-liked or to realize more material benefits? I suppose what I'm asking is how much of an influence, if any, do you think the moral and spiritual factors are in our time?

BEAUFORT: I think they're still very substantially influential. I'm not a social historian; I'm not a sociologist. All I'm willing to say is that I believe that for the most part the people in the United States are motivated by many such things or other and many finer things than Willy Loman was motivated by: love of country, religious principles, and ethical values. . . . I mean you only have to consider in any situation the response of the American people to a disaster and the need for help to see that we are not an indifferent people. We are a concerned people. Oh, I don't mean to say that we never manifest indifference, we do; but all I'm trying to say is that you couldn't, at least I couldn't, accept Willy Loman as the reflection of the mean of American society in terms of the individual citizen. It just wouldn't be possible.

GELB: Arthur Miller, how valid and pertinent are Mr. Beaufort's observations?

ARTHUR MILLER: The trouble with Willy Loman is that he has tremendously powerful ideals. We're not accustomed to speaking of ideals in his terms; but, if Willy Loman, for instance, had not had a very profound sense that his life as lived had left him hollow, he would have died contentedly polishing his car on some Sunday afternoon at a ripe old age. The fact is he has values. The fact that they cannot be realized is what is driving him mad—just as, unfortunately, it's driving a lot of other people mad. The truly valueless man, a man without ideals, is always perfectly at home anywhere . . . because there cannot be a conflict between nothing and something. Whatever negative qualities there are in the society or in the environment don't bother him, because they are not in conflict with what positive sense one may have. I think Willy Loman, on the other hand, is seeking for a kind of ecstasy in life, which the machine-civilization deprives people of. He's looking for his selfhood, for his immortal soul, so to speak. People who don't know the intensity of the quest, possibly, think he's odd. Now an extraordinary large number of salesmen particularly, who are in a line of work where a large measure of ingenuity and individualism are required, have a very intimate understanding of this problem. More so, I think, than literary critics who probably need strive less after a certain point. A salesman is a kind of creative person (it's possibly idiotic to say so on a literary program, but they are), they have to get up in the morning and conceive a plan of attack and use all kinds of ingenuity all day long, just the way a writer does.

GELB: What about this, Mr. Miller? John Beaufort made the statement that if Willy Loman represented the whole mass of American civilization today, the country would be in a terrible state. He would not for a moment accept Willy Loman as an average American man.

MILLER: Well, it's obvious that Willy Loman can't be an average American man, at least from one point of view; he kills himself. That's a rare thing in society, although it's more common than one could wish. But this "being average" is beside the point. As a matter of fact, the standard of averageness is hardly valid. It tells neither whether a character is a truthful character, as a character, nor a valid one. It's ridiculous. Hamlet isn't a typical Elizabethan either. Horatio probably is. What's the difference? It has no point unless we are not talking about literature but about patriotism. I did not write *Death of a Salesman* to announce a new American man, or an old American man. Willy Loman is, I think, a person who embodies in him some of the most terrible conflicts running through the streets of America today. A Gallup poll might not indicate that they are the majority conflicts; I think they are; but then what is the difference?

GELB: Earlier, Martin Dworkin said that he feels the play makes a statement about the average American man because Willy Loman is such a particular Willy Loman. Do you feel that the best way to present a universal is in terms of a really specific story?

MILLER: It is the best way! It is the hardest way too! The ability to create the universal from the particular is not given to many authors, nor to any single author many times. You have to know the particular in your bones to do this. But it is the best way. As the few plays that are repeatedly done over generations and centuries show, they are generally, in our Western Culture anyway, those plays which are full of the most particular information about the people.

GELB: What about this question of hope and hopelessness? I mean, is there a chance to make the positive value in drama dramatic? Or is drama, by its very nature, only an attack upon things?

MILLER: Not only drama, but literature in general—and this goes back a long, long distance in history—posits the idea of value, of right and wrong, of good and bad, high and low, not so much by setting forth, but by showing so to speak, the wages of sin. In other words, when, for instance in *Death of a Salesman*, we are shown a man who dies for the want of some positive, viable human value, the play implies—and it could not have been written without the author's consciousness that the audience did believe something different. In other words, by showing what happens where there are no values, I at least, assume that the audience will be compelled and propelled toward a more intense quest for the values that are missing. I am assuming always that we have a kind of civilized sharing of what we would like to see occur within us and within the world. I think that the drama, at least mine, is not so much an attack but an exposition of "the want." This kind of drama can be done only if the audience itself is constantly trying to supply what is missing.

GELB: Although critic John Beaufort and playwright Arthur Miller seem to be in some disagreement over the character of Willy Loman, I think it is even more significant to note that Mr. Beaufort, in his earlier comments, came up with the very conclusion that Mr. Miller wanted from his play—the conclusion that there is a better way than Willy's way, that we can act on more meaningful values. In other words, John Beaufort supplies some of what Arthur Miller seems to be suggesting as the missing moral links between the Death of a Salesman and the Life of a Man. The day I first interviewed Arthur Miller was shortly after the Russians had launched the first satellite. This led me to ask Mr. Miller as to whether or not the various sciences, from nuclear physics to psychology, hadn't made the contemporary artist's job too difficult by giving him too many facts and views to consider. Under this deluge of knowledge, weren't apathy, anxiety and cynicism the natural results? Could any creative writer take even most of the available information and insights into consideration and still write creatively?

MILLER: Well, whether it can be done remains for me or somebody else to prove. But let me put it this way: we're living, or I'm living anyway, with a great consciousness of the incredible force of objective thought. As we speak, there is an object flying around in the sky passing over this point every, I think it's one hundred and some minutes, which was put up there by thinking men who willed it to go up there. The implications of this are as enormous as any statement by or on the part of Zeus, or Moses, or Shakespeare, or any feeling man. Now, it may be a great bite to take, but I think the only thing worth doing (whether one can do it or not is an entirely different story, but aims are important) today in the theatre, from my point of view, is to synthesize the subjective drives of the human being with what is now demonstrably the case. Namely, that by acts of will he can and has changed the world. It is said that nothing is new under the sun. This is! It's right under the sun, and it's new! But it's only one of many things that are new. I've seen communities transformed by the act of a committee. I've seen the interior lives of people transformed by the decision of a company, or of a man, or of a school. In other words, it is old fashioned to simply go on asserting the helplessness of the individual.

GELB: You're not in the large "artistic" camp then of those who write of, by, and for despair.

MILLER: Well, for myself I can't write anything if I'm sufficiently unhappy. A lot of writers write best when they're most miserable. I suppose my sense of form comes from a positive need to organize life and not from a desire to demonstrate the inevitability of defeat and death.

GELB: Do you think this becomes a kind of final analysis of many issues in life—social, political, economical, psychological? You made a statement putting you on the side of life against death. Aren't many "final answers" dependent upon whether this is or is not a basic commitment?

MILLER: It is a commitment on my part. I don't see the point in proving again that we must be defeated. I didn't intend that in *Salesman*. I was trying in *Salesman*, in this respect, to set forth what happens when a man does not have a grip on the forces of life and has no sense of values which will lead him to that kind of a grip; but the implication of it was that there must be such a grasp of those forces—or else we're doomed. I was not, in other words, Willy Loman. I was the writer, and Willy Loman is there because I could see beyond him.

DAVID W. THOMPSON: In summary then, "the curious thing" about Arthur Miller's *Death of a Salesman* is, as Mr. Watts said, that it really is "a tragedy for extroverts." In older drama, for example in Molière, a bumbling, simple-minded hustler is always a figure of fun. He is the object of satiric criticism. Mr. Miller does criticize his salesman but earnestly, without a trace of the older comic view. And what is really curious is that the play, besides criticizing Willy Loman's dishonesty and vulgarity, asks that a great deal of sympathy and attention be paid to the failure himself. Willy is shown to be wrong in every respect of human decency but is still expected to be a great tragic figure. This asking for more sympathy than the facts seem to deserve is what gives, as Mr. Vidal said, "a certain sentimentality" to the play. As Mr. Beaufort put it, "I think that Willy Loman is not a tragic character. I think that he is a sad character. I think he is a vicious character. The trouble with Willy Loman, as a figure in dramatic tragedy, is that he never starts with any ideals to begin with. . . . He has no moral values at all."

This word "values" set off the big controversy in today's program. In his reply to Mr. Beaufort's charge, Mr. Miller at first insisted that Willy Loman "has tremendously powerful ideals. . . . The fact is that he has values . . . (he) is seeking for a kind of ecstasy in life." (One might note here in passing that the universal, primitive egotism of a child always leads to a generalized "seeking for a kind of ecstasy in life"—its worth depends entirely upon what specific values and forms mark that search, especially in adult life.) Later, Mr. Miller seemed to contradict himself by saying that his play shows "what happens where there are no values," and that Willy Loman has "no sense of values" which will lead him to "a grip on the forces of life." This contradiction, of course, proves very little, except perhaps that Mr. Miller, fortunately for us, is a playwright and not a dramatic theorist.

There was, after all, general agreement among the participants as to Mr. Miller's important, even leading, position as a contemporary American dramatist. There was no denying that his *Death of a Salesman* is a powerful play giving a true-to-life portrayal of a certain type of American, who, as Mr. Dworkin said, is as old as the Sam Slick Yankee trader and as current as the modern huckster. If some of us, like Mr. Vidal, and Mr. Beaufort, feel the play is marred by a certain senti-mentality in its demanding so much sympathy for Willy, this may only mean that we are neither salesmen nor extroverts.

Perhaps in older, tougher days the subject of a foolish, childish salesman, plus Mr. Miller's keen sense of realistic detail, would have produced a biting social satire. Today, however, it is certainly not Mr. Miller's fault that his audience, composed mainly of hucksters, will accept criticism only in a sympathetic "tragedy for extro-verts."

Ruby Cohn

THE ARTICULATE VICTIMS
OF ARTHUR MILLER

Both *All My Sons* and Miller's best-known play, *Death of a Salesman* (1949), presumably dramatize WASP families, since Miller does not specify racial or religious origins. Mary McCarthy has scolded Miller for concealing the Jewishness of the Loman family,[1] and Leslie Fiedler has claimed that Miller creates "crypto-Jewish characters ... who are presented as something else." Miller has countered that "Jewishing" the families would undercut their all-American typicality, and Miller views the drive toward success as all-American.[2] In *Death of a Salesman* Miller uses an appropriately informal syntax and many casual repetitions to suggest an all-American quality. It is hardly relevant to claim, as does George Steiner, that "The brute snobbish fact is that men who die speaking as does Macbeth are more tragic than those who sputter platitudes in the style of Willy Loman."[3] *Macbeth* today can be food for farce, not tragedy, as illustrated by the success of *McBird* and the failure of *Makbeth*. And platitudes can be meaningful if the total play rises above them.

Whatever Miller may have written afterwards, *Death of a Salesman* is larger than Willy Loman, and a variety of dialogue contrasts with his platitudes. Leonard Moss mentions a hundred odd repetitions of the word "man," about a hundred of "boy" and "kid" (with its easy, undiscriminating bisexual affection), about fifty variants of the verb "to make."[4] But this flatness is relieved by Charley's cynical urban idiom, Uncle Ben's rugged phrases, Linda's sententious or sentimental outbursts, Happy's wise guy banter, Biff's lyricism about Nature, and, most important of all, the range of Willy Loman's clichés.

Like Buechner's Woyzeck, Willy's feelings overflow his language. But Woyzeck is sparing of words, and Willy is lavish. He himself admits: "I talk too much. . . . I joke too much!" And Miller dramatizes the "too much" in comparison with the dialogue of the other characters. As in *Woyzeck,* there is no raisonneur or norm character; there are only different inadequacies expressed through different idioms. Unlike

From *Dialogue in American Drama* (Bloomington: Indiana University Press, 1971), pp. 70–79.

Buechner, Miller does not use folk songs and the Bible to cement his modern Tower of Babel. And yet, the moral logic of the play reveals the bankruptcy of Willy's language.

The original title of *Death of a Salesman* was *The Inside of His Head*, and Miller's dramatic achievement has been the skillful manipulation of Willy's last hours to reveal what goes on inside his head. In Act I four extended memory scenes are climaxed by Biff's discovery of the woman in his father's hotel room. Near the end of Act II Willy has a fantasy of asking his dead brother Ben for advice about his own suicide. Through blocking, lighting, and music, Miller sets off these verbal excursions into Willy's memory and fantasy, so that we never confuse them with the suspenseful present.

We are able to shuttle between past and present because of the "partially transparent" Loman house. Jo Mielziner's set for the original New York production of *Salesman* is a descendant of Strindberg's set for *Ghost Sonata*. Perhaps under Strindberg's influence, O'Neill built similarly in *Desire under the Elms*; Williams continued the mode in *Glass Menagerie* and *Streetcar Named Desire*. And *Salesman* is the last of the series.

The English critic Dennis Welland has summarized the thematic importance of these transparent settings: "The cataclysms that cause the fall of the frontage of the houses of Eugene O'Neill's Ephraim Cabot and Ezra Mannon, of Tennessee Williams's Amanda Wingfield and Stanley Kowalski, and of Miller's Willy Loman, are psychological rather than meteorological. . . . The 'exploded' house set is integral to the impression at which all these plays aim, for not only does it mirror the family combustion that has come more and more to dominate the American theatre, but it is peculiarly suited to their dramatic idiom."[5] Particularly astute is Welland's recognition that the exploded house is background for an exploding idiom. *Desire*, *Salesman*, and *Menagerie* abound in expletives and sentence fragments. Without the blatant subjectivism of expressionist drama, these plays nevertheless seek to make a similarly general statement, transcending realism. Miller has called attention to his "expressionistic elements . . . to create a subjective truth" in *Death of a Salesman*.[6] And the father of such elements is Strindberg in his *Dream Play*.

Miller has often acknowledged his debt to Ibsen rather than Strindberg, and yet *The Dream Play* is the ancestor of *Death of a Salesman*, where dream is theme, refrain, and technique. Rather than a tragedy of failure, as the play is often described, *Death of a Salesman* dramatizes the failure of a *dream*. The intrusion of Willy's past and fantasy into his present resembles a dream, and the word "dream" recurs, from the early scenic direction: *"An air of the dream clings to the place, a dream rising out of reality."* through the introduction of Willy's sons: "[Biff's] *dreams are stronger and less acceptable than Happy's."* to the triple evocation in the Requiem:

BIFF: He had the wrong dreams.
HAPPY: He had a good dream.
CHARLEY: A salesman is got to dream, boy. It comes with the territory.

Miller's play is as much about the salesman's dreams as about his death, but death lies imminent in Willy's dreams.

Though Willy is prey to the American dream of success, and to the tribal dream of success through heirs, the dream itself is vague in detail. Only obliquely does Willy's success dream come "with the territory," through salesmanship; rather, Willy feels that success will come in some undefined way, through the most insistent phrase in the play—being "well liked."[7] The phrase is Willy's, but it is echoed by Linda, Biff, and Happy. Only Charley challenges this central aspect of Willy's dream, and he does so with a pithy Jewish inflection: "Why must everybody like you? Who liked J. P. Morgan? Was he impressive? In a Turkish bath he'd look like a butcher. But with his pockets on he was very well liked." While Willy tries to win friends and influence people, Charley insists that money talks; each of them voices a different aspect of the success dream.

Willy is sufficiently sure of his dream to reject Charley—advice and money. But at the same time he is so insecure in his dream that he carries on a lifelong debate with his brother Ben. Both Charley and Ben—a small businessman and a ruthless adventurer—are foils for Willy, and their respective idioms contrast with his simple clichés of success through popularity. Charley's salty prose has been quoted, and Ben speaks in active epigrams: "Never fight fair with a stranger, boy." But monosyllabically and boisterously, Willy preaches popularity more loudly than he is able to practice it. Though Willy sometimes claims to be well liked, he confides to Linda that people laugh at him instead of liking him. Even his infidelity is the result of making a woman laugh. Certainly he often makes *us* laugh—in large part by the juxtaposition of his ephemeral dream against the irritating concreteness of his Chevvy, Studebaker, and Hastings refrigerator. We may not know what Willy sells, but we know what he buys: "The refrigerator consumes belts like a goddam maniac." The death of the salesman is foreshadowed in the comic deaths of his installment-plan purchases, which we witness only through dialogue.

A sequence of shiny, treacherous machines is suggested through the play's abrupt opening and Willy's first memory scene. In these two important early scenes, Biff's boyhood popularity is contrasted with Willy's laughableness. The memory scene begins when Willy praises Biff for polishing his car, but he soon gives advice about the girls with whom Biff is "makin' a hit." At the end of Willy's recollection of Biff's day of success, Willy boasts and complains in typical self-contradiction: "Oh, I'll knock 'em dead next week. I'll go to Hartford. I'm very well liked in Hartford. You know, the trouble is, Linda, people don't seem to take to me." As he describes how people laugh at him, a woman's laugh is heard, introducing Willy's memory within a memory. Unlike the girls who pay for Biff, Willy's Woman has to be bought with silk stockings, while Linda mends her stockings at home. When Willy returns to his first memory, all is soured—Biff is failing math, he steals, the mothers complain that he is too rough with the girls. The emotional shift—conveyed entirely by dialogue—foreshadows the play's climactic confrontation between Willy and Biff.

The opening scenes of Act II not only develop the precarious quality of Willy's dream; they also set up father-son foils to Willy-Biff. Old man Wagner's son Howard is successful by inheritance, and his idiom reflects his security. Charley's son Bernard is successful by hard work, and his idiom reflects his studiousness. Both sons succeed within the framework of American capitalism. Yet Biff is a failure because he remained a slave to his father's "phoney dream" even after he has rejected his father as a "phoney fake." His idiom reflects his immaturity; even his name is a boy's nickname.

In the swift sequence of scenes in Howard's office, Charley's office, Frank's chop-house, Miller skillfully disintegrates Willy's dream for us (though not for him). The scene in Howard's office offers a paradigm for the whole play: Howard is no more faithful to his father's memory than Willy is to the memory of his father's flutes; Howard is as blind and provincial about his children as Willy is about his; Howard speaks inconsiderately to his wife, as Willy does to Linda. The tape-recorder is a symbol of both Howard and Willy, with ready-made phrases uttered mechanically. Howard and Willy show two sides of American progress: one is failure and the other success, with little to choose between them.

In Howard's office Willy evokes the memory of the great salesman, Dave Singleman, whose name denies "a dime a dozen." Singleman is singular, unique. He achieved the popularity to which Willy aspired; it is his death, narrated by Willy, that evokes the play's title: "When he died—and by the way he died the death of a salesman, in his green velvet slippers in the smoker of the New York, New Haven and Hartford, going into Boston—when he died, hundreds of salesmen and buyers were at his funeral." And that is the kind of funeral Willy envisions for himself. After leaving Biff his insurance, Willy addresses the fantasy figure of his dead brother Ben: "Ben, that funeral will be massive! They'll come from Maine, Massachusetts, Vermont, New Hampshire! All the old-timers with the strange license plates—that boy will be thunderstruck, Ben, because he never realized—I am known! Rhode Island, New York, New Jersey—I am known, Ben, and he'll see it with his eyes once and for all." Geography and repetition sound lyric notes for Willy, but the old-timers with the strange license plates are dead, if they ever existed; only the family and faithful Charley come to Willy's actual funeral.

The imaginary funeral underlines the poverty of Willy's imagination. Compare his listing of states with the vision of Genet's Solange for the funeral of a maid: "The funeral will unfold its pomp. It's beautiful; isn't it? First come the butlers, in full livery, but without silk lining. They're wearing their crowns. Then come the footmen, the lackeys in knee breeches and white stockings. They're wearing their crowns. Then come the valets, and the chambermaids wearing our colors. Then the porters. And then come the delegations from heaven." (Frechtman translation) Pomp and circumstance create a mythology, so that servitude bursts its bonds to achieve royalty—in the imagination of a maid.

Willy's linguistic poverty, by contrast, reflects both the poverty of his world and the poverty of his dream. Henry Popkin has described Willy's world as "full of aspirin, arch supports, saccharine (all the wrong cures for what ails Willy), Stude-bakers, Chevrolets, shaving lotion, refrigerators, silk stockings, washing machines."[8] But the first three items are (perhaps) remedies, and most of the others break down. Willy's life embodies the contradiction between these concrete trivialities and his grandiose verbal projections. In past, present, and fantasy, Willy usually expresses himself through repetition and cliché, a formulaic chant which is unaf-fected by the stubbornness of things. "*An air of the dream*" may "ris[e] *out of reality*," but Willy's vague dream is at odds with concrete reality. He has achieved neither popularity nor success as a salesman, and he has failed as gardener, car-penter, and father.

Willy's opening words suggest his immaturity: "Oh, boy, oh, boy." To the figure of Ben he confesses that he feels "kind of temporary" about himself. His repetitions of "The woods are burning" indicate some perception of the Inferno in which he lives, but his perception is limited. Willy's Hell may be paved with good intentions, but even they appear to be rationalizations after the fact; Willy dreams of success for Biff because he himself is a failure. Willy refuses Charley's charity because he himself cannot accept the truth of his failure. Though he has been toying with the idea of suicide, Willy actually kills himself only when he can disguise his death as a gift to Biff.

Miller and others have written many pages about Willy Loman, the low man. Consistently conceived, Willy does not speak out of character.[9] But Miller disturbs his own thematic consistency by his climactic scene—Willy's memory of Biff's discovery of a woman in his Boston hotel room. Willy's dream, vague in detail, is the American dream of success. Though Willy dies without recognizing the triviality of his dream, the play makes *us* aware of that triviality. Before the climax, Miller dramatizes Biff's recognition of the impossibility, if not the insubstantiality, of Willy's dream. We see Willy rejected by Howard, and we hear of Biff's parallel rejection by Oliver.

The scene of Biff's self-recognition is a recognition of the phoniness of his father's dream. Rhythmically colloquial—"He thinks I've been spiting him all these years and it's eating him up."—pointedly economical—"We've been talking in a dream for fifteen years."—the dialogue is nervous with questions, interruptions, and muted repetitions.

WILLY: What happened? He took you into his office and what?
BIFF: Well—I talked. And—and he listened, see.
WILLY: Famous for the way he listens, y'know. What was his answer?
BIFF: His answer was—(*He breaks off, suddenly angry*). Dad, you're not letting me tell you what I want to tell you!

WILLY (*accusing, angered*): You didn't see him, did you?

BIFF: I did see him!

WILLY: What'd you insult him or something? You insulted him, didn't you?

BIFF: Listen, will you let me out of it, will you just let me out of it!

HAPPY: What the hell!

WILLY: Tell me what happened!

BIFF (*to Happy*): I can't talk to him!

The repetitions of "listen" stress Willy's inability to listen to any contradiction of his dream. Uttered without strain, Biff's "I can't talk to him" summarizes the scene and Biff's whole life.

Biff's recognition scene dovetails neatly with Willy's next memory scene, but the two are not related thematically. A phoney dream of success should be exploded by a scene about the phoniness of success, and not about illicit sex. The final tableau of the scene leaves us with a strong impression of Willy's self-contradiction—begging on his knees as he threatens Biff with a beating. But there are flaws in the woman's dialogue—she insists that Willy open the door and she pointlessly questions Biff: "Are you football or baseball?"

As the climax violates the thematic drive of the play, so the Requiem violates its form. *Death of a Salesman* is not rigidly contained by Willy's mind, but the Requiem is jarringly and flagrantly outside his mind. More important, the Epilogue provides us with few new insights, and those are confusing. We have already heard the divergence of Willy's sons in their judgement of their father; Happy remains subject to Willy's dream while Biff attains self-recognition in Oliver's office; this bifurcation scarcely needs to be spelled out again. Charley, on the other hand, changes surprisingly; having repeatedly urged Willy to give up his phoney dream as a traveling salesman, Charley is suddenly sentimental about that dream. Earlier, he had said to Willy: "The only thing you got in this world is what you can sell," but by the Requiem the "what" gives way to a shine and a smile—an utterly incongruous coupling on the sharp tongue of the cynical businessman.

It is Linda, however, whose words in the Requiem are most confusing. We have witnessed her devotion to her husband, and we can sympathize with her grief. However, it is difficult to understand her lack of understanding. When Linda found the rubber pipe near the gas jet, she worried, but she did not wonder *why* Willy wanted to kill himself, discouraged and exhausted as he was. Desperate (and deluded) by the end of the play, Willy finally carries out his threat. Her bereavement evokes our pity, but her astonishment is astonishing. Like Charley's final speech, hers sentimentalizes the tragedy in its flagrant bid for tears.

Though Miller's stage directions specify that Linda "*lacks the temperament to utter*" the longings she shares with Willy, she is quite articulate—too articulate for her final lack of understanding. Willy treats her badly, but she defends him eloquently. Far from the Jewish Mother who has been detected beneath Linda's syntax, Willy's wife is a tear-making tool for Miller, from her "Attention must be paid" speech, through her remonstrances with her sons, to the final ironic chant: "We're free. We're free . . . We're free . . ." Bound to Willy's dream, she defends it against the temptation represented by Ben. She claims attention for Willy as a "human being," but she magnifies Willy's importance through her use of generalizations, passive constructions, resonant "that man"s, and her pretentious or sentimental epigrams: "Life is a casting off." "A man is not a bird, to come and go with the springtime." "He's only a little boat looking for a harbor." At such lines, one can sympathize with Willy's efforts to shut her up; and yet she is, more perniciously than Willy realizes, his "foundation and . . . support."

Near the beginning of the play, Willy grumbles: "Figure it out. Work a lifetime to pay off a house. You finally own it, and there's nobody to live in it." Linda almost echoes him at the end: "I made the last payment of the house today. Today, dear. And there'll be nobody home." What neither of them learns is that a house is not a home when clichés boomerang transparently. Ironically, however, much of the play's strength lies in the carefully rhythmed poverty of Willy's language. His mass-produced phrases belie his claim to special attention. His sentimental fantasies are inevitably punctured by concrete reality. But rather than risk complete deflation, he risks—and loses—his life.

Somewhat superfluously, Miller told an interviewer that he was not Willy Loman but a writer; "Willy Loman is there because I could see beyond him."[10] And it may well be that Willy's durable stage thereness rests on the fact that all of us see, and especially hear, beyond him. Willy's vocabulary is totally familiar—endearingly so because it is so limited. Willy's questions seem totally familiar—again endearing because limited. It is easy to pity and even love Willy, who is our father, brother, cousin, friend. But never *me*.

Compared to O'Neill's Hickey, Willy is bankrupt of words. Hickey begins by being well liked and successful; he has the gift of gab, and he spends it lavishly. Willy is not frugal of words, but he has so few of them that he keeps repeating his small stock. Hickey's relentless flow of words finally turns us against him, but we remain attached to Willy because we can talk and think rings around him. *Death of a Salesman* triumphs because Willy falls short of us, but within touching distance.

NOTES

[1] Mary McCarthy, *Sights and Spectacles* (New York, 1956), xxiv–xxv, and Leslie Fiedler, *Waiting for the End* (New York, 1964), 91. Miller has denied this, since his family did not speak Jewish, but Jewish inflections in English nevertheless permeate his plays. See Robert A. Martin, "The Creative Experience of Arthur Miller: An Interview," *Educational Theatre Journal* (October, 1969), 315.
[2] Cf. Introduction to the *Collected Plays* (New York, 1957), and Martin interview.
[3] George Steiner, "The Retreat from the Word," *Kenyon Review* (Spring, 1961), 211.
[4] Leonard Moss, "Arthur Miller and the Common Man's Language," *Modern Drama* (May, 1964), 52–59.
[5] Dennis Welland, *Arthur Miller* (New York, 1961), 64–65.
[6] Introduction to the *Collected Plays*, 39.

[7] Cf. Arthur Ganz, "The Silence of Arthur Miller," *Drama Survey* (Fall, 1963), 224–237 for a critique of Willy's dream and an analysis of his likeability.

[8] Henry Popkin, "Arthur Miller: The Strange Encounter" in Alan Downer, ed., *American Drama and Its Critics* (Chicago, 1965), 234.

[9] Biff and Happy, respectively, speak such flawed lines as: "It's a measly manner of existence." and "That's what I long for."

[10] Philip Gelb, "Morality and Modern Drama: Arthur Miller," *Educational Theatre Journal* (October, 1958), 199.

Dan Vogel

WILLY TYRANNOS

Ever since Arthur Miller's *Death of a Salesman* opened to Broadway success in 1949 and after it has been revived effectively on stage, screen, and television, controversy has raged over its stature as a tragedy. For many, the play is simply not a tragedy at all, because its hero, Willy Loman, cast as a type of tyrannos, is too commonplace and limited, its atmosphere is too dependent upon the delusions and weaknesses of an American materialistic society, and its problem is too ignoble for the arousal of total catharsis. Since it does not pit the hero against irresistible universal forces, it is but a fine, if pretentious, play of social protest, according to Joseph Wood Krutch.[1] A distinguished array of critics joins Krutch on this side of the argument—Richard Foster, Eleanor Clark, George Jean Nathan, William McCollom, Elder Olson, Herbert Muller. The latter's estimate is typical: *Salesman* merely tells the story of "a little man succumbing to his environment, rather than a great man destroyed through his greatness.... There is no question of grandeur in such a tragedy.... The hero may excite pity, but nothing like awe." But, judicious as always, Muller does go on to equilibrate the matter: *Salesman* is a "different kind of tragedy ... characteristically modern," but it is a work of "uncertain intention" and less than universal in its achievement of catharsis.[2]

On the other side John Gassner, Eric Bentley, and Willy's creator, Arthur Miller, man the critical ramparts. In their animadversions on the remonstrances of the anti-*Salesman* critics, they were not reluctant to insist that total catharsis can arise from the tragedy of a Willy Loman, or to speak of him in the same breath with untouchable heroes of yesteryear, or even to compare him with the archetype himself, Oedipus. "The common man is as apt a subject for tragedy in its highest sense as kings were,"[3] declared Miller, and placed him alongside the Greek heroes and Job. In the same vein, Gassner asserted:

From *The Three Masks of American Tragedy* (Baton Rouge: Louisiana State University Press, 1974), pp. 91–102.

I fail to comprehend why a character's failure to measure up to the "stature" of Hamlet or Lear must be a deterrent to "pity" and "fear." The case of Willy Loman in the successful production of *Death of a Salesman* would disprove this assumption. It is precisely because Willy was a common man that American audiences felt *pity* for him and *feared* for themselves. Willy was a sort of suburban Everyman with whom audiences readily established a connection, if not indeed an actual identification.[4]

The universality of the catharsis is testified to by Eric Bentley: "We all find that we are Willy, and Willy is us; we live and die together; but when Willy falls never to rise again, we go home feeling purged of (or by) pity and terror."[5]

Underlying the controversy, then, is a familiar challenge for democratic tragedy that for the Greeks was a foregone habit: magnitude of plot and character. Though Miller pooh-poohs the traditions of tragedy ("I had not understood that these matters are measured by Greco-Elizabethan paragraphs"),[6] his dramaturgical instinct forced him to agree with them on this point of magnitude. However, "if society alone is responsible for the cramping of our lives," wrote Miller, "then the protagonist must needs be so pure and faultless as to force us to deny his validity as a character. From neither of these views can tragedy derive, simply because neither represents a balanced concept of life."[7] Society must be seen as having more magnitude than that: " 'Society' is a power and a mystery of custom and inside the man and surrounding him."[8] In the confrontation of the individual and society, one can discern the ancient *agon* of the external power's tendency toward determinism and the hero's response to the imposition. One begins to see, then, why so many critics, and Miller himself in his introduction to his *Collected Plays*, perceive a relationship between the Greek tyrannos, Oedipus, and the American Everyman, Willy Loman.

The social frame of limitation of Willy's world does not restrict the drama to a commonplace or materialistic plot, because in his bumbling, inarticulate way, Willy Loman personifies his creator's concept that even the commonplace hero has "the human passion to surpass his given bounds, the fanatic insistence upon [his] self-conceived goal."[9] Though Oedipus' search for the truth is a conscious exercise of a powerful regal mind dealing with a problem of broad dimension and import, and Willy's quest for the truth is restrained by commonness of mind and a restricted sphere of life, yet Gassner perceives that "Willy pursues the 'truth' and struggles against it within his personal and social limits no less arduously and catastrophically than Oedipus."[10] In the generations between these two heroes, the family bloodline may have thinned a bit, but the lineaments of the tyrannos have not been elided.

It is not what society demands that makes the action, it is what Willy *thinks* it demands, and that is the unpreventable element that is the all-powerful motivation of his tragedy, as it was for Oedipus in his situation. It would seem, then, that Miller's vision of tragedy is as broad as his predecessors'. It is not society that is the primary

flaw, but man's innate, eternal, inevitable tendency to self-delusion, ironically in-
duced by uncontrollable external powers.

This commonalty of virtuous, ironic grotesquerie relates the king of Thebes to
the Brooklyn salesman, the great intellect to the plodding huckster, the toy of the
gods to the discarded drummer. It is worth reading what Thomas Lask perceived
in this relationship:

> Certainly it is not easy to see in Willy the lineaments of an Othello or
> Oedipus. Intolerable in real life, he is almost so on the stage. Coarse, vulgar,
> banal, self-deluding, full of stupid pride, intellectually hollow, his mind is a
> compendium of yesterday's tabloid editorials. He seems scarcely the stuff of
> tragedy.
>
> Yet, to my mind, Willy represents all those who are trapped by false
> values, but who are so far on in life, that they do not know how to escape
> them. They are men on the wrong track and know it. They are among those
> who, when young, felt they could move mountains and now do not even see
> those mountains.
>
> Aristotle said the tragic hero must be neither all good nor all evil, but
> rather a median figure. Everything about him is paltry except his battle to
> understand and escape from the pit he has dug for himself. In this battle he
> achieves a measure of greatness. In the waste of his life, his fate touches us
> all.[11]

Just so far extends Miller's depiction of a tyrannos and of a concept of tragic
magnitude. Perhaps no other American tragedian needs so badly the perspective-
righting insight of Aristotle when he said of Euripides that though he may not have
managed the subject well, yet he was so effective that he "is felt to be the most
tragic of poets" (*Poetics*, Chapter 13).

Just as Miller had to narrow the cosmic proportions of a tragedy of a tyrannos
to fit a democratic literature, so he had to revise the pattern of his drama. Unlike
Aristotelian peripety, Willy Loman's wheel of fortune had already turned down-
ward for him when the play opens. Willy is over the hill; his peripety is nearly
complete. Material success is past; the faith in himself that had sustained him in the
past has flagged badly; the hope of greatness in the name of "Loman" is now, as Biff
tells his father, but the dream of a desperate, unhinged mind. The rest of the play
is the fearful spectacle of watching the underpinnings of his already broken world
shatter one by one. What is left for the peripety to show is the disintegration of the
hero's psyche.

The method that Miller uses we have, in certain ways, already examined in
other tragedies. It is the use of the past to explain the circumstances and the
catastrophe of the present. The past in *Salesman* is as destructive an imposition as
in New England and southern tragedies. Willy was the one who had opened up the
whole New England territory. He could always sell Hartford and Boston. We
witness the enactment of a memory when this was true. Speaking to the young Biff

and Happy, Willy of yesterday crows, "I thank Almighty God you're both built like Adonises. Because the man who makes an appearance in the business world, the man who creates personal interest, is the man who gets ahead. Be liked and you will never want. You take me, for instance. I never wait in line to see a buyer. 'Willy Loman is here!' That's all they have to know, and I go right through" (I, 146).[12] Today, Willy of the present, with what is left of his innate pride of salesmanship, says to Linda, his wife, "Oh, I'll knock 'em dead next week. I'll go to Hartford. I'm very well liked in Hartford" (I, 148). But with an inexorable sense of realization stealing over him, he verbalizes the growing doubt about himself in this very same piece of dialogue: "You know, the trouble is, Linda, people don't seem to take to me . . . I'm fat. I'm very—foolish to look at, Linda" (I, 148). Pity and terror begin to grow in the audience, who witness the torture of speaking an inner truth pushed down away from consciousness because of the very pain of it.

Right along with the torture of self-doubt and self-analysis the old Loman pride still persists. When someone calls him a walrus, he reports to Linda, he smacked him across the face. "I won't take that. I simply will not take that." But again, vacillating in pain and doubt, he admits to her, "They do laugh at me. I know that" (I, 149). There is a residue of strength in this suffering, bewildered character who has lost his way between past and present, between what he thought was good and valuable and is now turning to ashes in his mouth. Anguish and suffering are interspersed with flashes of the tyrannos.

The spectacle of self-doubt in the very grip of pride carries over to Willy's remembrance of things past, the symbols of the time when he was able to form his own world. These objects are his automobile, his house, and his son Biff. With Sophoclean irony, Miller uses the very emblems of success to symbolize the tragedy that is evolving.

The automobile is his society's symbol of Willy's profession and affluence. There are recollections of the beautiful big car that is an adventure and a ritual to polish, and the rite represented the togetherness of the self-made man and his stalwart sons (I, 143). But now the automobile has been transformed into a past memory which sharpens present pain. His New England car trip at the beginning of the play is truncated in Yonkers because the car "kept going off onto the shoulder," Willy reports to Linda. She desperately suggests that the mechanic doesn't know the car and didn't repair it properly. Willy replies, "No, it's me, it's me. Suddenly I realize I'm goin' sixty miles an hour and I don't remember the last five minutes. I'm—I can't seem to—keep my mind on it" (I, 132). Troubled by his loss of control over the car and all that it stands for in his life, he cries to his sons: "For Christ's sake, I couldn't get past Yonkers today! Where are you guys, where are you? The woods are burning! I can't drive a car!" (I, 152). Arthur Miller reports that in part *Death of a Salesman* "grew from images of futility—the cavernous Sunday afternoons polishing the car. Where is that car now?"[13]

Here is the house that Willy built. The stage directions introducing the first act describe it thus: *"An air of the dream clings to the place, a dream rising out of reality"* (I, 130). The sweet dream had once been realized, when the house had been located in a rustic section of Brooklyn. But now the neighborhood has been given over to tenement buildings, and there is hardly a piece of ground to grow a flower, and you have to crane your neck to see a star. Worst of all, the house is the scena before which is enacted the denuding of expectations. "Figure it out," Willy says. "Work a lifetime to pay off a house, you finally own it, and there is nobody to live in it" (I, 133). Of course, the "nobody" is Biff, his son. So the house comes through as the external manifestation of Willy's dream of the future, a successful Biff Loman, scion of the house of Loman. But Willy, in his own sphere, has misread the future of his house, quite like those other tyrannoi, the owner of Cabot's farm and the squire of Sutpen's Hundred.

For Willy, the pride, the disappointment, the suffering are never so deeply felt, or so variously, as in relation to Biff, the almost tangible clay that Willy, tyrannos in his own house, had hoped to mold in his own image. Biff embodied, Miller wrote, "a need to leave a thumbprint somewhere in the world. A need for immortality, and by admitting it, the knowing that one has carefully inscribed one's name on a cake of ice on a hot July day."[14] We come to recognize, together with John Gassner, the heroism of this battered man's "refusal to surrender all expectations of triumph for, and through, his son. . . . Unwilling to resign to failure," Willy persists in pushing until there dawns upon him the "truth about himself and his situation."[15] Anagnorisis, in other words.

Realism demanded of Miller a concept of anagnorisis that he admittedly extrapolated from Ibsen's legacy to "forge a play upon a factual bedrock"; that is, not upon what people felt (or say they felt), but upon what they did.[16] In this light we must reinvestigate one of the most serious charges leveled at *Salesman*, that its hero is incapable of anagnorisis. For example, Joseph A. Hynes, using quoted words from a Miller essay, remarked, "For Willy Loman 'victory' would have been realization not only of Biff's love for him, but of 'who he was.' But such a 'victory' Willy could not possibly have, simply because he was created 'incapable of grappling with a much superior force'—whether Biff's love or his own dream, the two forces which 'his witlessness, his insensitivity,' and his love for Biff prevent his seeing sanely."[17] It is to Miller's credit that he turns Willy's witlessness and insensitivity into means that tease the audience into an eventual anagnorisis together with the protagonist and then into a burst of pity and awe.

Willy will not let go of the echoes, and we reminisce together with him about the halcyon days. Willy recalls the glory when Biff Loman was "like a young god. Hercules—something like that. And the sun all around him. Remember how he waved to me? Right up from the field, with the representatives of three colleges standing by? And the buyers I brought, and the cheers when he came out—Loman, Loman, Loman, God Almighty, he'll be great yet. A star like that, magnificent, can never really fade away" (I, 171). But the dream is fading, rapidly and sadly. It is a kind of David-and-Absalom reenactment going on before us, of an indulgent father who cannot understand how his indulgence engenders ingratitude, disrespect, and failure in his son.

Hence, as Thomas Lask said, the bullying, the ragging, and the coarseness against those who persist in seeing the truth of it all, that dreams are but dreams and that life has a way of playing with you and not you with it. The coarseness is but the sign of the bewildered tyrannos. Willy calls Biff "a lazy bum," but a few lines later insists "Biff is not lazy" (I, 135), and then taunts him and his brother Happy with their whoring and their fancy cars (I, 152); and in his extremity extends his desperate arrogance even to Linda, to the point that Biff complains that his father wipes the floor with her (I, 162). Yet, in the hands of Arthur Miller, none of this alienates the audience; rather, it conjoins us with the protagonist. Linda herself expresses for us the sympathy we feel for the cracking protagonist: "He's not the finest character who ever lived," she cries to her sons, "but he's a human being and a terrible thing is happening to him. So attention must be paid. He's not to be allowed to fall into his grave like an old dog. Attention, attention must be finally paid to such a person" (I, 162).

When Biff can no longer take the bullying and what he believes to be the pipe dreams of his father, he bursts out, "I never got anywhere because you blew me so full of hot air I could never stand taking orders from anybody! That's whose fault it is" (II, 216). This is not a petulant shift of responsibility, for we must admit Biff is right. Biff is the crowning creature of the father-tyrannos, and this apex of a self-created edifice of the future becomes the instrument whereby Willy is hurtled to his anagnorisis. The conflict between Willy and his son rises in a crescendo of traded recriminations until Biff forces his father to face up to the reality about both of them:

> BIFF: Pop! I'm a dime a dozen, and so are you!
> WILLY (*turning on him in an uncontrolled outburst*): I am not a dime a dozen! I am Willy Loman, and you are Biff Loman!
>
> .   .   .   .
>
> BIFF: I am not a leader of men, Willy, and neither are you. You were never anything but a hardworking drummer who landed in the ash can like the rest of them! I'm one dollar an hour, Willy! . . . I'm not bringing home any prizes any more, and you're going to stop waiting for me to bring them home! (II, 217)

The pitch is too high for the two of them. There is a moment of suspension, and then Biff breaks down. Weeping, Biff moves slowly offstage.

> WILLY (*after a long pause, astonished, elevated*): Isn't that—isn't that remarkable? Biff—he likes me! . . . He cried! Cried to me. (*He is choking with his love, and now cries out his promise*): That boy—that boy is going to be magnificent! (II, 218)

It would be unrealistic if a protagonist of such limitations would quickly give up his old dreams and adjust at once to a new perception. Thus we hear again a litany of Biff's magnificent future, but at the same time we note something new. Willy discovers that there is a greater force than even the drive for success: love. Like the first and last plays of the ancient Oedipus trilogy, these are the forces that sustain the final actions. Willy Tyrannos is about to arrive at Colonus.

Fearfully alone now, his psyche crumbling, Willy calls upon his brother Ben, who had flitted through so many of the dream sequences as the epitome of success, hurrying on to an Alaskan gold field or an African diamond mine. But Willy's last invocation of this shade is never completed. Willy waves away all the shadows and echoes that have haunted and taunted him, telling them at last to keep silent. There is a moment of stillness, in which Willy sees into the ultimate necessity. He knows what he has to do and he goes ahead and does it—in the very symbol of his success. The offstage sound is that of an automobile speeding off and crashing into eternity (II, 220). The peripety of a man's mind is concluded.

Unlike the suicide attempts reported to us earlier in the play, this last suicide try is quite different in motivation. Those came at the nadir of Willy's bewilderment and despair; they were cowardly and escapist. This one is purposeful, self-sacrificial, and epiphanic. It is the supreme act of love for his son, and Willy Loman goes to his death with the music of unheard but remembered cheers for Biff resounding in his head. Does he have the insurance money in mind? Of course he does, being Willy. But if the money contributes to the time when "that boy will be magnificent," Willy won't be around to witness it and crow about it, and he knows that, too.

Miller summarized his tragic protagonist's anagnorisis by pointing out that Willy "achieved a very powerful piece of knowledge, which is that he is loved by his son and has been embraced by him and forgiven." The process of arriving at this knowledge engenders pity. The total commitment to a mistaken way of life, which demands in recompense the total commitment of a sacrificial catastrophe, arouses the terror.

"Requiem," the last scene of *Death of a Salesman,* parallels the choric themes at the end of *Oedipus at Colonus.* Willy's influence, so tragic in life, is effectuated properly only in death. We see this final glow emanating from the tragedy of Willy Loman in the last conversation between his two sons:

> BIFF: Why don't you come with me, Happy?
> HAPPY: I'm not licked that easily. I'm staying right in this city, and I'm gonna beat this racket! (*He looks at Biff, his chin set.*) The Loman brothers!
> BIFF: I know who I am, kid.

And when Happy persists in his tyrannical dream, Biff dismisses him "with a hopeless glance" ("Requiem," 222). In life, Willy taught Biff lessons of fraudulence; in death, he teaches him lessons of truth.

The audience, too, has learned the meaning of the tragedy of this salesman, the man who selected the wrong alternative, who misinterpreted his life as a tyrannos and thereby became a tragic figure. Arthur Miller overcame the limitations of his setting, the role of society, the commonness of his hero, to awaken catharsis in us. At the end we remember Willy Loman as what Bernard Knox said of the departed Oedipus, "a spirit which lives on in power in the affairs of men after the death of the body. His tomb is to be a holy place [and] in his grave . . . he will be powerful."[18]

This is the proper epitaph of all the other American tyrannoi as well.

NOTES

[1] Joseph Wood Krutch, "Why O'Neill's Star Is Rising," *New York Times Magazine,* March 19, 1961, p. 108.

[2] The essays by Richard J. Foster, Eleanor Clark, and George Jean Nathan are in John D. Hurrell (ed.), *Two Modern American Tragedies: Reviews and Criticism of* Death of a Salesman *and* A Streetcar Named Desire (New York: Scribner's, 1961). See also William C. McCollom, *Tragedy* (New York: Macmillan, n.d.), 16–17; Elder Olson, *Tragedy and the Theory of Drama* (Detroit: Wayne State University Press, 1961), 249–50; Herbert J. Muller, *The Spirit of Tragedy* (1956; reprint, New York: Washington Square Press, 1965), 272.

[3] Arthur Miller, "Tragedy and the Common Man," in Richard Levin (ed.), *Tragedy: Plays, Theory, and Criticism* (New York: Harcourt, Brace, 1960), 171.

[4] John Gassner, "Tragedy in the Modern Theatre," *Theatre in Our Times* (New York: Crown, 1954), 64.

[5] Eric Bentley, "Better Than Europe?," in Hurrell (ed.), *Two Modern American Tragedies,* 132.

[6] Arthur Miller, *Collected Plays* (New York: Viking, 1957), 31.

[7] Miller, "Tragedy and the Common Man," 3.

[8] Miller, *Collected Plays,* 30.

[9] Ibid., 33.

[10] John Gassner, "Tragic Perspectives: A Sequence of Queries," in Hurrell (ed.), *Two Modern American Tragedies,* 26.

[11] Thomas Lask, "How Do You Like Willy Loman?," *New York Times,* January 30, 1966, Sec. 2, p. 23.

[12] The text of the play used here is the one in Miller's *Collected Plays.* Both act and page number are cited in parentheses.

[13] Miller, *Collected Plays,* 29.

[14] Ibid.

[15] Gassner, "Tragic Perspectives," 26.

[16] Miller, *Collected Plays,* 19.

[17] Joseph A. Hynes, " 'Attention Must Be Paid . . . ,' " in Gerald Weales (ed.), *Death of a Salesman: Text and Criticism* (New York: Viking, 1967), 286.

[18] Bernard Knox, "Sophocles' Oedipus," in Cleanth Brooks (ed.), *Tragic Themes in Western Literature* (1955; reprint, New Haven: Yale University Press, 1960), 23.

A. D. Choudhuri

DEATH OF A SALESMAN: A SALESMAN'S ILLUSION

A man can't go out the way he came in, Ben, a man has got to add up
to something.   —LOMAN, *Death of a Salesman*

Democracy proclaims the individual in society to be free, and American democracy, in addition, approves the myth of his infinite success and happiness. And yet the law and social conventions constrain and frustrate him in what he has come to believe as the birth-right of a member of the greatest open society. Miller has seized this open contradiction to dramatise the individual torn between the expected and the actual. His approach to, and treatment of, the theme is sociological, although the characteristic indignation of social protest plays is subdued, and a large amount of human sympathy and pity for the underdog, perplexed in the grip of unexpected circumstances and too powerful forces, is the final impression of his theatre. Most of his characters are undistinguished citizens who do not understand themselves or the overwhelming social forces that destroy them; their defects and redeeming qualities are not above criticism, but they have a certain quality of character which may be described as obstinacy, thoughtless obstinacy, driving them to destruction and their action and behaviour to a sort of tragic expressiveness. This sense of tragedy, however, is essentially social in nature and rarely touches the larger sphere beyond it. This kind of mundane moral vision, bereft of any reference to the cosmic universe, finds its grandeur in the affirmation of human dignity. A sense of moral compassion, which has its affinities more with a larger human vision than with a strict sense of right and wrong, lights up his handling of themes and characters, and makes his drama more significant than periodic pieces dramatizing contemporary social tensions and prejudices. It perhaps needs pointing out that Miller seizes the conflicts of his society to interpret them in the light of human values so much so that his vision transcends the immediate and the contemporary; it projects values associated with tragic imagination, values that are limited to man's position in society, values that are rarely concerned with the cosmic relevance of man. He strikes an affirmative note in the tradition of the social drama, but his moral imagination extends beyond the anxieties of the protest plays.

From *The Face of Illusion in American Drama* (Atlantic Highlands, NJ: Humanities Press, 1979), pp. 94–111.

Miller's theatre is essentially a critique of the values and prejudices of mid-century American society, of the dilemmas and anxieties that divide the community into polarities, but it is also an attempt to define the dignity of man in terms of his social ambitions and commitments, his sense of guilt and ignorance. The classic drama describes the tragic path of self-discovery of the hero and the discovery of the missing link to assert the sense of human grandeur. *All My Sons, Death of a Salesman* and *A View from the Bridge* describe the ignorant helpless struggle of blind groping men who neither understand themselves nor the forces that finally crush them. In the altered social condition when social pressures are too complex to be fathomed by undistinguished citizens, Miller accepts the struggle of their self-destructive assertion as human beings to be equivalent to the tragic discovery of the classical theatre. Oedipus' discovery of his parentage and his incestuous living with his mother brought clear perspectives on his life's problems, and he sought to redeem the sins by acts of denial, acts invested with moral dignity in the eyes of society and himself. The heroes of Miller's drama, except in *The Crucible,* are creatures afflicted by dilemma and confusion, sightless people groping about in darkness. The struggles and fumblings of these men, little men as they are, their desperate and vague search for the identity of the forces, the explanation of their 'bad luck', take, in the eyes of Miller, the shape of tragic dimension. In the uncertain volatile democratic age when values are changing so fast and establishment of human dignity seems to be so much more difficult, the waste of human efforts for self-fulfilment certainly calls for pity and compassion. The unfulfilled dreams and the lifelong futile struggle—don't they contain between them the substance of the tragic material?

Miller seems to ask this question. The absorbing fable of the modern man's search for his place in society, his confrontation with social conventions, the conflicts it generates in himself are loaded with tragic significance in this godless age. The modern playwright is, perhaps, within his right to treat these themes as tragic. To a wage earner in an industrial society larger references to questions like cosmic significance of man's activities seem to be far-fetched, and even out of place. Harassed by a sense of his insignificance in the face of the impersonal forces of society, there is some justification in his total absorption with his own little dreams and activities. It certainly narrows the field of tragic values, but in modern democracy, particularly in an industrialised community, this may be a valid enough canvas to evoke tragic feelings. The intensity of the feelings is there if it is an absorbing work, pity and compassion for the ruin of possibilities may be there, and there may also be a sort of tragic dignity associated with a man's desperate energy to find a foothold in his life. In fiction Balzac has unforgettably painted the tragic waste of undistinguished people in search of their little private dreams. He understood that in a democracy undistinguished little citizens like Pere Goriot or Pons had as much a right to tragic passions on the strength of their total commitment to their private dream as the classical heroes. The classic drama with its assurance of a divinely ordered universe and man's place in this universe, its sense of certitude in divine justice, its delight in the basically harmonious universal laws produced its heroes, and aesthetic structure. The unsettled society of today and the changing values give us Willy Lomans, Eddie Carbones or Joe Kellers. Their universe is narrowed down to their worries about their jobs, or passion for a woman, or profit from war contracts. Every ounce of their energy is devoted to their objectives, and their almost stupid tenacity to pursue their objects has something of the tragic potential in it. They force to assert their human dignity or fulfilment on an unwilling society. The affirmative note of Miller's theatre derives its energy from their exertion and pains. The paradox of the situation lies in the hero's efforts to project an image of himself which his society rejects and yet he remains to the end unaware of the reasons of the rejection. He is much too absorbed in his own world and feelings to care for forces that are really controlling his activities.

The tragic vision that emerges out of Miller's theatre is intimately associated with the dramatisation of the abstraction of human values in conflict with the social experience. He sees in the democratic society a tendency to bulldoze the individual into a faceless non-entity. All his heroes cry for their identity, as though all their efforts and assumptions were directed to this end. John Proctor cries, 'How may I live without my name?' and tears up his confession; Eddie Carbone demands, 'Gimme my name' and is destroyed; Loman cries out, 'I am not dime a dozen. I am Willy Loman'; Joe Keller commits suicide to save his name. Their greed for profit in business, their care for their job, their sexual passion are only different expressions of their search for dignity. Miller, by and large, equates their search for financial security with the search for identity of a modern man. As these people wear no badge of honour, the only distinction available to them is money. In older civilisations a man could achieve power and distinction by virtue of his noble birth or title or dedicated social service. But the businessman's ethos dominates the American mind so much that only money gives a citizen social distinction, and money seems to be the prime source of status. The state does not confer titles or honour, nor does society recognise the superiority of birth or family. All citizens being equal, the only distinguishing mark between them is financial success. Lomans and Joe Kellers are only following the lead their culture provides them with: one is a mediocre credulous salesman and the other a businessman who believes to be following the business ethic of maximum profit.

Americans enjoy the highest standard of living, and it costs more to live in America than in any country in the world: 'the cost is not only in dollars and cents', novelist Henry Miller says, 'but in sweat and blood, in frustration, ennui, broken homes, smashed ideals, illness and insanity. We have the most wonderful hospitals, the most fabulous prisons, the best equipped and highest paid army and navy, the speediest bombers, the largest stockpile of atom bombs, yet never enough of any of these items to satisfy the demand. Our manual workers are the highest paid in the world; our poets the worst.'[1] Henry Miller in this attack on American values poses a central question: does standard of living mean *only* more comfort, more earning and more spending? Has it anything to do with a man's inner happiness, his sense of fulfilment, his satisfaction in living a fruitful life? This question, perhaps, would be asked by any thoughtful American living in mid-century: the massive structure of the technological civilisation has assured material prosperity; but at what cost? and what for? Has it given the individual a fuller appreciation of life, a more meaningful enjoyment of his material possessions? Does the purposeless chase of material comfort itself constitute a worthwhile goal in life?

Willy Loman's entire life is a question mark in that direction, although he did never suspect that he was asking this question throughout his career as a salesman. In fact he was not selling automobiles, he was selling himself to ensure personal fulfilment, and peace and happiness in the family. And at both the levels he failed as millions do in a competitive commercialised society. He failed to gain the minimum sense of security and prosperity in his profession, and he lost the respect and affection of his children for whom he cared so much. Willy Loman, however, is largely responsible for his failure. And his failure sums up the case of a misfit who cannot comprehend the intricate mechanism of the modern business world, and believes in a desperate way in its goodness and justice. His failure is all the more pitiable because in an age of rigid organisation he was content to cherish and follow the declared ideal of the great open society: he was hardworking, he was honest, he trained his sons to be 'well liked'—and yet everything he touched came to nothing. It is almost a typical case of the American dream transformed into American illusion! Arthur Miller dramatises not only the longings and disappointments of a little man in America and the inhuman attitude of the business world towards a man not useful to the organisation, but what is more important, he focuses our attention on the credibility gap between the American dream and the American reality. The stage directions make it abundantly clear that the dramatist's central concern was related to this important aspect of modern society. The play begins with: 'A melody is heard, played upon a flute. It is small and fine, telling of grass and trees and the horizon. . . . An air of the dream clings to the place, a dream rising out of reality.' The play ends with: 'Only the music of the flute is left on the darkening stage as over the house the hard towers of the apartment buildings rise into sharp focus.' It began with dreams and longings of the human heart and the curtain comes down on shattered dreams; the longings are still there, but side by side stand the hard facts of reality. The playwright has taken particular care throughout to underline the sense of inadequacy in Loman's life, his idealised attitude towards a society he never understood, and above all to convey the image of a trapped animal in a rigid social structure. Loman encounters many pitfalls in his character; he is neither an ideal father nor an ideal husband. These are the defects of his weakness, and, in spite of them, his substantial loyalty to his wife and children and to the cherished ideals of his society are unquestionable. He trusts them with the naiveté of a child, and a large part of his failings as a man may be directly traced to his uncritical acceptance of contemporary social values.

Arthur Miller, however, is not primarily concerned in this play with the demonstration of the economic injustice of the community Loman lives in. Nor is he interested in solving an important social problem: the central energy in *Death of a Salesman* is derived from an exploration of a particular aspect of culture, twentieth-century technological culture, in which illusions take the place of dreams and fantasy substitutes reality. This phenomenon, ignorance of reality or non-recognition of facts, has been a potent source of European theatre since the Greeks; but what lends weight to Miller's discovery is that it is not an exceptional experience to a few but is common enough in industrial civilisation. Miller points out, with remarkable artistic perception, the hold of illusion on individuals and its disastrous consequences, the dreams that are intertwined with illusions, the gulf that separates the actual practices from the professed ideals of society. In fact one may not be very far from the truth if one describes the play as a dramatic exercise in exploring the broad spectrum of illusion as a cultural product of the American society. One of the refreshing qualities of this play is that it does not visualise the consumer society as a backdrop to be used for focusing the inadequacies and failings of Willy Loman; it visualises his life and the social forces within which he operates as a single unit, as an inextricably interwoven area which defies separate analysis. Dreams of a better future slowly take the shape of wishful fantasies, so much so that the sharpness of the conflict between illusion and reality, between Loman's little dreams and the impersonal forces of society, seems to be apparently lost in comprehensive images of extraordinary poetic force. The comments and behaviour of other people, who cross Loman's life frequently, provide us with pointers to the social side of the picture. Such a comment comes from Linda when she says, 'Willy Loman never made a lot of money. His name was never in the paper. He's not the finest character that ever lived, but he's a human being, and a terrible thing is happening to him. So attention must be paid. He's not to be allowed to fall into his grave like an old dog. Attention, attention must be finally paid to such a person.'

The social relevance of the play, however, gains in poignancy and concentration as it gradually demonstrates Loman's utter incapacity to understand himself and the complex social forces controlling his life. This paradoxical dramatic objective of concentrating on the individual while making the social significance of his life progressively relevant is achieved by the adept artistic fusion of Loman's past and present, his moments of pride and failure; and throughout the play we watch the slow but sure grip of illusion on Loman's thoughts and activities. Rebuffed by society, discarded by his employer, Loman discovers spiritual nourishment in his fantasies like a man caving into his own world to protect the remnants of his dignity and importance. It is to be noted, however, that Willy Loman never knew himself, and he had been nurturing his illusions up to the very end. He came very near to revealing the dominating dream of his life when he tells Ben: 'A man can't go out the way he came in, Ben, a man has got to add up to something.' He unconsciously recognised this *something* which makes one's existence fruitful and meaningful, but consciously he was thinking of the twenty thousand dollars his family would receive from the insurance company after his death. He died thinking that all the valuable things in life—honour, recognition, dignity, sense of importance, peace of mind—are purchasable commodities. With twenty thousand dollars, 'like a diamond shining in the dark, hard and rough', the family would buy dignity and opportunity, dreams and security. And, perhaps, unknown to Loman, illusions! With that sense of pathetic optimism he rushed to his grave.

How does Miller organize the material through the medium of drama? What is the style or technique he employs to achieve the maximum dramatic expressiveness of the story? It is easy to see that in *Death of a Salesman,* as in *All My Sons,* Miller uses the 'retrospective' structure of Ibsen's drama: present situations are explained in the light of past incidents, the gradual revelation that leads to a clearer understanding of the present crisis. But he reads something more in Ibsen's plays. 'If his plays', Miller says in his introduction to the *Collected Plays,* 'and his method, do nothing else they reveal the evolutionary quality of life. One is constantly aware, in watching his plays, of process, change, development . . . dramatic characters, and the drama itself, can never hope to attain a maximum degree of consciousness unless they contain a viable unveiling of the contrast between past and present, and an awareness of the process by which the present has become what is.' To achieve this 'evolutionary quality of life, of process, change, development', Miller draws upon the devices of the Expressionist Theatre: and thus he attempts to visualise the psychological reality along with the objective reality of actions. The remarkable fusion of these two techniques seems to answer Miller's demand for presenting the objective as well as the subjective reality of the situation. It is to be noted that the opening conversation between Willy and Linda presents a perfectly naturalistic dialogue which points to the overstrained anxiety of the salesman, and also his nostalgic longing for the past. This conversation is followed by the dialogue between Happy and Biff who are apprehensive of their father's mental strain and their own future. Even before the two brothers finish their conversation we see Willy in the kitchen muttering to himself, imagining young Biff listening to his advice. Biff and Happy, as in their high school days, materialise and the conversation between the father and sons, later joined by Linda is surely as good as a flash-back shot in a cinema. This fantasy is interrupted when Happy comes down from the stairs and Charley, his next-door neighbour, comes up to suggest a game of cards. Up to now there is the clear division between scenes of actuality and those of fantasy: the opening conversation is followed by Willy's recollection scene of the happier early days which fades out to give place to Happy and Charley's actual appearance. Then Ben appears and the kitchen-room is at once converted into a dramatic space in which the distinction between actuality and dream is sacrificed to present the picture of a mind which has lost all sense of time sequence.

As action progresses the playwright makes increasing use of situations in which past and present, dream and actuality co-exist as in a montage. In Act I the dialogue between Willy and Ben in the kitchen is the only instance when, as Miller himself describes, 'the boundaries between now and then' are destroyed. But in Act II there is more frequent use of this device, bringing home the sense of confusion in

Willy's mind. The dream scenes, however, confine themselves to past days and serve as explanatory episodes. They are nostalgic in effect. The two dream scenes in Act II—the dialogue of Ben and Willy following the scene at Howard Wagner's office, and the dream at the restaurant when young Bernard informs Linda of Biff's failure in the examination—not only contrast the actual situations that precede them, they also answer questions the actual situations raise. The dream episode, just after Wagner fires Willy, describes how he declined Ben's offer to start a new life at Alaska and also his thoughtless infatuation with his sons. This explains, partly, Willy's present misfortune. The second episode, visualising Biff's failure in Maths, confirms Willy's opinion that he is intentionally destroying himself. The dream episode in Act I also explains and comments on Willy's attitude to his sons and his trust in the myths of the American business world. But the scenes in which reality and fantasy intermingle have the most powerful dramatic impact. We see before us the disintegration of a mind for whom all sequence of time and space has been dissolved. The scene in which Ben appears while Willy and Charley are playing cards (Act I) reveals the humorous as well as the pathetic. In Act II there are, however, three scenes in which the distinction between past and present is blurred: at the restaurant the hotel bedroom episode when Biff discovers his father's unfaithfulness, in the kitchen garden when Willy discloses his plan of suicide to Ben, and again in his home when he meets Ben before he rushes out. These scenes, interlocking past and present, generate a kind of dramatic tension which forcefully projects Willy's internal world. Miller picturesquely describes this as 'a mobile concurrency of past and present' which depicts the desperation of Willy who has 'destroyed the boundaries between now and then'.

This novel and remarkable technique brings about a sort of dramatic density, further buttressed by the excellent use of dramatic irony. All through the play irony plays a vital part in sharpening our sense of enjoyment. Willy neither understood himself nor the world. He was, however, vaguely aware of the contradictory world around him, though he was unable to read the meaning of the chaos of his experience. The situation is indeed ideal for the use of dramatic irony, and Miller fully exploits it to his advantage. Of course, Willy's whole life is a study in irony: his trust in the clichés and legends of the business world is ironical; he loves his family and children, but he cannot keep them together; he loves Linda and yet is unfaithful to her; he loves his children but they do not respect him. There are numerous scenes in which the edge of irony is sharp enough to reveal the gap between illusion and reality: at the end of the dream scene (Act I) Willy gives the woman fresh silk stockings, and in the immediately following actual scene Linda is seen mending a pair of her silk stockings; Charley and Bernard are not 'well liked' but Willy in Charley's office (Act II) asked Bernard for the secret of his success; Willy went to the hotel to have a grand dinner and to evoke a sense of comradeship with his sons, but he came home crushed and alienated. Two situations at the end of the play demand special attention. Willy died with the illusion that Biff really loved him and thought that the insurance money would really make a man of him! The other ironical situation is the funeral scene which is attended only by his family and Charley. No salesmen came from Maine, Massachusetts, Vermont, New Hampshire, New York or New Jersey to attend the funeral of Willy Loman. He had told Ben in the garden (Act II) that the funeral would be an event in the life of the family. His life and death were equally unrecognised!

Some of the images have the extraordinary power to evoke a tender and nostalgic mood, bringing in a sort of poetic dimension to the entire picture. In Act I as Willy is talking to himself he is recalling those happy days when Biff and Happy were two young boys loyal to their father and full of promise. As Biff and Happy sleep the 'apartment houses are fading out, and the entire house and surroundings become covered with leaves', leaves of memory that bury the harsh reality of the present and make the past more real than the present. A little later we see Charley and Willy playing cards and Ben ('When I was seventeen I walked into the jungle, and when I was twenty-one I walked out. And by God I was rich.') suddenly materialises. Willy says that he remembers Ben walking away down some open road and the family moving from one place to another in a wagon, father stopping in the towns and selling the flutes that he had made on the way. This image of a man walking away down some open road and the family moving in a wagon from Boston to Ohio and Indiana and all the Western states is part of the picture of the American dream, and hardly fails to evoke nostalgic racial memory. Again, the image of a man making flutes, symbol of carefree happy life, and selling them sharply contrasts Willy's life of drudgery in the city. One other image at the end of the play is worth noting. Biff and Happy left Willy alone in the restaurant. Willy understands, although he refuses to accept it fully, that his life and efforts have been fruitless. In an effort to defy fate and convince himself of his usefulness he brings home seeds to plant in the garden: seeds that will grow into carrots, beets and lettuce: an attempt to create something fresh and living in his life. And ironically enough, it is when he is planting these seeds of life that he decides to kill himself!

But there are other images which project his idealised past or hopes so as to accentuate the starkness of his present position. Often they are ironic in effect, bringing home Willy's failures and inadequacies. In Act I Linda says, 'Willy, darling, you're the handsomest man in the world', but 'the laughter of a woman' interrupts her. We see Willy and the woman in a hotel room, Willy giving her stockings, and just after that Linda is seen mending a pair of her silk stockings. Images criss-cross one another focusing the unreality of a dream and yet intensifying their inherent tension. In Act II at the restaurant Willy feels that Biff has a spite against him and is ruining himself deliberately. Immediately follows the picture of Biff's shock at the discovery of his father's adultery. This juxtaposition of opposites places side by side the strength and weakness of Willy as a father and as a husband. The implicit irony shocks us into a fuller understanding of this little man's dilemmas.

Is he a tragic figure? Is not there too much of a sense of pity and compassion associated with Willy Loman to make him a tragic figure? He clings to the illusions up to the last moments of his life and certainly this obstinacy denotes his capacity for endurance until it is beyond his breaking point. Suffering itself gives a certain dignity to a man, but if it is only mute suffering without comprehension, without any understanding of the causes of his suffering; in short, without a recognition of the forces of destruction within and outside himself, he is to be viewed with more pity and concern than respect. And yet, even with all the pity the situation generates, Willy Loman's suicide does not actually make him merely more pitiable; in fact it adds to his stature. What is it at the back of our mind that refuses to accept Loman's suicide as an irrefutable proof of his defeat? His suicide may look like the logical conclusion of a losing game, but viewed from a different angle, this final act of sacrifice may impress us as the first and last protest of a helpless man against the illogicalities of a society which refuses him a normal happy life. This protest is somewhat of an affirmation of his dreams: dreams of security, and happiness for his family. These dreams are no more than illusions, the mood and the total impression of the play make this clear enough to the audience; but his decision to commit suicide takes on the strength of a desperate powerful protest against the odds of life. He remains a salesman to the end, selling his life for those he loved. Moreover, Loman impresses us not only as an individual, his representative capacity cannot be missed by anyone: Loman is certainly not a heroic character, but as a representative typical insignificant salesman (and who is not a salesman in America today?) he acquires a certain importance: and his death may be interpreted as an assertion, the strongest possible assertion, of his human dignity. Loman has neither the capacity nor perhaps the inclination to go beyond the terms of his existence, terms determined by the ethos of a ruthlessly competitive society. He has to act within the rigid framework of ideas and activities allotted to him by the gods in the commercial houses. He played his part as well as he could, and his suicide was not within the terms of the agreement, written or unwritten, with society. He made his choice as a free man: a man who was at least free to make an end to his life. In the last hours of his life he makes his first important decision, i.e., to protest against an ignoble existence. By that he acquires dignity and even distinction in our eyes. His death is a positive assertion of his right to live as a free man, and also his irrefutable claim as a hero of tragic potential.

The search for identity, one of the distinguishing features of any tragic hero, hardly figures in Loman's thoughts and actions: he is incapable of a conscious analysis of the situation, and he has accepted the American myth that if a man is 'well liked' everything will lead to success. And in spite of his labours at being loved by others he finds himself progressively pushed into a corner. He clings to his dreams of success in profession and happiness in family. The image of himself that he constructs with so much labour is one supplied by advertising agencies: his culture hands over to him this picture and he gratefully accepts it. This acceptance, however, means the death of reality and non-recognition of fact. And the most vital energy of the dramatist has been directed towards constructing images in which fact and fiction coalesce to highlight Loman's losing struggle with reality. For one thing, the images give us ample knowledge of what passes through the tormented mind of a desperate man at the end of his tether, but rarely do they light up the significance of a situation. They are a series of incandescent pictures meant to bring home the strength of the hold of illusions on Loman's mind. These images, in which reality and illusion are so artistically intertwined, are no more than picturesque descriptions of his losing battle with life, his absorption with the idea of success, his tenacious hold on his dreams. The images, again, demonstrate his wild ambitions as well as his failures, and we are not allowed to forget the scenes of guilt, of occasional failings either in profession or in family surroundings. All these strengthen the impression of the littleness of Loman, though the little man's social reference is significant enough to make him a representative figure of modern industrial civilisation—a man whose dreams have been reduced to illusions, and yet the culture of the consumer society compels him, in a way, to cling to his dreams. He cannot confess failure in public, nor does he confess it to himself. The structure of the images allows two contradictory perspectives on one circumstance and the bridge between these perspectives is constructed by the imagination of the audience. The dramatic tension of the play largely depends on the inherent tension in these images, subdued though they are with the melancholy light of poetry. Their expressionistic quality further imparts a sense of unreality, even of futility, of everything that happens to Loman, and this makes us aware of the magnitude and intensity of the part played by illusion in contemporary American life. Loman's efforts may well be described in terms of structures of illusion—of which he was never conscious—although the audience enjoys every bit of irony of the situation. The images are important for their illustrative quality of the conflict of illusion and reality in the life of this average American. They give a convincing vision of the paradoxes in Willy Loman's existence—his total unthinking commitment to the advertised ideals of the great open American society, and his shocked discovery of its shrinking vision. Loman could never think of all this clearly, but the images bring to us the total futility of all his dreams: the barren ideals and treacherous illusions!

It is necessary to emphasise that Loman is gregarious by nature—a salesman can hardly afford to be lonely. Post-war drama, and fictional literature for that, focuses its particular attention on the lonely man. But Miller, in his choice of a salesman as the hero of the play, wants to demonstrate the progression of loneliness in a basically sociable man. Ben is the ideal of Loman's aspiration, and he appears at the end of Act I. Before that we always see him in the company of his family or friends. Act II, however, is an essay in disillusion; shock after shock make his life unbearable, and as he loses interest in the objective world his subjective world gains increasing importance for him, the bridge between the two being more and more tenuous. At the end we see a completely isolated man, lonely in his struggle with a hostile invisible enemy. One has, however, to remember that he fully shoulders the responsibility of his failure and does not blame anybody for it: his sense of remorse for his inability to make life fruitful points to a significant aspect of the contemporary cultural perspective. And the intensity of the dramatist's social thinking becomes proportionately clearer with the progressively shrinking picture of the objective world in Loman's thoughts: paradoxically enough, as the subjective world of Loman assumes larger proportion in the play the unspoken social significance of the whole thing becomes more and more insistent and broadens the focus of the theme by relating his world of imagination to the world outside. The play does not really challenge the whole American money-ethos, as some critics have been at pains to point out; Willy Loman never aspired to be a millionaire, his facile use of words like 'success', 'number one', 'greatest society', etc., are indications of his unthinking acceptance of the cultural values of his community rather than of any real craving to be number one in society; he wanted to have a normal happy life, sons settled and retired life in his own house—he liked to imagine that he could use his hands well, was proud to build the stoop ('there's more of him in that front stoop than in all the sales he ever made'.—Biff).

His superficial conviviality certainly betrays the cash-nexus attitude of the salesman, but it also demonstrates his deeper craving for genuine human relationship—which he was not permitted to cultivate. His sense of self-respect (often a pretension) does not allow him to accept a job offer from Charley, but he does not hesitate to accept loans from him. His confused tired mind was incapable of formulating anything of a higher than everyday level, and his entire life speaks for his enjoyment of mediocre success and comfort. Money was certainly valuable to him, but he valued to a greater extent honour, security, respect and recognition. His real enemy was, if we express the gist of his efforts and thinking, the values of contemporary American society, and not merely the economic organisation of the country. It is worth noting that he does not very frequently use words like 'money' or 'dollar'; it is only at the end he talks about the twenty thousand dollars from the insurance company, which will ensure security and future prospects for his family.

He had deep affection for his wife and sons. Linda's statement that he sacrificed his whole life for his sons was not far from the truth. Willy's one desire was to shine in his sons' eyes. He did not know himself nor did he understand his sons. He did not realise that he was largely responsible for their failure. He made them believe that they were born to be number one. Their youthfulness appeared to him to be a sure indication of exceptional qualities, their unwillingness to work hard to be the natural contempt of the brilliant for the plodding. He never tired of saying, 'Be liked and you will never want', and the two mediocre sons grew into crude uneducated fellows at a loss to define their own inadequacy. Happy remains totally blind to reality, trapped in the dream of being number one. But Biff finally awakens to the truth about his father and himself. In the funeral scene Biff says, 'He [Willy] had the wrong dreams. All, all, wrong . . . the man didn't know who he was.' Nothing truer has been said about Willy. And Happy's outburst, 'It's the only dream you can have—to come out number-one man', shows that he remains to the end as much illusion-ridden as his father. Willy, of course, lived and died in illusion. The irony of his illusion at the end is crushing: he died with the comforting discovery that Biff really loved him and his suicide was an act of love for his son, who would benefit to the extent of twenty thousand dollars. But he died with the illusion that twenty thousand dollars would be the making of Biff! Up to the very end he clung to his illusions.

Willy's is the typical case of a man of limited abilities attaching himself to images which his society has created. His success-worship, material ambition, faith in the magic of 'personal attractiveness', admiration of youthful flair rather than of quiet diligence are the stereotypes of mid-century American culture; there he is only an undistinguished member of a great conformity society. Loman's distinction, and the dramatic possibility of this character lies in the intensity of his fruitless struggle to achieve his end in the face of sure defeat, and his bewilderment over the failure to achieve success even when he follows all the accepted prescriptions for it. This dual character of the man—his wholehearted commitment to the contemporary business ethic and his bewilderment—makes the audience uneasy and arouses feelings of pity, and even of respect for this commercial traveller. For, even the limited one-track mind of Loman had its moments of doubt, although he always rationalised them with images of assurance. Miller, with a sure intuitive grasp of the total picture, dramatises these moments of Loman's weakness, and brings out, in a brilliantly expressive technique, the conflicts of illusion and reality inherent in the theme. It is assuredly an expression of the dilemmas and illusions of a commonplace salesman, and although there is little of verbal poetry in Miller's theatre (Miller indeed is awkward at it!), this is the only play in which genuine poetry is put into the perception, mood and architecture so much so that at moments it attains a poignancy and lyrical quality hardly achieved in post-war drama. The scenic juxtaposition of the alluring dreams of his troubled mind and the harsh reality crowding in on him has been simply superb. The sufferings and delusions of the man could hardly have been communicated more forcefully: and the conflict of illusion and reality (which is the abstract substance of the play) gains a singularly effective visual demonstration. The tragedy of the life of a little man, and the pretences of a culture of success and efficiency are the two sides of a composite picture that the playwright handles synchronously. Is this the American dream?—Miller seems to question—this life of illusion and frustration?

In focusing our attention on the power of illusion on the lives of common men in America today Miller is not really proving himself a prophet of doom. Far from it; his distrust of determinism and his belief in the freedom of human will are too insistent for that. 'Determinism, whether it is based on the iron necessities of economics or psychoanalytic theory', Miller states in his 'Introduction' to *Collected Plays*, 'seen as a closed circle, is a contradiction of the idea of drama itself as drama has come down to us in its fullest development'. *Death of a Salesman*'s particular appeal lies in its successful projection of the private concerns of Willy Loman as part of the values of the business world in America, in dramatising his illusions as a necessary product of the culture of his country. The grip of illusion on the psychology and behaviour of Loman is not seen in isolation from contemporary social forces, but his dreams and the reality of the technological culture are viewed as constituent parts of the same design. The fusion of these two areas heightens the dramatic character of the entire picture, and also imparts a sort of poetic ambience to the work. And in a sense this blending of the two forces defines the special character of the play.

Because of this successful coalescence of the two aspects of the picture, Willy Loman imperceptibly grows in stature as a representative of all Lomans. His obstinate clinging to his unrealisable dreams, to false values, to inflated ideas about himself come to us as a determined pattern of thinking of a large section of the community. Loman's misfortune, his human qualities and failures, his pride and his stupidity assume a larger dimension: his failures and pitfalls are largely the product of his own weaknesses, but one is reminded, progressively, of the responsibility of a money-centred culture, a culture that produces hollow dreams and false ideals. Against the background of this widespread culture of illusion, Loman's dreams and efforts take on a strangely unreal character, and his failures represent the failures of millions. The simultaneous focusing on the individual aspect and the social scene brings into sharper relief the importance of Loman; and intensifies the tragic quality of the play.

NOTES

[1] Quoted by Carl Shapiro, 'The Greatest Living Author' in Henry Miller's *Tropic of Cancer*, Grove Press, 1961, p. xxi.

Robert N. Wilson

THE SALESMAN AND SOCIETY

When failure takes Willy Loman in, we are obliged to follow him into the "longed-for valley," for we are all implicated in Willy's dream of success and his nightmare of defeat. Shaw, commenting upon the domestic drama of Ibsen, points out that we cannot be detached or merely amused; referring to the play within a play in *Hamlet,* Shaw calls the audience "guilty creatures sitting at a play." Why do we feel guilty? Why is *Death of a Salesman* so painfully close to home that we flinch and weep for our parents, and perhaps for ourselves? I suggest that the immense power of Arthur Miller's American tragedy is rooted in two primary sources: the psychological depth in which he explores family relationships, and his sociological grasp of certain fundamental elements of life, particularly occupational life, in the United States.

The Psychodynamic Elements

Daniel Schneider, in his remarkably perceptive study *The Psychoanalyst and the Artist,* finds the heart of the play in the relationship between the salesman, Willy, and his two sons. He starts with the symbol of the heavy sample cases that weigh on Willy as the play begins: "There is at the outset a cogent symbolization of the substance of the play: the salesman comes home carrying wearily the two battered, black sample cases that are his cross. They are like the two sons he has carried through life; they are a burden we want him to set down with honor, but we sense almost at once that they are to be his coffin."[1]

Schneider sees the presentation of historical events in the play, for example the conversations with Willy's older brother Ben or Biff's afternoon of football glory, as hallucinations in the present rather than as flashbacks to the past. These hallucinations constitute the return of the repressed, in psychoanalytic terms the invasion of the ego by primitive impulse. Here is the inrush of the unconscious self,

From *The Writer as Social Seer* (Chapel Hill: University of North Carolina Press, 1979), pp. 57–71.

unknowingly compromised and buried; it is the return Jung so terrifyingly characterized as "with knife in hand." Weakened by fatigue and oppressed by his length-
ening catalogue of failures, Willy becomes increasingly vulnerable and disorganized.
What we witness is a human being coming apart before our eyes. In Willy's own
words, "The woods are burning!"

Is Willy's disintegration the stuff of classic tragedy? Clearly, Willy is not in
actuality noble or larger than life. But he is a hero in his dreams, and this play is after
all concerned with a variety of feckless dreams. One might even contend that
twentieth-century American society differs from the society of Aristotle's *Poetics*
precisely in that here and now all men are enjoined to seek the ennoblement of
economic achievement. In any event, Willy is, in Meredith's fine phrase, "betrayed
by what is false within." And he is betrayed, of course, not only by his own intrinsic
flaws but by the manifold falsenesses he has long encouraged in his sons. There is
an inevitability about his collapse that is beautifully caught by Schneider's comparison of the sample cases to coffins.

Schneider isolates the sons' disillusionment with their father as the dominant
conflict in the play. Willy is a god who decays before the boys' eyes, a decay
strikingly shown in Biff's collapse after he finds his father in a Boston hotel room
with a mistress. The father has been sexless in being godlike, and this image is now
destroyed. Schneider sees this as a variation of the Oedipal theme: the father has
played god (for instance, in "fixing" things for the growing boys when they run into
trouble, the trouble having arisen in part from the sons' efforts to follow Willy's
warped dicta for "success") and then fails to measure up to godhood. One might
add the reciprocal disillusionment of Willy with his sons, a revelation so hard to
bear that in panic he adopts every strategy for concealing it from himself. Like all
families, the Lomans share certain almost essential fictions about one another; but
since their fictions are exaggerated and grotesque, the truth is correspondingly
painful in intensity. The mute conspiracy that supports the fictions and the devas-
tation brought by the unmasking are astonishingly similar to the themes of the family
drama in O'Neill's *Long Day's Journey into Night*.

Willy's steady fall in the second act, when he is told he is no good as a salesman
and simultaneously is driven to face his sons' unworthiness, culminates in symbolic
murder. Instead of having an anticipated celebration dinner at which Willy's authority and old paternal role might be reaffirmed, the father and sons break up:
Willy is symbolically castrated and rushes to the bathroom while the sons assert
their own sexuality by picking up two girls. The mother accuses the sons of killing
their father by their whoring. Schneider discovers in this sequence the ancient
archetypal drama celebrated in the Oedipus myth and in Freud's notion of the
primal horde. "This is as close to the original battle fought eons ago by man and his
sons as has ever been put upon the stage. It is this very thinly and yet very adroitly
disguised Oedipal murder which gives the play its peculiar symbolic prehistoric
power. It is not only modern man exploited; it is also Neanderthal man raging
against the restraint of civilization's dawn."[2]

Finally, Schneider thinks the tragedy is concerned with a hidden motivation—

the guilt of a younger son for hating his older brother. Willy envies the rich and mysterious Ben; Hap envies Biff. Willy's failure is in the defeat of his effort to overtake Ben by becoming a successful salesman. "In a sense," the psychoanalyst says, "every first son 'strikes it rich' in a younger son's eyes."[3]

This psychodynamic analysis, then, treats the play as primarily a family drama, attentive to unconscious motivations and preeminently psychological in import. Schneider sees the social conflicts as secondary and external to the clash of character and the working out of timeless universal forces. He says relatively little about the American society and the American values that constitute the environment of the family plot. But I shall argue that the society in which the Lomans move is more than a fortuitous historical frame, that its nature is integral to the action of the play. Willy's role as salesman is equal in significance to, and in the end inseparable from, his role as father and husband. For here the public and the private, the domestic and the occupational worlds, merge, and are alike confounded by Willy's posturing dreams.

The Necessity to Strive

Willy with his sample cases is not only the father, with his burdensome sons, parental responsibilities, and vast vulnerabilities. He is is also, and as importantly, a salesman sui generis. Those cases straining his arms and seeming to drain him of vitality are not merely symbols; they contain real goods for sale, and Willy in trying to peddle them is a pathetic archetype of the American dream of success. Despite the fact that most Americans are not salesmen by a strict occupational definition, that, unlike Willy, we work in large organizations and are hourly or salaried employees, we have in all of us something of the salesman and dream his dream of a success obtained through individual desire and energy. What Erich Fromm termed the "marketing orientation" is woven into the fabric of our national life; in this disposition of personality, the individual's credo is "I am as you desire me." So Willy attempts to be the person he thinks others desire: for his customers, the jovial yet dignified drummer; for his sons, the firm yet indulgent and all-protective father; for his wife, the ever-dependable breadwinner. He tells Biff and Happy about his friends: "And they know me, boys, they know me up and down New England. The finest people. And when I bring you fellas up, there'll be open sesame for all of us, 'cause one thing, boys: I have friends. I can park my car in any street in New England, and the cops protect it like their own."[4] In this society we all feel, more or less keenly, that we must sell ourselves, must be responsive to the demands of others, must make a good impression in order to be (as Willy puts it) not just "liked, but *well* liked."

When we see *Death of a Salesman* we are truly "guilty creatures at a play." Willy's failure is our failure, for we are also involved in the cult of success, and we, too, measure men by occupational attainment rather than by some sympathetic calculus of the whole human being. We are all partners in the American Dream and parties to the conspiracy of silence surrounding the fact that failures must by definition outnumber successes, given our cultural ground rules and our singular interpretations of the words "success" and "failure." Surely part of the undeniable power Miller's play exerts is rooted in the author's audacity in breaking this conspiracy of silence, in revealing to us a failure almost too painful for audiences to bear. How many times has one heard contemporaries exclaim that Willy reminds them of their own fathers, and that they find a deep loving sorrow in the reminiscence. One of the master themes in twentieth-century American literature is the articulation of the individual's quest for a vocational identity and a satisfying public image of self with the private world of family relationships. O'Neill, Fitzgerald, Hemingway—all grapple with the devilish ambiguities and profound disappointments that seem intrinsic to the striving for success and its attendant lack of domestic tranquility.

Success and Failure

We need to look more closely into the nature of success and into its social context in the United States. In this effort we can begin with a model first advanced by Robert K. Merton in his germinal essay "Social Structure and Anomie."[5] Merton distinguishes two major features of the social structure—cultural goals and institutional norms. Cultural goals consist of the ends toward which we strive, in Willy Loman's case the image of the master salesman, esteemed by all and almost effortlessly able to move his goods and earn a comfortable living. Thus Willy remembers his early ambition to seek his fortune in Alaska and what redirected him toward the life of a salesman.

> And I was almost decided to go, when I met a salesman in the Parker House. His name was Dave Singleman. And he was eighty-four years old, and he'd drummed merchandise in thirty-one states. And old Dave, he'd go up to his room, y'understand, put on his green velvet slippers—I'll never forget—and pick up his phone and call the buyers, and without ever leaving his room, at the age of eighty-four, he made his living. And when I saw that, I realized that selling was the greatest career a man could want. 'Cause what could be more satisfying than to be able to go, at the age of eighty-four, into twenty or thirty different cities, and pick up a phone, and be remembered and loved and helped by so many different people? Do you know? when he died—and by the way he died the death of a salesman, in his green velvet slippers in the smoker of the New York, New Haven and Hartford, going into Boston—when he died, hundreds of salesmen and buyers were at his funeral. Things were sad on a lotta trains for months after that.[6]

Willy's goal, then, reiterated in many guises throughout the course of the play, is to achieve as a salesman; but perhaps more important, it is to be "remembered and loved and helped by so many different people."

Merton asserts, "Aberrant behavior may be regarded sociologically as a symptom of dissociation between culturally prescribed aspirations and sociologically structured avenues for realizing those aspirations."[7] Willy finds that available institutional norms, or "structured avenues," are not open to him. Unable to discover the means to realize himself as a latter-day Dave Singleman, he does indeed become aberrant, but in a fashion we find all too poignantly understandable. Willy exemplifies the dissociation between goals and means that Merton identifies: "Contemporary American culture appears to approximate the polar type in which great emphasis upon certain success-goals occurs without equivalent emphasis upon institutional means."[8]

Merton's argument is essentially that American emphasis on success—particularly as gauged by the accumulation of wealth—outruns the availability of means for achieving success, at least among large sectors of the population. Individuals in the lower-middle and lower social strata are especially exposed to this discrepancy, and the lower-middle class is of course precisely Willy Loman's milieu. All audiences of *Death of a Salesman* are aware of Willy's unrealistic dreams, his half-knowing deception of himself and others. He harbors inflated hopes for his own success. When the hopes must be relinquished, when he is reduced to begging for "a little salary," they still persist in displaced form as dreams for his sons' achievements. Here he is entirely consistent with the familiar parental syndrome of projecting success hopes upon one's children; to pass the baton to the next runner in this fashion is also consonant with the stress on the unceasing struggle for achievement and on the assumption of individual responsibility for one's vocational destiny. Willy knows in very general terms where he wants to go—to be rich like his elder brother, Ben, or to be revered like Dave Singleman. But he hasn't the faintest idea of how to get there. Quite prepared to sell himself as well as his goods to pursue the chimera of being universally well liked, Willy lacks the interpersonal competence on which he pins his faith just as he lacks the technical competence to make big sales. He cannot adopt a meaningful strategy for achievement; stale slogans—"The world is an oyster, but you don't crack it open on a mattress!"—are the failing substitute for intelligent planning or commercial skill. As one of my affluent Ivy League undergraduates once disdainfully expressed it, "Willy just doesn't pack the gear." Yet the point is perhaps not to condemn the foolishness of his great expectations. It is, rather, to analyze the origins of the dream, the imperative for clinging to it in the face of overwhelmingly negative evidence, and the tenacity with which Willy holds his system of beliefs. Who taught this man to hope so gloriously, to dream so boldly?

Our culture has consistently exhorted the individual to strive for transcendent success. Today's inciting language is probably less vulgar (and also less honest) than the strident nineteenth-century pronouncements of an Andrew Carnegie—"Say each to yourself: 'My place is at the top.' Be king in your dreams"—or a Russell H. Conwell—"I say that you ought to get rich, and it is your duty to get rich"; "The idea is that in this country of ours every man has the opportunity to make more of himself than he does in his own environment, with his own skill, with his own energy, and with his own friends." But one may doubt that the substance of the message has changed much. The transition from Andrew Carnegie to Dale Carnegie, epitomized by David Riesman as "from the invisible hand to the glad hand," entails less emphasis on capital formation and more on the charms of leadership style, but the aim is still to be a winner in a very competitive game, whose rules are as vague as its scoreboard is explicit. In Merton's axiom of striving, one should regard the situation as fluid, never foreclosing one's chances, and should identify oneself with those at the top whom one will sooner or later join. And we are enjoined, further, to think that energetic ambition is in some sense a moral obligation, a responsibility devolving solely on the individual, to be honored even in the situation of patent failure.

Willy Loman is an exemplar of just these values. In fact, each of the figures in *Death of a Salesman* may be viewed as enmeshed in this set of circumstances, and each takes some path of action in the effort to deal with them. Merton sets forth a number of alternate strategies an individual might adopt in trying to cope with the American success ethic. He arranges them in a seemingly simple but remarkably stimulating model:

Conformity—accepting both conventional cultural goals and approved institutional means of reaching them

Innovation—accepting the goals but rejecting the fully legitimate means

Ritualism—rejecting or withdrawing from the goals, but dutifully adhering to the means

Retreatism—shunning both the goals and the means; essentially, not playing the game

Rebellion—substituting new values in the realms of both goals and means

Obviously, very few people could be expected to cling uniformly to a single one of these strategies throughout life; almost all actual behavior is composed of mixed strategies, and people shift their emphases in tune with life's exigencies. Nevertheless, it is fair to say that each of Miller's characters seizes one of these patterns as his dominant mode for coming to grips with the imperatives of success. A brief sketch of their choices may supplement Schneider's psychological analysis of the drama—the love and hate among brothers, fathers, and sons—with a sociological context.

Willy Loman's path is primarily that of conformity. Indeed, one of the saddest aspects of his story lies in his stubborn, futile effort to do what is expected of him; then, having played by the rules as he conceives them and having held a bright image of achievement in mind, he is unfairly deprived of his just reward. Thus Willy laments, in dialogue with his wife:

WILLY: Figure it out. Work a lifetime to pay off a house. You finally own it, and there's nobody to live in it.
LINDA: Well, dear, life is a casting off. It's always that way.
WILLY: No, no, some people—some people accomplish something.[9]

Especially in his earlier years, Willy embraces the dominant values of his culture and struggles to reach them through legitimate techniques. He has never really *been* very successful, but he has admired those who made it and he has held out hope. His sense of the imperative is so overpowering that he is forced to lie to himself and his sons, to buck himself up with a threnody of exhortation and might have been. He doggedly believes in his society as the land of opportunity. But Willy does not realize that "personality" and friendship are not enough. In the contemporary United States occupational conduct is more clearly governed by "universalism" (not who you are, but what you can do) and "functional specificity" (not the valuing of the total man, but of his specific skills and contributions to some enterprise). So Willy's best friend Charley tries to enlighten him:

> WILLY: Charley, I'm strapped, I'm strapped. I don't know what to do. I was just fired.
> CHARLEY: Howard fired you?
> WILLY: That snotnose. Imagine that? I named him. I named him Howard.
> CHARLEY: Willy, when're you gonna realize that them things don't mean anything? You named him Howard, but you can't sell that. The only thing you got in this world is what you can sell. And the funny thing is that you're a salesman, and you don't know that.
> WILLY: I've always tried to think otherwise, I guess. I always felt that if a man was impressive, and well liked, that nothing—
> CHARLEY: Why must everybody like you? Who liked J. P. Morgan? Was he impressive? In a Turkish bath he'd look like a butcher. But with his pockets on he was very well liked.[10]

Willy, however, cannot bring himself to understand. He talks of his n'er-do-well older son, Biff: "Biff Loman is lost. In the greatest country in the world a young man with such—personal attractiveness, gets lost."[11]

As life closes in on him in the form of time payments, disappointing children, failing energies, and the bald truth that the Dave Singleman legend is not to be his, Willy slips more nearly into *ritualism*. He still plays the game and abides by the rules but doesn't truly hope for economic success; he emphasizes his manual talents more strongly and his wish to raise chickens at a little place in the country. Finally he follows an unusual form of *innovation:* desperately wanting the success goals for his sons, he uses illegitimate means to provide them with money—that is, the proceeds of his life insurance policy, the only tangible thing he has to give them. From another perspective, Willy's suicide could be seen as the ultimate in *retreatism,* the final turning away from a life and a society that have perhaps failed him as much as he has failed them. Suicide, given Willy's hopes for his boys and his dutifulness toward his wife, may be for him the closest approximation of the more common kinds of retreatism such as Skid Row.

Willy's friend and neighbor, Charley, exemplifies *conformity,* accepting both the goal of success and the approved routes to its attainment. He and his son, Bernard, form a counterpoint to Willy and his boys; Charley and Bernard are realists, appraising their circumstance with clear eye and hard head. Their facility in "making it" is presented to us in recurrent contrast to the windy, aimless thrashing about of the Lomans, impaled between dreams and incompetence. We are offered few details of Charley's successful coping. He appears as a shrewd if largely un-heeded counselor to Willy, and as a businessman comfortable enough to subsidize Willy's declining months. Bernard's career, traced in somewhat more detail, is the classic American success story of our era. Thematically, it is sharply opposed to the drifting non-careers of Biff and Happy Loman. At least two facets of Bernard's history are especially significant in the light of contemporary social structure. The first is the value he places on education, which is, as we know, more and more often *the* path to occupational achievement. Bernard learns his lessons well; he is groomed by the school system and his parents to value both academic attainment per se and the complex of motivations surrounding it. A "good boy" conforming to all expectations, he reaps a good boy's rewards. The second striking element in Bernard is the symbolic import of his career, the meaning of appearing as a lawyer before the Supreme Court. Here Miller has chosen both a high-prestige profession—in some ways today the case type of conforming careerism—and an institution, the Supreme Court, that stands at the very peak of American occupa-tional esteem. Finally, the scene between Bernard and Willy in Charley's office and the ensuing conversation Willy has with Charley underline again the distinctions between a fulfilling and an unfulfilling conformity. We have once more the contrast of charm versus competence, seeming versus doing.

> WILLY: The Supreme Court! And he didn't even mention it!
> CHARLEY: He don't have to—he's gonna do it.[12]

Willy's brother, Ben, represents *innovation* in Merton's analysis. He has fully adopted the goal of material success but has apparently taken unusual and not entirely approved means to realize the goal. He has gone outside the framework of his society as an adventurer in the Alaska of that day, presumably the twenties and thirties. His business ethics are questionable, as indicated in the scene in which he trips Biff with his cane and comments, "Never fight fair with a stranger, boy. You'll never get out of the jungle that way."[13] Like many innovators—the Robber Barons of the late nineteenth century, the gangsters of the twentieth—Ben has a glamorous aura. People like Ben have often been admired in American life, espe-cially by the conforming or ritualistic Willys, who see in the Bens a confirmation of the cultural promise. Thus Willy describes Ben's success: "What's the mystery? The man knew what he wanted and went out and got it! Walked into a jungle, and comes out, the age of twenty-one, and he's rich!"[14]

It is true, as Schneider observes, that the heart of *Death of a Salesman* is the complex relationships between Willy and his sons and between the two sets of brothers (Willy and Ben, Biff and Happy). The dynamics of this interplay, punctu-ated by affection, jealousy, high expectations and cruel recriminations, are the threads that lead us through Willy's disaster. But the primary sociological point is

these relationships all find their focus, their emotional field of force, in the occupational world and the success ethic. We have seen how Willy and Ben take
different paths and how Ben represents for Willy a brutal, flashy alternative to the
success image of Dave Singleman. How do Biff and Happy respond to the challenges inherent in Merton's model of ends and means?

The Loman brothers grow up nourished by their father's misguided but
potent success dream. Throughout their lives Willy devotes himself to coaching
them, almost like an older teammate, in the techniques for winning the striving
game. He stresses, of course, those tactics he believes to be the keys to achievement: popularity, congeniality, physical prowess, attractiveness—in a phrase, the
cult of personality. Willy never tells the boys they need skill or industriousness;
indeed, he sedulously encourages them, especially Biff, in cutting corners and relying
on personal magnetism to carry the day. One might say he determinedly sells them
the bill of goods he has once been sold, infecting the next generation with the
vocational pathology whose symptoms bring him down.

Biff, the older son, appears to fit the pattern of *retreatism*. We feel occasionally that if Biff had more energy and stability of purpose he might pursue *rebellion;*
yet his rebellion only flickers in the desert of his nomadic drifting, as in his dream
of an outdoor life far from the rat race. Although Biff pays sporadic lip service to
the cultural goals, partly in a futile effort to buck up the sagging Willy, he really has
withdrawn his allegiance from both common goals and common means. His wandering in the West is an escape from the competitive occupational world, just as it
is an escape from the father whose infidelity makes him feel sexually betrayed. He
vaguely yearns for something different but does not have the qualities to articulate
and search out that "something." Biff's attitudes and behavior add up to a bitter
caricature of a man, trapped by the success ethic, floundering as his father floun-
ders: "I tell ya, Hap, I don't know what the future is. I don't know—what I'm
supposed to want. . . . And always to have to get ahead of the next fella. And
still—that's how you build a future. . . . I've always made a point of not wasting my
life, and everytime I come back here I know that all I've done is waste my life."[15]

Happy seems harder to place in Merton's terms but is generally *conforming.*
Although his sharp business practices may incline toward *innovation* on the style of
his Uncle Ben, his is a kind of empty conformity. Happy gets, in modest measure,
what he thinks he wants, but his life is somehow flavorless, without bite or savor.
He is the one character many critics of the play have found puzzling and inconsistent
with the master themes of the drama. Schneider goes so far as to suggest that the
play might be seen as a dream of Happy, that he stands outside the main flow of
action.

Linda, wife and mother, is obviously the linchpin that holds the Loman family
together, as nearly as they may be said to cohere. Of course, in her role she does
not confront the occupational strife as a direct participant; nevertheless, the strains
of all three male Lomans lap over into her life. Hers is the voice of sweet reason,
of the wise, resigned observer. But with all her understanding of what makes Willy

run, she is powerless to stop the onrush of failure and doom. Linda's chosen path is *ritualism*. She keeps on keeping on but asks wearily, "Why must everybody conquer the world?"[16]

Final Comparisons

One might argue, with justice, that *Death of a Salesman's* only peer as the American play of the twentieth century is Eugene O'Neill's *Long Day's Journey into Night*. As I noted earlier, there are many thematic similarities in the two. They are, of course, "about" the same thing—life-long quest of a certain image of self and other, set in the twin frameworks of family role relationships and occupational success striving. Both demonstrate how these spheres interpenetrate, particularly the way in which a culturally enjoined success ethic informs and corrodes family life. The Lomans and the Tyrones, though unlike in many ways, are both nuclear families and almost totally self-absorbed. The family members, with few ties to any rich life outside, feed upon one another; demanding too much of one another and of themselves, they are embittered by the inevitable gulf between ideal image and functioning reality. Both families subsist on fictions, shared delusions that seem necessary to the preservation of any family life at all. Perhaps all families require the maintenance of certain myths about themselves; but the Tyrones and the Lomans are extraordinary in the pervasiveness and grandeur of their domestic myths. In each play, crises arise and create a breaking through of the delusive fabric. Thus Biff, at last determined to expose Willy's comforting lies for what they are, says, "We never told the truth for ten minutes in this house!"[17] The dramas are also akin in that the action pivots on a troubled target member—Willy Loman, Mary Tyrone—whose torments throw the tangle of domestic affection and accusation into sharp relief.

In the end, Willy's tragedy lies as much in the bringing down of his dreams as in the bringing down of the man. In some curious way, perhaps the dreams were the best part of the man. Willy chased the same green light Jay Gatsby chased. Willy and Gatsby share the same epitaph—"nobody came to the funeral." Willy's whole being has been based on the moving power of a friendship and a presence that do not exist. And so his last dream of all comes to nothing: "Ben, that funeral will be massive! They'll come from Maine, Massachusetts, Vermont, New Hampshire! All the old-timers with the strange license plates—that boy will be thunder-struck, Ben, because he never realized—I am known! Rhode Island, New York, New Jersey—I am known, Ben, and he'll see it with his eyes once and for all. He'll see what I am, Ben!"[18]

Thomas Mann once remarked to Arthur Miller that *Death of a Salesman* is uniquely American in its directness, its transparency; everyman is here revealed to us in the simple, tangible story of a salesman who cannot sell. The play is now more than a quarter of a century old, and Willy Loman's America has been in many ways transformed. Yet the values portrayed and betrayed are with us still, and the pain and terror are not diminished by a fraction. Linda and Charley, who see Willy unblinkered, affirm that he is a tragic hero. Their words are now familiar, engraved on the consciousness of those who care about the American theatre and care about the texture of our national life:

> LINDA: I don't say he's a great man. Willy Loman never made a lot of money. His name was never in the paper. He's not the finest character that ever lived. But he's a human being, and a terrible thing is happening to him. So attention must be paid. He's not to be allowed to fall into his grave like an old dog. Attention, attention must be finally paid to such a person. . . . A small man can be just as exhausted as a great man. . . .
>
> CHARLEY: Nobody dast blame this man. You don't understand: Willy was a salesman. And for a salesman, there is no rock bottom to the life. He don't put a bolt to a nut, he don't tell you the law or give you medicine. He's a man way out there in the blue, riding on a smile and a shoeshine. And when they start not smiling back—that's an earthquake. And then you get yourself a couple of spots on your hat, and you're finished. Nobody dast blame this man. A salesman is got to dream, boy. It comes with the territory. . . .
>
> LINDA: Help me, Willy, I can't cry. It seems to me that you're just on another trip. I keep expecting you. Willy, dear, I can't cry. Why did you do it? I search and search and I can't understand it, Willy. I made the last payment on the house today. Today, dear. And there'll be nobody home. We're free and clear. We're free. We're free . . . We're free . . .[19]

NOTES

[1] Daniel Schneider, *The Psychoanalyst and the Artist* (New York: Farrar, Straus, 1950), p. 247.
[2] Ibid., p. 251.
[3] Ibid., p. 254.
[4] Arthur Miller, *Death of a Salesman* (New York: Viking Press, 1949), p. 31.
[5] Robert K. Merton, *Social Theory and Social Structure* (New York: Free Press, 1957), pp. 131–60. I should here give credit to my former student David Perlmutter, who first perceived the quite astonishing parallel between Merton's scheme and action of *Death of a Salesman*.
[6] Miller, *Death of a Salesman*, p. 81.
[7] Merton, *Social Theory*, p. 134.
[8] Ibid., p. 136.
[9] Miller, *Death of a Salesman*, p. 15.
[10] Ibid., p. 97.
[11] Ibid., p. 16.
[12] Ibid., p. 95.
[13] Ibid., p. 49.
[14] Ibid., p. 41.
[15] Ibid., pp. 22–23.
[16] Ibid., p. 85.
[17] Ibid., p. 131.
[18] Ibid., p. 126.
[19] Ibid., pp. 56, 138, 139.

Jeremy Hawthorn
SALES AND SOLIDARITY

The very title, *Death of a Salesman,* directs our attention to the relationship between the personal and the commercial, the individual and the employee. In 1948, when the play was first performed and the Cold War had well and truly started, Miller's work evoked the same sort of interest as had been aroused by *She Stoops to Conquer* nearly two centuries previously, and for not dissimilar reasons. Both plays concern themselves directly with issues so central to their respective societies that their audiences responded to them as to personal revelations. As we saw earlier with Lucy Snowe, in her surprise to discover Polly's thoughts so similar to her own, a society which privatizes and represses certain feelings does not allow its members to discover that their secret fantasies and their apparently idiosyncratic impulses are common to many. One of the most positive aspects of art and literature is that they work against such concealments, allowing the individual to discover himself or herself in other people—and vice-versa. It is because Arthur Miller confronts problems central to his time and his society in *Death of a Salesman* that he is able to touch the private and personal concerns of his characters—and his audience—so effectively.

Part of Miller's genius perhaps consisted in his having chosen a *salesman* as hero. The very name of the profession triggers off just the right contradictory responses: representative on the one hand of the capitalist ethic, commerce, free enterprise, individual initiative and personal achievement (along with the geographical and social mobility so much a part of the American Dream), but on the other hand with a reputation for double-dealing, hypocrisy, easy morality and the ethics of the rat-race. When American voters were asked whether or not they would buy a used car from Nixon, they were being encouraged to recognize precisely the same sort of untrustworthiness in the politician as they knew had to be guarded against in the salesman.

From *Multiple Personality and the Disintegration of Literary Character: From Oliver Goldsmith to Sylvia Plath* (New York: St. Martin's Press, 1983), pp. 108–16.

Willy Loman's fragmentation, then, has to be seen as an exaggerated version of what people already associated with salesmen; people whose private thoughts were at variance with their public professions. As with all such forms of knowledge, however, this awareness of the gap between the commercial and the human is a partial one for most people in a capitalist society; it is there to be used in practical situations, it will be admitted when people are explicitly asked about it, but its implications are rarely followed through. The reasons for this can be found within Miller's play: there is a continuous barrage of propaganda to deny that this is the case, sometimes direct propaganda, but more often than not indirect and subtle.

Let me, prior to looking in detail at *Death of a Salesman,* give an example of what I mean. Barbara O'Brien's book *Operators and Things* is an account of a schizophrenic breakdown suffered by the writer, a breakdown which took the form of her experiencing severe hallucinations, in which various odd and threatening individuals gave her orders and advice which she, believing in their real existence, followed. O'Brien starts her account with a description of the pressures she felt subject to at work, a description which calls to mind Golyadkin's and Aikeky Aikeyevitch's office nightmares, and which suggests that some forms of social pressure are crystallized in tensions at work. O'Brien picks out one business technique which she names 'hook operating.'

> I've made some sharp revisions in my ideas of how people get ahead fast in business since the day I looked at Ken [*a colleague*] and saw how clear it all was. The thing you need is a special kind of skill that Ken didn't have and could never have developed. It's the technique of the Hook Operator. (O'Brien 1976, 30)

According to O'Brien, success in business follows implementation of the techniques of hook operating. The hook operator, once he (and it normally is he, not she) enters a business organization, noses out the person with power. He then finds his weak spot and wounds it either to discredit another person (the rival), or to make himself essential to the 'Powerman.'

Such a summary does scant justice to O'Brien's lengthy account of the techniques of getting ahead in business, but it does indicate its main points. In the organization in which she worked there were two such operators: Gordon and McDermott. Of them she comments:

> [. . .] there are too many men like Gordon and McDermott for me to feel now that all of them are twisted. In a way, they have adapted themselves superbly to a certain type of business environment. Both Gordon and McDermott cut the most direct road they could find to where they wanted to go. That they both knifed a few men getting there was totally unimportant to either of them.[. . .] Christian principles are not the principles on which the Hook Operators build their lives, although this fact, so glaringly obvious to others, is rarely apparent to the Hook Operators. I think that the strangest thing I knew

about either Gordon or McDermott was that both were extremely religious men. (O'Brien 1976, 35)

There are two crucial insights in this passage, to which I wish to draw attention. Firstly, that the *primary* contradiction is not in the people themselves but in the type of business environment to which they have adapted, and secondly that this adaptation has turned them into divided and contradictory people, although they don't know this and feel themselves to be perfectly normal and consistent.

O'Brien's breakdown is a classic example of how the person who tries to remain consistent, in an environment which demands inconsistency, is driven mad. Her breakdown took the form not of a personality split in the manner of my earlier case-histories, but of hallucinations in which, among other things, personified hook operators appeared and explained the world to her. However, what I find most interesting of all in her account, and most directly relevant to Willy Loman's case, is that in spite of the fact that she is amazed to discover that neither McDermott nor Gordon recognize the contradictions in the values according to which they live, she too ends up by blaming her breakdown, in a curiously confused passage, not on her situation but upon herself:

> I seem to be blaming my community for a personal tragedy. I am not. There was nothing particularly wrong with it and there was a great deal in it that was right. It was a civilized community. The tragedy was that, overnight, certain jungle qualities appeared faster than I could adjust to them. The error lay, not in the community in which I was reared but in the way in which I, as an individual, adapted to it. I departmentalized, burying elements inside of me which should never have been buried and as a consequence lost wholeness to gain acceptance for a part of me. (O'Brien 1976, 140)

As I say, this seems to me to be confused, indeed, almost neurotic in its refusal to place the blame where all her earlier arguments lead—in the ethics of the business community. To call the community civilized is directly at variance with what she has earlier described as the perfect fit between the techniques of the hook operators and the business community to which they are adapted. It is odd that, in the passage just quoted, the civilized community is distinguished from 'certain jungle qualities' which just 'appeared'—the vague grammatical formulation serving to obscure whether or not the jungle qualities are part of the so-called civilized community or, as is here hinted if not explicitly stated, somehow extraneous to them.

I find this process of equivocation and contradiction very significant indeed. Let me explain why by drawing a parallel with Miss Beauchamp's case. We can hypothesize that a key contradiction in her case—if not the key contradiction—lay in the ambivalent attitude towards sexuality of her society. If you were respectable, then you were not sexually excited by improper conversation and behaviour. Finding that she was sexually excited by these, Miss Beauchamp had, we may hypothesize, two alternatives. Either she could decide that the accepted views of her society were wrong: nice girls *were* also subject to sexual excitement as a result of behaviour not considered proper, or she could decide that society was right and that therefore she was not a nice girl. We can further hypothesize that Miss Beauchamp felt incapable of condemning society and its double standards vis-a-vis sexual morality and behaviour, and so she was forced to conclude that the fault lay in her. However, being unable to accept either that she had not been sexually aroused by Mr Jones, or that she was not respectable, she resolved the irresolveable by becoming two people: one respectable person and one person subject to improper sexual excitement. (I should make it clear that although I find this a defensible interpretation of part of Miss Beauchamp's personality fragmentation, it is clearly not the whole story.)

In Barbara O'Brien's case we can see that, by refusing to locate that double-standard she deplores in society, by failing to see that her society claims to be a Christian society but also runs its businesses according to the law of the jungle, she forces herself to ascribe her breakdown to her own inadequacy. The pattern is directly applicable to Willy Loman's case. He is neither unimaginative enough to act as did McDermott and Gordon and proceed oblivious of the fact that there are contradictions in his life (although it is perhaps the case that he tries to do this but fails), nor can he recognize the larger double standards central and essential to his job and the capitalist social system. He believes the version of the American Dream that comes from the Chevrolet advertisements in the glossy magazines, and he tries to fit his actual life experiences into this mythic pattern. When the two won't fit he refuses to acknowledge the fact until he is first of all split into two people and, finally, destroyed. (Although he commits suicide it is also legitimate to see his death as something that is imposed upon him by outside forces.) Like Barbara O'Brien, Willy Loman refuses to blame his job or his society for inculcating false and contradictory values, perhaps because these values have become so much a part of his view of himself that to attack them would involve reconstructing enormous aspects of himself. We can see a similar pattern in Virginia Woolf's *Mrs Dalloway*, in which novel Septimus, the 'mad' character, at one point muses that as his brain is perfect, 'It must be the fault of the world then—that he could not feel.' But the medical profession takes it upon itself to prove that it is in fact Septimus, not the world, that is at fault, and he too commits suicide. We can perhaps venture a generalization here: if a person is subjected to intolerable and contradictory pressures from society, family or work, but insists upon seeing these pressures as normal, uncontradictory and manageable, then he or she will be forced to conclude that the fault is in him or herself.

This leads us to the vexed issue of ideology, around which there has been much debate in recent years, and to which I have at this moment scant desire to add much comment. *Death of a Salesman* is a play which forces us to consider the issue of ideology however, as Willy Loman's breakdown is so clearly associated with the ideological pressures placed upon him by his work and his society. One of Willy's problems is that like Septimus he refuses to compartmentalize; he tries to behave to others and to himself in a consistent way. Paradoxically, of course, this has the effect of splitting him in two. During my discussion of Dostoyevsky's *The Double* in an earlier chapter I quoted from Ludwig *et al.* (1972) to the effect that the separate functioning of different personalities may represent a more effective way of handling anxiety than a coalescence of identities in one, integrated personality. I commented then that it may not just be a better way of handling anxiety, but a better way of handling contradictions in society. The point is germane to a discussion of Willy Loman's case. Willy's problem is not that he is divided, but that he cannot keep his separate identities apart. It is not that he is affected by the Chevrolet advertisement or by dreams of his son becoming a great football player—that much must have been true of millions of Americans—but that when his actual experiences fail to measure up to these ideologically imposed myths he attempts to paper over reality with the myth. Another way of putting it is to suggest that Willy's problem is not that he is divided, but that he is not divided enough: we can recall that Wemmick's life starts to become problematic for him only when his 'country' personality intrudes into his 'town' existence. Willy's mistake is, as Charley points out at the end of the play, that he allows the dreams necessary to his work to start to take over his whole person.

> Nobody dast blame this man. You don't understand: Willy was a salesman. And for a salesman, there is no rock bottom to the life. He don't put a bolt to a nut, he don't tell you the law or give you medicine. He's a man way out there in the blue, riding on a smile and a shoeshine. And when they start not smiling back—that's an earthquake. And then you get yourself a couple of spots on your hat, and you're finished. Nobody dast blame this man. A salesman is got to dream, boy. It comes with the territory. (Miller 1968, 111)

If it is significant that Herbert Pocket and Pip make their fortune abroad, it is equally revealing that Willy Loman's dream is associated with the myth of the frontiersman, the man who solves all the contradictions of his social relationships by geographical movement, by lighting out to a new territory, in which things can all start afresh. But Willy's 'territory' is not virgin land: it is the capitalist jungle, and its problems cannot be solved through individual effort.

As Charley points out, the salesman is, as it were, almost the personification of pure exchange: he does not engage in productive labour, he doesn't help people directly, he sells, and he also sells himself. Thus when people stop smiling back it means not only that you are failing at your job, but also that you are forced to see the other side of that freedom from human contact that in one part of the myth you prize. As Charley says, you have got to dream, 'It comes with the territory', you have to lead a fantasy life because your workaday life is denuded of all real human contact. It is important to recognize, therefore, that Willy's dreams are not just personal idiosyncrasies, but necessary products of his job as a salesman. We can suggest, though, that whereas the dream usually functions as a *compensation* for the life the salesman has to lead, Willy tries to impose it on that life, to see his whole existence in terms of this compensatory dream. And, paradoxically, by trying to lead a consistent, undivided life, he ends up separating it into dream and reality.

Biff comes to see this. He says that Willy had the wrong dreams, and he looks at the pen he has just stolen, a theft which at this point in the play seems to epitomize a particular set of qualities: individualism, self-seeking and hardness. He asks himself

> what the hell am I grabbing this for? Why am I trying to become what I don't want to be? What am I doing in an office, making a contemptuous, begging fool of myself, when all I want is out there, waiting for me the minute I say I know who I am! (Miller 1968, 105)

The insight here is, I feel, only partial, and its incompleteness is perhaps as much Miller's as it is Biff's. Biff still believes that the escape from such contradictions is an individual thing, dependent upon 'knowing who you are', even if he does recognize that there are pressures on people to be what is unnatural to them. The idea that one might have a very good perception of who one is, but still be unable to allow this perceived identity full play in a society that is not run on exclusively human lines is missing. There is thus a case for arguing that although *Death of a Salesman* attacks the American Dream through Willy, there is a certain amount of ideological recuperation through Biff. If all we had to do was recognize who we were, and act upon it, then clearly Willy is personally responsible for his collapse.

In many ways the play is split between a recognition of the falsity of the dream of individual salvation, with the implication that the society that fosters such dreams is at fault, and a view that is itself fundamentally individualistic, that human beings have to work out their own salvation and choose the right life for themselves. Thus in the early conversation between Biff and Happy about going out West, the unreal nature of this solution to their problems is clearly signposted:

> BIFF [*with enthusiasm*]: Listen, why don't you come out West with me?
> HAPPY: You and I, heh?
> BIFF: Sure, maybe we could buy a ranch. Raise cattle, use our muscles. Men built like we are should be working out in the open.
> HAPPY [*avidly*]: The Loman Brothers, heh? (Miller 1968, 17)

This solution, clearly shown as an impossible dream at this stage of the play, is the one actually chosen in a modified form by Biff at the end of the play.

Willy is a man who has never realized that his dreams are dreams, and may offer him some comfort for the life he has to lead, but can never actually be lived. In one sense this is what marks out his moral stature: he refuses to accept the existence—or the power—of the sordid commercial values that dominate his working life. When he gets no help from Howard, the son of his old boss who he actually named, he is surprised; he believes that his human relationship with Howard and his father means that he can expect human treatment by them. Charley tells him the truth:

Willy, when're you gonna realize that them things don't mean anything? You
named him Howard, but you can't sell that. The only thing you got in this
world is what you can sell. And the funny thing is that you're a salesman, and
you don't know that. (Miller 1968, 76)

Such blindness, we are led to feel, is to a certain extent one of Willy's endearing
qualities; to fail in a society in which the price of success is so high may indicate a
humanity that is not to be despised. And Willy's belief that human values really
count that much in the commercial world is, after all, a belief that is fostered in his
(and our) society. As the authors of *Love and Commitment* put it:

The profusion of images of love in our culture makes it appear as if they can
penetrate any social context. They never depict exchange occurring in solidarity contexts. Moreover, there is no social context which these images
cannot encompass. For example, we are shown interracial couples drinking in
harmony in neighborhood bars in working-class communities. More insidi-
ously, these images portray solidarity and exchange as perfectly compatible
[...]. (Schwarz and Merten 1980, 254)

They go on to suggest, in a comment to which I have already made reference, that
whereas in contemporary American culture solidarity is vulnerable to transformation by exchange principles, people are led to believe that it is the reverse that is
actually the case. This is what Willy believes: that his human relationships with
others are more important (which they are) and more powerful (which, immediately, they are not) than the arguments of cash and commerce.

In my earlier discussion of Barbara O'Brien's book, I quoted a comment of
hers in which she referred to 'jungle qualities' which appeared in her business
community. The word 'jungle' appears a number of times in *Death of a Salesman*
and represents precisely those same qualities of unprincipled self-seeking and ambition described by Barbara O'Brien. The character who personifies them in the
play is Ben who, in a mock fight with the young Biff, trips him up and threatens his
eye with an umbrella:

BEN [*patting* Biff's *knee*]: Never fight fair with a stranger, boy. You'll never get
out of the jungle that way. (Miller 1968, 38)

If Willy imposes his human dream on the inhuman world, Ben imposes the values
of his inhuman world on his human relationships.

Willy's problem, though, is that the inhuman world keeps tripping him up,
holding an umbrella to his eye, and demanding that he recognize its existence. Thus
Willy gets agitated and angry when he senses that reality is going to break into his
dream:

LINDA: When you write you're coming, he's all smiles, and talks about the
    future, and—he's just wonderful. And then the closer you seem to come,

the more shaky he gets, and then, by the time you get here, he's arguing,
and he seems angry at you. (Miller 1968, 42)

The reality of Biff and Happy cannot mesh in with the fantasy picture of them that
Willy has, a picture which clearly Willy has not constructed from nothing, but which
he has absorbed from the myths of his culture. When I hear the following imaginary
speech of Willy's to his young sons, it reminds me of nothing more than those car
advertisements in glossy American magazines of the 1940s and 1950s:

> WILLY: I been wondering why you polish the car so careful. Ha! Don't leave the
> hubcaps, boys. Get the chamois to the hubcaps. Happy, use newspaper
> on the windows, it's the easiest thing. Show him how to do it, Biff! You
> see, Happy? Pad it up, use it like a pad. That's it, that's it, good work.
> You're doin' all right, Hap. [*He pauses, then nods in approbation for a
> few seconds, then looks upward.*] Biff, first thing we gotta do when we
> get time is clip that big branch over the house. Afraid it's gonna fall in a
> storm and hit the roof. [. . .] (Miller 1968, 21)

The gap between the world of advertisements and reality is more or less explicitly
referred to when Willy contradicts himself so starkly about his refrigerator and his
car. Willy tells Linda that the 'Chevrolet [. . .] is the greatest car ever built', then a
few moments later, learning that he still owes money on the carburettor (something they don't normally talk about in car advertisements), he explodes, 'That
goddam Chevrolet, they ought to prohibit the manufacture of that car!'

What Willy says of the refrigerator is true of himself:

> Once in my life I would like to own something outright before it's broken! I'm
> always in a race with the junkyard! I just finished paying for the car and it's on
> its last legs. The refrigerator consumes belts like a goddam maniac. They time
> those things. They time them so when you finally paid for them, they're used
> up. (Miller 1968, 56)

On the day that Linda makes the last payment on the house, she also buries
Willy. He too has been a victim of planned obsolescence; when he has no more
cash value, his humanity is discarded. As Willy says to Howard, he has been used
like an orange; the fruit has been eaten and the peel—Willy himself—is thrown
away.

Willy Loman's fragmentation, then, cannot be seen simply as the result of a
fatal flaw in him, an inability to work out who he is or what he wants. He swallows
the tales he is told, but he cannot digest them. Only by blackmailing people to share
his fantasies can he maintain them for a limited period, but eventually, like all those
who try to live in a divided society as if it were undivided, he is crushed. Ben
survives, because the laws of the jungle can be imposed upon the human world in
his society, whereas Willy discovers that in America the laws of the truly human

cannot be imposed upon the jungle. As Schwarz and Merten put it, solidarity cannot penetrate exchange relationships; love does not conquer all.

In Brecht's *The Good Woman of Setzuan* the heroine, Shen Te, learns the lesson indicated by Ludwig et al.; the separate functioning of alter identities can in certain circumstances be a more effective way of surviving than the creation of a consistent and integrated personality. In her and Willy Loman's divisions we see comparable insights into the nature of societies which, paradoxically, insist that their members divide themselves in order to stay whole. But in the last resort, whereas Brecht moves from this insight to a clear indication that society must needs be changed, Miller's conclusion retreats from the implications of his earlier analysis.

REFERENCES

Ludwig, Arnold M.; Brandsma, Jeffrey M.; Wilbur, Cornelia B.; Bedfeldt, Fernando; and Jameson, Douglas H. 1972: "The Objective Study of a Multiple Personality." *Archives of General Psychology* 26 (April).

Miller, Arthur 1968: *Death of a Salesman*. Reprinted. Harmondsworth: Penguin Books.

O'Brien, Barbara 1976: *Operators and Things: The Inner Life of a Schizophrenic*. Reissued. London: Routledge & Kegan Paul.

Schwarz, Gary, and Merten, Don (with Fran Behan and Allyne Rosenthal) 1980: *Love and Commitment*. Beverly Hills and London: Sage.

C. W. E. Bigsby
ARTHUR MILLER

The origins of Miller's best-known play lie in a brief short story which he wrote at the age of seventeen and which his mother rediscovered at the time of its first production. Called 'In Memoriam', it is based on Miller's own experience with a Jewish salesman when he was working for his father for a few months after graduating from high school. The story is concerned with a single day during which the young narrator accompanies the salesman, carrying some of his samples for him (in this case, coats). The man is old and tired and has to humble himself by asking his young companion for the car fare. The salesman sells nothing and is mistreated by the buyers. The story ends with his reported death and the narrator's sentimental response. In fact, Miller observes in a note scrawled on the manuscript, the man had thrown himself in front of a subway train.

Clearly the experience and the story do contain the seeds of the later play. As the narrator observes of the old man,

> His was a salesmans [sic] profession, if one may call such dignified slavery a profession, and he tried to interest himself in his work. But he never became entirely moulded into the pot of that business. His emotions were displayed at the wrong times always and he never quite knew when to laugh. Perhaps if I may say so he never was complete. He had lost something vital. There was an air of quiet solitude, of cryptic wondering about both he and his name.

He is described as looking out of place in clothes which seemed to have been chosen by someone else and with a name which seemed not wholly to belong to him. 'His last name was Schoenzeit, the first I never learned, but it had to be Alfred. He always seemed to need that name.' His growing desperation is apparent in his whole manner. 'I knew that he felt as though his life was ended, that he was merely

From *A Critical Introduction to Twentieth-Century American Drama, Volume 2: Tennessee Williams, Arthur Miller, Edward Albee* (Cambridge: Cambridge University Press, 1984), pp. 173–86.

being pushed by outside forces. And though his body went on as before his soul inside had crumpled and broken beyond repair.[1]

However, it is instructive to note the differences. Unlike the salesman Willy was to be located firmly in the context of his family life while Miller was concerned to project his illusions and frustrations onto a national level. He became both a vital character and a patent symbol. And unlike the protagonist of the short story Willy was not Jewish. Indeed, Mary McCarthy was later to attack the play as a story about Jewish characters in which their Jewish identities had been suppressed. Miller has denied this, pointing out that when the touring company, quite coincidentally, was found to consist entirely of Irish actors, including Mary McCarthy's brother, it was greeted by two Boston newspapers as an Irish drama.

Death of a Salesman—the story of an ageing salesman, baffled by a lifetime of failure in a society which apparently values only success—has proved one of the most powerful and affecting plays in American theatrical history. The confusions and dreams of a single individual on the verge of psychological collapse were made to embody the collapse of national myths of personal transformation and social possibility. Miller's achievement lay in his ability to distil in the person of Willy Loman the anxieties of a culture which had exchanged an existential world of physical and moral possibility for the determinisms of modern commercial and industrial life—the country for the city. The dislocations of Willy's private life—discontinuities which open up spaces in familial relationships no less than in memory and experience—are equally those of a society chasing the chimera of material success as a substitute for spiritual fulfilment. All the characters in the play feel a need which they can articulate only in terms of the rhetoric of a society which has itself lost touch with its youthful ideals. Aware of a profound sense of insufficiency they seek to remedy or at least to neutralise it in the public world of consumerism and status. For the most part they are blind to the consolation and even transcendence available through personal relationships. The love which they feel for one another is real enough. To some degree it shapes their actions and determines their desperate strategies, which are none the less real for their failure to be realised. But it fails to hold them back from the fate in which they wilfully conspire. And this is the basis of the irony which slowly erodes their confidence and their hopes.

And yet the play's success in virtually all societies in the four decades following its first performance shows that it is something more than a dramatisation of the American dream, its corruptions and coercions. Willy proved an international figure, as appealing and recognisable to a Chinese audience in 1983 as it had been to an American one in 1949. Willy's dreams are too recognisable, his blindness to the reality and necessity of a proffered love too familiar, for his plight not to demand the attention for which his wife calls. Like most plays it perhaps has its flaws but the human reality of Willy Loman is such that few works have provoked the shock of recognition which has greeted and continues to greet Willy's anguished debate with himself and with the world in which he has never felt at home.

Willy betrays himself and others. Desperate to sustain his self-esteem he has an affair with another woman, buying her attention with a gift of stockings while his wife sits at home mending her own. And when his son, Biff, catches them together he believes that the moment of disillusionment links them together in a more profound way than had the love which he felt but which he could never adequately express. Biff's 'failure' thus becomes a living reproach which fuses love and guilt together in such a way as to threaten the spontaneity and integrity of his responses. Increasingly anxious to justify his life and expiate what he sees as his responsibility for his son's wilful self-annihilation, he plans a suicide which will create the fortune that his life could never accumulate. The proceeds of his insurance policy will thus stand as a justification of his dreams while offering some kind of belated restitution to the wife and son he had betrayed. Desperate for love they are to be offered cash. The irony of Willy's life is that he has accepted other people's estimations of his value. He has the power to construct himself as he has the skill to fashion wood but he cannot bring himself to believe in the worth of a sensibility so constructed and a life forged out of nothing more substantial than an honest perception of the real. The play is Miller's requiem for a country which, no less than Willy, had all the wrong dreams as it is a gesture of absolution towards those who allow themselves to be too fully known. Though in a sense it is a story of defeat, its very lyricism implies the persistence of other possibilities and of a relationship with language, experience and the physical world which goes beyond the terrible banality and threatening pragmatism of a dream tainted at source. Willy is a kind of Everyman. Miller may have taken care to root him in a specific social and historical world but the specificity is raised to another level by the authenticity with which he repro- duces the tangled emotions and diffuse longings of those who translate into the language of national myth what has its origin in more fundamental necessities. Willy Loman lives and dies in an attempt to sustain a sense of personal dignity and meaning. Yet if that is a struggle which has its correlative in terms of American notions of self-fulfilment and social status it is equally a battle waged by everyone who tries to locate a sense of significant purpose in a life which seems to consist of little more than a series of contingent events. And if that in turn seems in some final sense a losing game then a certain dignity is perhaps to be derived from the courage with which it is conducted and the poetry which can on occasion be forged out of the prose of experience.

Death of a Salesman is built around the relationship between Willy and his son, Biff. In his notebook Miller wrote himself a memo: 'Discover . . . The link between Biff's work views and his anti W feelings . . . How it happens that W's life is in Biff's hands—aside from Biff succceeding. There is W's guilt to Biff in re: The Woman . . . There is Biff's disdain for W's character, his false aims, his fictions, and these Biff cannot finally give up or alter.'[2] Here, as elsewhere in Miller's work, the relationship between father and son is a crucial one because it focusses the question of inherited values and assumptions, it dramatises deferred hopes and ideals, it becomes a microcosm of the debate between the generations, of the shift from a world still rooted in a simpler rural past to one in which that past exists simply as myth. It highlights the contrast between youthful aspirations and subsequent compromises and frustrations. It presents the submerged psychological tension which complicates the clear line of social action and personal morality. The family, so much an icon of American mythology, becomes the appropriate prism through which to view that mythology. The son's identity depends on creating a boundary between himself and his father, on perceiving himself outside the axial lines which had defined the father's world.

Biff and Willy's relationship is bedevilled by guilt. Willy feels guilty because he feels responsible for Biff's failure. Having discovered Willy with a woman in a Boston hotel room, he had refused to retake a mathematics examination, thereby abandoning his chance of reaching university and his access to a better career. But Biff equally feels guilty because he recognises a responsibility which he cannot fulfil, the responsibility to redeem Willy's empty life. In a telling speech, included in the notebook but excluded from the published and performed versions, Biff outlines his feelings explicitly.

> Willy—see?—I love you Willy. I've met ten or twelve Willys and you're only one of them.—I don't care what you do. I don't care if you live or die. You think I'm mad at you because of the Woman, don't you. I am, but I'm madder because you bitched up my life, *because* I can't tear you out of my heart, because *I keep trying* to make good, *do something* for you, to *succeed for you.*[3]

If Biff loves Willy he also plainly hates him. Like the other characters he is composed of contradictions. Indeed, in his notes, Miller saw the conflict in Biff between his hatred for Willy and his own desire for success in New York as crucial to an understanding of the play as he did 'the combination of guilt (of failure), hate, and love—all in conflict' that Willy hopes to resolve 'by "accomplishing" a 20,000 dollar death.'[4] Indeed, the ironies of the play flow out of contradiction in *Death of a Salesman*, much as they do in another sense in *Waiting for Godot*. Action is immediately aborted, assertions withdrawn, hopes negated. Thus Willy complains of Biff that 'the trouble is he's lazy', only to reverse himself a few seconds later. 'There's one thing about Biff—he's not lazy.'[5] Happy asserts that money holds no interest for him and that he would be happy with a free life in the West, only to ask immediately, 'The only thing is—what can you make out there?'[6] The response to Biff's 'Let's go' is the same as that proffered in *Waiting for Godot*. They do not move. And so Happy regards himself as an idealist while taking 100-dollar bribes, Biff as rejecting a material life while stealing from his employer. For Willy, constant contradiction is a linguistic reflection of the collapse of rational control, but, more fundamentally, for all the Loman men it is indicative of a basic contradiction between their aspirations and the reality of their lives, between their setting and the essence of their dreams. They are denied peace because the philosophy on which they have built their lives involves competition, a restless pursuit of success, a desire to register a material achievement which they can conceive only in financial terms because they have neither the language nor the capacity to assess its significance in any other way. Hence Biff, who tries to retrace the steps of his father into the past and the West, is unable to accept a simple sense of harmony with his surroundings as adequate to the definition of success which his father has instilled in him, though that harmony is precisely what his father longs to achieve. As Biff explains to his brother,

> This farm I work on, it's spring there now, see? And they've got about fifteen new colts. There's nothing more inspiring or—beautiful than the sight of a mare and a new colt. And it's cool there now, see? Texas is cool now and it's spring. And whenever spring comes to where I am, I suddenly get the feeling, my God, I'm not getting anywhere! What the hell am I doing, playing around with horses, twenty-eight dollars a week! I'm thirty-five years old, I oughta be makin' my fortune. That's when I come running home. And now, I got here, and I don't know what to do with myself.[7]

And so the lyricism, which is a powerful and crucial dimension of the play, defers to materialism, to a pragmatism which disrupts an incipient harmony and opens up a gap between Biff and his setting which, once closed, would not only offer him a simpler relationship between himself and the natural world but also still the conflict between his sensibility and his actions. He is, however, held back not only by the surviving dream of material success, a dream which he might be able to abandon, but also by the guilt which he feels toward Willy. He continues to feel responsible to a man who has warped his life but to whom his fate is ineluctably joined. In Miller's earliest draft the point is even more explicit:

> w: . . . What do you want to be?
> b: I want just to settle down and be somebody! Just a guy working in a store, or digging earth, or anything . . .
> w: Then do it, do it.
> b: You won't let me do it.
> w: Me? When did I control you?
> b: You do control me. I've stood in the most beautiful scenery in the world and cried in misery. I've galloped elegant horses and suddenly wanted to kill myself because I was letting you down. I want you to let me go, you understand. I want you to stop dreaming big dreams about me, and expecting anything great of me. I'm manual labor, Pop; one way or the other I'm a tramp, that's all. Can you make your peace with that . . . ? I ask one thing. I want to be happy.
> w: To enjoy myself is not ambition. A tramp has that. Ambition is *things*. A man must want *things, things*.[8]

In the final version these perceptions no longer need to surface in language. Biff and Willy remain bewildered for most of the play, unable to analyse the pressures at work on them, unable in particular to confess to the guilt, the love and the hate that connect and divide them. Willy's concern with things, meanwhile, is evident in his fascination with his refrigerator and his car but, most significantly, in his acquiescence in his own reduction to inanimate article to be marketed on appearance and image.

In his first stage direction Miller insists on Willy's 'massive dreams and little cruelties', but in truth the play is concerned with suggesting that the adjectives might be legitimately reversed. And Biff, like his father, is still trying to buy love. As Miller wrote of the scene in the restaurant in which Biff and Happy abandon their father, 'Biff left out of guilt, pity, an inability to offer himself to W.' He recognises that Willy's desire that he should succeed is, in part at least, evidence of his love and, as Miller reminded himself, Biff 'still wants that evidence of W's love. Still does not want to be abandoned by him.' However, it is a love which threatens to destroy him, since it expresses itself in a desire on Willy's part to bequeath his son the thing he values most of all—his dream. The drama of the play emerges from the fact that Biff now gradually recognises the necessity for this abandonment. Indeed he has returned home with an intention not that remote from that of Chris Keller or Gregers Werle. 'He has returned home', Miller insists in his notes, 'resolved to disillusion W forever, to set him upon a new path, and thus release himself from responsibility for W and what he knows is going to happen to him—or half fears will.' There is the same passion for truth which springs from guilt and self-interest as had characterised the protagonists of *All My Sons* and *The Wild Duck*. But now Miller seems to recognise the necessity for this break with illusion. For here, it is finally not truth which kills as it had been in *All My Sons*; it is a continued commitment to illusion. Biff breaks free; Willy does not. In his own eyes his death accomplishes the success that had evaded him in life, and, more importantly, it finally purges him of the guilt that he has felt for what he takes to be his son's failure. Since Biff had abandoned his potential career after finding Willy with another woman, Willy had thereafter felt responsible for his son's failure. And this is the principal tension of the play. In order for Biff to survive he has to release himself from his father and the values which he promulgates; in order for Willy to survive he has to cling to Biff and the conviction that material success is still possible. Thus guilt becomes the principal mechanism of human relationships. As Miller notes, 'Biff's conflict is that to tell the truth would be to diminish himself in his own eyes. To admit his fault. His confusion, then, is not didactic, or restricted to Willy's elucidation of salvation, but towards a surgical break which, he knows in his heart, W could never accept. His motive, then, is to destroy W, free himself.' In the final version it is not so clear. He is intent to save Willy's life as well as his own. His motivation is less obvious, his concern for his father largely genuine. And yet, of course, in saving Willy he will be freeing himself, so that the self apparently lies behind all actions.

This was certainly to be the conclusion that Miller reached in *After the Fall*, but here that conclusion is masked by a social drama. For the fault does not only lie in the individual; it also patently lies in self-interest systematised into capitalism. Willy Loman is thrown on the scrap heap by his employer after thirty-six years, and, though Miller has objected that in the persons of his next-door neighbours, Charley and Bernard, he has created two characters who retain their humanity, it is Charley who advises Willy that human concerns can play no role in business. When Willy objects that he had actually selected his employer's first name when he was born, Charley replies, 'when you gonna realize that them things don't mean anything? You named him Howard, but you can't sell that. The only thing you got in this world is what you can sell. And the funny thing is that you're a salesman and you don't know that.'[9] It is Charley who boasts that his son's success had been a consequence of his own lack of concern, announcing that, 'My salvation is that I never took an interest in anything.'[10] And, though his own compassionate treatment of Willy would seem at odds with this, the system of which he is the most admirable representative can clearly accommodate itself to individual acts of charity provided that these don't threaten its structure. The fact is that Charley underwrites the system that destroys Willy. Bernard, a successful lawyer, makes too brief an appearance to know whether his affability towards Willy goes any deeper than appearance. His success is certainly a consequence of hard work but the question of the human value of that success, central to the play's theme, goes largely unexamined. After all, elsewhere in the play Miller seems to be posing the question as to whether material success bears any relationship to basic human needs, but in the person of Bernard he seems to suggest the possibility of having one's cake and eating it.

Biff and Willy feel a profound if unfocused sense of dissatisfaction with their lives. Beneath the monotony of daily survival is a yearning spirit, a perception of some kind of spiritual need which they can only express through material correlatives or through stuttering encomiums to beauty or belonging. One of the problems of the play, indeed, derives from the fact that their lack of success actually confuses spiritual with financial failure. The more significant question is whether material success would have blunted or indeed even satisfied that need and, though this might have brought Miller perilously close to cliché, his portrait of Bernard— moral, hard-working, successful, attractive—is perhaps in danger of validating the dreams which Willy had had for Biff. Willy had, admittedly, regarded such success as an inevitable product of life in America and had taught Biff to take what he could not earn, and yet in some way the adequacy of that success is not challenged in Bernard's case. Indeed he seems to represent the apparently untroubled serenity which is the reward of honest toil. Indeed, it was not until *After the Fall* that he chose to question the adequacy of that portrait, taking as his protagonist a lawyer whose success, like that of Bernard, is marked by his appealing a case before the Supreme Court. Then he was to query the value of success even when it is the product of effort and application. Uncle Ben might be a portrait of a Horatio Alger figure, stumbling over wealth, but Bernard is in many ways an idealised figure. The danger is that he is not only a model for Willy of what his sons might have become; he also becomes a model for Miller.

The dice are loaded against Willy. In the original notes he was literally to have been a little man. Miller chose to transform that into an obesity apparent in the text

but ignored when Lee J. Cobb was cast for the central role: 'I'm fat. I'm very—
foolish to look at, Linda...as I was going in to see the buyer I heard him say
something about—walrus. And I—I cracked him right across the face.'[11] Even
allowing for the exaggeration of self-pity, this offers a clue to his failure as a
salesman. His misfortune was that he chose a career in which appearance was
everything, at a time and in a country in which appearance was primary. As Biff was
to have said in an early draft, and as is apparent but not voiced in precisely these
words in the final version, 'The pity of it is, that he was happy only on certain
Sundays, with a warm sun on his back, and a trowel in his hand, some good wet
cement, and something to build. That's who he really was.'[12] As a salesman he
has always to dissemble, to smile, to put up a front. He is an actor who has
increasingly lost his audience. His life is a falsehood. But perhaps there is a certain
naivety in the assumption, no less Miller's than that of one of his characters, Charley,
that the situation is fundamentally different for others, for his contrast of the life of
the salesman with that of a man who can 'tell you the law' seems to be justified
by the character of Bernard. The real force of the play suggests otherwise. For
Miller implies that Willy had the wrong dreams, not simply that his methods of
fulfilling those dreams were wrong. With Eugene O'Neill he seems to suggest that
Willy's mistake was to imagine that he could gain possession of his soul through
gaining possession of the world. In that respect he was paradigmatic. Charley and
Bernard are successful and humane, but they, too, live a life whose intimacies seem
lacking. Where is the love between them? The problem is that the light is never
swung in their direction and thus it is possible to see in them a vindication of the
material success which they represent.

Biff's anger at his father derives partly from Willy's weakness and helplessness,
partly from his bitterness, but partly also from his love for him, a love which won't
cut Biff loose from his own sense of guilt. To absolve his father would be to admit
to his own weakness and culpability. As Miller wrote in his notebook,

> Biff's conflict is that to tell the truth would be to diminish himself in his own
> eyes. To admit to his own fault. The truth is that though W did overbuild B's
> ego, and then betrayed him, Biff feels guilt in his vengeance on W knowing that
> he also is incompetent. Through this confession of his having *used* W's be-
> trayal, W sees his basic love, and is resolved to suicide.[13]

Again the final version of the play deflects this confession into action, intensifying the
force by refraining from discharging its energy through words. Thus Biff, having
denounced his father and admitted to his own inability to command more than a
dollar an hour, breaks down in tears, 'holding on to Willy, who dumbly fumbles for
Biff's face'.[14] And love, which Miller has said was in a race for Willy's soul, becomes
the very mechanism which pulls Willy towards his death. Thus Linda, whose love
for Willy has revealed itself in an encouragement of his dreams combined with a
practical capacity which has enabled him to sustain his illusions in the face of reality,
proves finally to be deadly. Her actions are motivated by a compassionate concern

but there is a clear connection between her refusal to challenge those illusions and his death. Nor is she free of responsibility for the warped values of her children. She is simply too passive a force. Her culpability lies in her acquiescence, which is simultaneously an expression of her love. In her own way she is as obsessive as Willy. She has reduced her own life to a single focus—Willy. And so she tells Biff to leave home and completely ignores Happy's announcement of his impending marriage. Doubtless she recognises it for the self-deceiving gesture which it is, but she seems to feel no obligation towards her sons. Though she is never swept up in Willy's dreams she refuses to judge them. Her almost complete failure to understand Willy, as opposed to sympathise with and admire him, is thus finally a sign of the inadequacy of that love. It is not strong enough to make demands, to wrestle Willy away from his illusions.

Once to have been called *The Inside of His Head*, *Death of a Salesman* is a memory play. The past we see is as it is recalled by Willy Loman, as he tries to track down the moment when things began to go wrong. And not the least of Miller's achievements lay in the originality of the staging through which he created a theatrical correlative for Willy's tortured mind. The action had to move easily between past and present. The realistic texture of Willy's environment was crucial but so were the distortions created by his memory, the fragments of the past through which he sorted with increasing desperation. The result was a blend of realism and expressionism which dramatised personal psychology in the context of social change. In a sense the environment—the trees and open spaces of the real or remembered past, the oppressive constrictions of an urban environment—is a principal character in the play and a primary achievement of Miller, his director Elia Kazan, and his designer Jo Mielziner. Instantaneous shifts of scene were achieved through the ingenuity of Mielziner who, in one scene, contrived a small elevator to enable the actors playing Biff and Happy to move directly from a bedroom in the 'past' to a kitchen in the present. Writing in the introduction to his *Collected Plays* Miller has confessed to standing 'squarely in conventional realism', but has equally insisted that where necessary he has 'tried to expand it with an imposition of various forms in order to speak more directly, even more abruptly and nakedly of what has moved me behind the visible façades of life.'[15] The experiments are perhaps seldom radical since until later in his career he was too concerned with establishing the social context and implications of his plays to stray too far from a form which gives physical expression to the wider world. He is fully aware that the innovative power of realism has long since been blunted but he has always been drawn to find some way to relate the private anguish of his characters to the environment which presses upon them and which in part they themselves shape and deform. His resistance to the total determinism of naturalism, however, is in a sense symbolised by his reaction against the totally realistic set and it would not be unreasonable to see the incomplete walls and insubstantial props as evidence of his belief in change and even transcendence.

In *Death of a Salesman* the production style was necessitated by the need to create a 'continuous present'. In allowing past and present to collapse towards one another Miller was able to trace causalities and hence identify the possibility of change. However, it was also necessitated by his desire to represent the psychological state of a man whose inner and outer life are in a state of collapse, and it was precisely the fact of Willy's disintegrating mind, of his literal inability to sustain temporal or spatial boundaries, which suggests a pathological state apparently inimical to the tragic status claimed for the play and at odds with a reading that would make it simply a critique of American values. Eric Bentley even suggested that in so far as it is a tragedy this potentially destroys the social play as the social play destroys the tragedy, Willy being either the victim of his own flawed character or of society, but scarcely both. Such a stance, however, seems to ignore the degree to which tragedy seldom if ever acknowledges an impermeable membrane between the self and its setting, projecting psychological disruptions outwards into the social world and vice versa. However, talk of tragedy was ill-advised. Willy never really shows any evidence of self-knowledge or awareness of the reality of the situation in which he is involved. His dreams, described by Miller as massive, are in reality petty and sustained by sacrificing not only himself but those around him. In fact it is Biff, and not Willy, who provides the moral, though scarcely the theatrical, focus of the play. He does acquire self-knowledge and develops as a character through understanding the mechanism by which he has suffered and of which he has been a primary agent. As I have argued elsewhere,[16] so long as Biff and Happy are regarded as expressions of Willy's own mind—the one representing a vaguely perceived spiritual need, the other a sexual and material drive—such a split between the dramatic and moral focus is insignificant. Once granted genuine autonomy, however, Biff's moral development merely underlines Willy's inappropriateness as a tragic hero. This is not a weakness in the play, however, but simply an indication that it is not best approached by trying to force it into a category of merely pedagogic significance.

Willy Loman's life is rooted in America's past. His earliest memory was of sitting under a wagon in South Dakota. His father had made and sold flutes as they travelled through what was still, just, frontier territory. And this remains the world of his aspirations, a natural world in which he can create things with his hands, in which his identity is forged by his own actions rather than imposed by a job which sends him wandering through New England cities selling things he has not made himself and which therefore have no organic connection with his sense of himself. But the past had not been wholly idyllic. Familial betrayal had existed even then. His father had abandoned the family for Alaska, presumably to make his fortune there. His brother Ben had left home when Willy was a very small child with the intention of finding their father but, in fact, wandering off into an Africa part real and part myth. Willy was thus born into a world in transition, a world in which the pressure of the material was already unmaking the pastoral myth as the cities were encroaching on the rural nature of nineteenth-century America.

So Willy's house, once situated in open fields, the location dramatised in the original production by a transparent gauze curtain covered with leaves which becomes apparent to the audience when Willy is recalling that pastoral past, is now surrounded by apartment houses. And the lyrical echo of his father's flute recalling 'grass and trees and the horizon'[17] is now superseded for Willy by the sound of cars and the noise of building. In visual terms the contrast is that between the blue light of the sky, a light which falls on the house, and what Miller, in a stage direction, calls the 'angry glow of orange' from the surrounding buildings. Willy has lost the space which he needs for his dreams to assume any reality, for his identity to resist the impress of a public world which recognises only role. Forced at moments to concede his own failure, his own inability to mould himself into an acceptable form, he has to fall back on his sons to fulfil the dreams which he himself has failed to realise. Deprived of love when young, offered only a model of acquisitive self-interest, he blindly passes on the same destructive lesson to his sons, unaware of the substantiality of the love which he is offered and which was a recognition of that very identity which he had sought in the external world. In the words of Linda's sad cliché he is indeed 'a little boat looking for a harbour', but he is living on borrowed time. Suicide is a logical projection of his many failures. Just as his insurance payments are overdue and he is relying on the period of grace, so he is inhabiting a personal period of grace prior to an inevitable termination. In fact, in his notebook, Miller toyed with the idea of using *A Period of Grace* as a title for the play. Willy, who has built his life on the conviction that "it's not what you do ... It's who you know and the smile on your face',[18] is left without meaning or direction when he can no longer smile, when he no longer commands respect or recognition. He survives but without a sense of himself. His sons are his only chance to succeed by proxy, the only mark he has left on a world resistant to his charm and his human needs alike.

But there is an ambiguity to the play's conclusion. Biff has acquired a crucial insight into himself. Presumably the striving is over, and he can now accept that simple harmony with the natural world which had always foundered on his persistent need for a material success which would appease his father and free him from his guilt. Certainly that is the only real value which has been identified—a lyricism strongly contrasted with the diminished world of urban America. He can return West to the one place where he was really happy. The problem is that on the one hand his flight to the West had originally also been a flight from responsibility, and on the other it is an ahistorical move. Like Huck Finn at the end of Twain's novel, he is lighting out for the territory ahead of the rest. But the rest will inevitably follow, and Miller admitted as much a few years later when, in *The Misfits*, the beautiful mare and its colt are rounded up by trucks and turned into dog food. Biff Loman has become Gay, an ageing cowboy as bewildered by the collapse of his world as Willy Loman had been. And so Biff, who at the end of *Death of a Salesman* has supposedly learned the lesson which Willy could not, seems to be committed to the old mistake of seeking in movement and in space what he should perhaps have sought in relationship. Indeed, when Miller returned to the stage in 1964, after a nine-year silence, it was with a play in which grace is the reward of suffering, and meaning the result of a love constantly renewed in the face of acknowledged imperfection. Like Steinbeck in *The Grapes of Wrath* he ends with a piety whose emotional force is undeniable but whose social utility is more problematic because he can conceive of no mechanism whereby Biff's moment of epiphany can be translated into social action. And that equivocation hangs suspended in the air, inhibiting the sense of completion towards which the play has seemed to move and projecting forward into all our futures a dilemma not so easily resolved by a moment of insight, by a seemingly purposeful action or by an articulate statement of intent. History has moved on and Miller's characters in *Death of a Salesman* seem close kin finally to Scott Fitzgerald's in *The Great Gatsby*. Corrupted by dreams which simultaneously denied them access to the potential redemption of human connectiveness, they had reached out for some substitute for the meaning which continued to elude them. They sought it mostly in an endlessly deferred future, a green light which beckoned them on towards a mythical world of romance and affluence. But at the end of the novel the narrator tries to find it in the past, a rural world where the dream was first born and where the corruption first started. Biff does much the same here, for the world of rural simplicity to which he will now presumably return had provided the context for his grandfather's desertion of Willy. It was also where Uncle Ben began his mythic climb to wealth and power, having abandoned his search for his lost father. The frontier bred the disease. And if it also represents a natural world of pure process then even that is under pressure. Like the land surrounding the Loman home it will presumably itself one day make way for the city and its cruelties. And so Biff, like Nick Carraway, seems poised for a deeply ambiguous and even ironic journey. So that if Willy, like Gatsby, believed in the green light, 'the orgastic future that year by year recedes before us', a future which 'eluded us then, but that's no matter—tomorrow we will run faster, stretch out our arms further . . . And one fine morning', he and Biff alike are also, perhaps, no more nor less than "boats against the current, borne back ceaselessly into the past."[9]

NOTES

[1] Arthur Miller, 'In Memoriam', in Humanities Research Center, the University of Texas at Austin, pp. 1–2.
[2] Arthur Miller, Notebook for *Death of a Salesman*, in Humanities Research Center.
[3] Ibid.
[4] Ibid.
[5] *Collected Plays* (London, 1958), p. 134.
[6] Ibid., p. 140.
[7] Ibid., p. 139.
[8] Arthur Miller, *Death of a Salesman*, early draft, in Humanities Research Center.
[9] *Collected Plays*, p. 192.
[10] Ibid., p. 191.
[11] Ibid., p. 149.

[12] *Death of a Salesman*, early draft.
[13] Arthur Miller, Notebook.
[14] *Collected Plays*, p. 217.
[15] Ibid., p. 52.
[16] C. W. E. Bigsby, *Confrontation and Commitment: A Study of Contemporary American Drama 1956–1966* (London, 1967).
[17] *Collected Plays*, p. 130.
[18] Ibid., p. 184.
[19] F. Scott Fitzgerald, *The Great Gatsby* (Harmondsworth, 1950), p. 188.

Leah Hadomi

DRAMATIC RHYTHM IN
DEATH OF A SALESMAN

The subtitle of *Death of a Salesman,* "Certain Private Conversations in Two Acts and a Requiem,"[1] as well as the title originally considered by the playwright, *The Inside of His Head,* already point to the play's thematic essence and major formal characteristic. Thematically, Miller's drama deals with the tension between the private inner world of the protagonist and external reality. Its principal structural characteristic consists of the integration of dramatic realism and expressionism.[2]

The conflicting inner selves that make up Willy Loman's many-sided persona represent his experience of the outer world refracted through the distorting medium of his fantasies. As the action of the play progresses, the connections between Willy's inner world and external reality—which are tenuous enough to begin with—grow increasingly unstable and volatile until he is driven to kill himself, the ultimate act of self-deception in his struggle to impose his fantasies upon a reality that consistently thwarts his ambitions and will.

The shifts in Willy Loman's mind between his dreams and actuality, on the level of his personal existence, and between fantasy and realism on the level of dramatic presentation, are conveyed in structural terms by the patterns in which the play's formal elements unfold to establish the dramatic rhythm of the work. In the analysis of Miller's play that follows, I take my cue from the conceptions of dramatic rhythm as set out by Paul M. Levitt and Kathleen George.[3] In my own consideration of the work, I shall examine the ways in which the rhythmic organization of the play is managed in respect of three structural elements in the play; characterization, symbolic clusters, and the plot.

I

Not only is Willy Loman the chief character of the play but it is primarily from his psychological perspective that the play's dramatic action derives its meaning. The

From *Modern Drama* 31, No. 2 (June 1988): 157–74.

actual events enacted in his presence become the trigger for Willy's recollections and fantasies which constitute the play's imaginary sequences. The significance of each of the play's episodes, as well as the structure of the plot as a whole, depends on the rhythmic alternations between actuality and the protagonist's mental responses to them. His ideal self-image and the reality of his actual behavior and circumstances are the poles of both his inner existence and his dramatic interactions with the other characters of the play. The personalities of each of the *dramatis personae* are connected specifically with a particular feature of Willy's inner self, with a particular stance he has adopted toward his environment, or with one of the values in which he has educated his sons. Thus the conduct of the play's other characters is in great measure both the effect of his illusory perception of external reality and the cause of his deepening submersion in the world of his fantasies. When reality becomes too painful, Willy retreats into a dream world consisting of his roseate recollections of the past and of fantasies in which he fulfills the aspirations the attainment of which has eluded him in life. Although his memories are based on actual events, these are falsified in his mind by wishful thinking about how they ought to have turned out. Hence in Willy's mind, reality as it is immediately experienced by him merges in his consciousness with his recollection of distant events to form a seamless continuum of past and present time.

The set in Arthur Miller's play furnishes, in the words of Edward Murray, "a flexible medium in which to enact the process of Willy Loman's way of mind."[4] The block of apartment houses and the Loman home provide the static elements of the set. The element of change is furnished by the shifts of the location of action from one part of the stage to another. Its role in Miller's work evokes an instance of Kathleen George's dictum that the polyscenic stage functions according to the same principles as do the other manifestations of dramatic rhythm in pointing to the stable and changing features of the plot.

However, the interplay between fantasy and reality in Willy Loman's mind enacted on stage represents only one aspect of the dramatization of the inner tensions of the protagonist. Willy is torn between his need, on the one hand, to give expression to his innermost longings by establishing a direct and harmonious connection with nature, and by manual labor; on the other, he wishes to maintain his place in society by creating a facade of emulous and combative self-assertiveness, which he tries to reconcile with his obsessive and desperate need to be admired and loved by others. Together these contrary tendencies account for the conflicts both in the ideal conception of himself and in the way he conceives of others, in relation to the idealized image of his own personality. Moreover, Willy's ideal self-image is as fragmented as his real personality. Rather than consisting of a single coherent self, it is compacted of a number of contradictory selves, each of which might alone have formed the core of an integrated personality relatively free of tension, but which together make up an unstable persona that ultimately costs the protagonist his life.

Willy Loman spends much of his time on stage in an ongoing inner dialogue with a number of characters. Some, like Willy's sons and his friend, Charley, belong to the immediate and concrete reality which is being dramatized. Three other figures emerge from Willy's recollection of the past and animate his inner world: his father, his older brother Ben, and old Dave Singleman. All three figures owe their presentation and description in the play to Willy's imagination, whose creation they essentially are. The characters that live through Willy's imagination are both the fruit and inspiration of this inner existence; and, by virtue of Willy Loman's function as the protagonist from whose perspective much of the play's action is seen, these characters furnish the focus of the clash of fantasy and reality in both Willy himself and the other *dramatis personae* of the play.

In Willy's consciousness each of the three men from the past has assumed the status of a personal hero and exemplar whom he aspires to emulate. And together they may make up the ideal end of the continuum between ideality and actuality along which Willy's fluctuations between fantasy and reality take place. Each in his own right also furnishes Willy with a separate "ego ideal" that occupies a distinct place on a descending scale of proximity to the real world.

Connected with Willy's past is the memory of his father, who never assumes substantial form in Willy's mind but nevertheless powerfully informs his fantasy, primarily through his imagined conversations with Ben. Thus, Willy's father, the least accessible and most dimly remembered of the protagonist's exemplars, functions as his "absolute" ego ideal. His brother, Ben, against whose adventurous life and grand mercantile enterprises in far-off places Willy measures his own inadequacy and petty destiny, is his "desiderative" ego ideal. And last, Dave Singleman, the quintessence of the successful salesman and Willy's inspiration and model for feasible achievement, serves the protagonist as his "attainable" ego ideal.

Of these three ideal figures, Willy's father is the most remote from actuality and belongs to the very earliest and vaguest childhood recollections. Though not one of the *dramatis personae,* and spoken of only twice in the course of the play—during Ben's first "visitation" in Act One (pp. 156–57), and then briefly by Willy in Howard's office in Act Two (p. 180)—his spirit dogs Willy and is repeatedly referred to on an auditory level by the sound of flute music, which is first heard as a sort of signature tune when the curtain goes up on the play, and is heard last when the curtain falls on the "Requiem." Hearing his father playing the flute is nearly the only sensory memory Willy has of him—that and his father's "big beard." What we know of the picture in Willy's mind of the man we learn from the description he receives from Ben's apparition. And what emerges from Ben's account is a part-mythic, part-allegorical figure. The image of him drawn by Ben is an emblematic composite of the classic types that are representative of America's heroic age: Willy's father is at once the untamed natural man and the westward-bound pioneer; the artisan, the great inventor, and the successful entrepreneur.

Willy's brother Ben represents an ideal which is closer to reality, that of worldly success, though on a scale so exalted as to be utterly beyond Willy's reach. To Willy's mind Ben is the personification of the great American virtues of self-reliance and initiative by which an enterprising man may attain untold wealth; and it is through Ben that Willy tries to maintain personal connection with the myth of the individual's triumphant march from rags to riches.

In Willy's consciousness Ben mediates between the domains of the ideal and the real. The aura of legend is nearly as strong in his brother as it is in his father. He, too, is a journeyer and adventurer. But what animates him in his rangings appears to be less a hankering for the open road and the "grand outdoors" than the idea of the fortune to be made there. Sentiment plays no part in the tough maxims he tosses out in accounting for his success. Nor does he let family feeling cloud his purpose or divert him from his quest for riches, as is evident from the ease with which he abandons his search for his father to pursue diamond wealth in Africa; or, again, in the offhand manner he receives the news of his mother's death. Even Willy gets short shrift from his older brother. Nevertheless it is Ben's qualities of toughness, unscrupulousness, and implacability in the pursuit of gain that Willy wishes for himself and wants his boys to acquire.

Of Willy Loman's three personal heroes it is Dave Singleman who stands in the most immediate relation to the actuality of Willy's life. Neither the ideal pattern of natural manhood personified by Willy's father, nor the incarnation of freebooting enterprise embodied by his brother, Singleman represents success that is potentially attainable. In Singleman the concept of success is cut down to Willy's size, reduced to an idea more nearly within his scope—that of getting ahead by being "well liked." Success as exemplified in Dave Singleman serves, as well, to sustain in Willy the feeling that, though wanting in the daring and toughness that is his father's legacy to Ben, he too possesses an essential prerequisite for material achievement, and one that he can pass on to his own sons. So, poised in Howard's office between the phantoms of his dead brother and of Biff in his teens, Willy proclaims in an access of confidence: "It's who you know and the smile on your face! It's contacts, Ben, contacts!" (p. 184).

Willy is not content merely to admire these men. He also internalizes their qualities and the ideas they represent, diminishing and trivializing them in the process. Thus the ideas of being in close touch with nature and taking to the open road that are inspired by Willy's memory of his father are diminished in his own life to puttering about in the back yard of his suburban Brooklyn home and making his routine rounds as a traveling salesman; the idea of venturesome private enterprise for high stakes represented by his brother depreciates to drumming merchandise for a commission; and even the example of Singleman's being "remembered and loved and helped by so many different people" (p. 180), over which Willy rhapsodizes to Howard Wagner, is degraded in his own aspirations to the condition of being merely popular and well-liked.

Three of the characters among the principal *dramatis personae* of the play, Biff, Happy and Charley, function in the real world as analogous to the ideal types in Willy's consciousness. Though none of them is a complete substantiation of Willy's ego ideals, there is in each character a dominant trait that identifies him with

either Willy's father, or Ben, or Dave Singleman, and that determines Willy's relationship to him.

   Biff most closely resembles his grandfather in rejecting the constraints imposed
by the middle-class routines of holding down a job and making a living, and in his
preference for the life of a drifter out West, working as a hired farm-hand in the
outdoors. He has a strong touch of the artist and dreamer in his temperament. He
is also the most complex character of the three, the most at odds with himself. In
this he closely resembles Willy. Like his father, Biff is torn between rural nostalgia
and his need for solid achievement, and is tormented by the knowledge of personal
failure. "I've always made a point of not wasting my life," he tells Happy, and then
confesses to him, "and everytime I come back here I know that all I've done is to
waste my life" (p. 139).

   Happy corresponds to Ben, if only in a meager and debased way. He shares
his uncle's unscrupulousness and amorality, but has little of his singleness of purpose;
and what he has of the last he dedicates to cuckolding his superiors at work and to
the pursuit of women in general, activities that make up the only field in which he
excels, as Linda recognizes when she sums him up as a "philandering bum" (p. 163).
He resembles Ben, too, in the shallowness of his filial emotions. The trite praise he
bestows on Linda—"What a woman! They broke the mold when they made her"
(p. 169)—is on its own vulgar level as perfunctory and unfeeling as Ben's more
elegantly phrased endorsement, "Fine specimen of a lady, Mother" (p. 155). However, some of his traits remind us of Willy, such as his bluster and nursing of injured
pride, his insecurity about making good, as well as his philandering.

   Charley is Dave Singleman brought down to earth. He has none of Singleman's
flamboyance that Willy so rapturously remembers from his younger days. Rather,
he is successful salesmanship domesticated. Singleman worked out of a hotel room.
Charley maintains an office with a secretary and an accountant. He is stolid but
honest and decent, and though not loved like Singleman, he is respected. And, by
Willy's own startled admission toward the end, he is Willy Loman's only friend. He
is also Willy's perfect foil, a man at peace with what he is and his place in the world.[5]

   Excepting Charley, the principal characters of *Death of a Salesman* share the
same condition of being torn between the conflicting claims of ideality and actuality;
and in this capacity the interrelations among them serve to extend and reinforce
the rhythmic articulation of the play on a variety of formal levels. Among the
consequences of the inner conflicts and contradictions of Willy Loman and his sons
is their uncertainty and confusion concerning their own identities, a circumstance of
which each shows himself to be aware at some point in the play. So Biff reveals to
his mother, "I just can't take hold, Mom. I can't take hold of some kind of a life" (p.
161); Happy tells Biff, "I don't know what the hell I'm workin' for... And still,
goddamit, I'm lonely" (p. 139); and Willy confesses to Ben, "I still feel—kind of
temporary about myself" (p. 159).[6]

   Willy Loman's attitude to the real characters of the play is determined by their
relation to the corresponding ideal types in his mind. None of the real characters

is an unalloyed embodiment of these exemplars, who have all been debased to varying degrees in their corporeal counterparts. So, for example, Willy's most complex and ambivalent relationship is with Biff, who is associated most closely with Willy's absolute ego ideal.[7] It is of his older son that Willy had always expected the most, and it is Biff's failure to live up to his expectations that grieves him the most. By comparison his relationship with Happy, of whom he expects much less, is straightforward and indifferent. Willy's relationship with Charley, too, is determined by Charley's proximity to the ideal and his own distance therefrom. Because Charley comes closest of anyone Willy knows to the attainable ideal he has set himself but failed to achieve, he treats him with a mixture of respect and envy. The last prevents Willy from accepting Charley's offer of a job, because doing so would be tantamount to an admission of failure, a reason never stated explicitly by Willy but of which Charley is aware, as we learn during Willy's visit to Charley's office in the second act (p. 192):

CHARLEY: What're you, jealous of me?
WILLY: I can't work for you, that's all, don't ask me why.
CHARLEY (*Angered, takes out more bills*): You been jealous of me all your life, you damned fool! Here, pay your insurance.

By taking money from Charley, instead, in the guise of a loan, Willy is able both to retain his self-esteem and to cling to his self-delusions. In a rare moment of candor Willy privately admits to Charley's virtues and superiority to himself ("a man of few words, and they respect him" [p. 149]), but for the most part he seeks to establish his own pre-eminence by belittling and hectoring him in petty ways, reminding Charley of his ignorance and inadequacy in ordinary matters: domestic repairs, diet, clothing, sports, cards, and so on.

To sum up, therefore, the function of all of the principal characters of the play (apart from Linda) is determined by the operations of Willy's consciousness, suspended between reality and dreams. The measure of their moral significance to Willy is contingent on the degree to which they have taken root in the ideal realm of his consciousness; and the extent to which they have done so is in inverse relation to their actual presence in the dramatic sequences that take place in current time and space. Thus, Willy's father, the absolute ideal figure of the play, assumes the status of a recognizable personality only through the account of him received from the shade of his deceased brother in a scene that unfolds entirely in the mind of the protagonist. Otherwise, he is mentioned only once in the real action of the play, when Willy offhandedly refers to him as a prelude to his pathetic boast to Howard, "We've got quite a little streak of self-reliance in our family" (p. 180). The name of Ben, too, is barely brought up—and then only in passing—in the real dialogue of the play; and it is only in the fantasizing episodes that he takes on palpable shape as a character in the play. And, finally, Dave Singleman, who serves Willy as a tangible, if illusory, example of success potentially within his grasp, comes alive in a present dramatic sequence of the play, even if only through the agency of words rather than action. Significantly, the short eulogy of him that Willy provides, and through which Singleman assumes dramatic life, comes at the moment that Willy is about to be fired and thereby deprived of the last vestige of his hope for the attainable success represented by Singleman.

The dramatic rhythm within and between the characters also finds expression in their attitudes to the opposite sex. Family relations and the role of women function as important compositional elements in the rhythm of the play. When connected to dramatic figures, functioning as Willy's ego-ideals, the women figures are either mentioned briefly or are meaningfully absent. Willy remembers sitting in his mother's lap; Ben remembers his mother as a "Fine specimen of a lady" (p. 155). Ben's wife bore him the legendary number of seven sons, and third male ideal figure is named "Dave Singleman". The remoteness and idealization of the women figures is paralleled by an abrupt attitude towards the women in the reality of the play—even in the indication of Howard's attitude towards his wife as revealed in the short incident of the tape recorder.

Willy and his sons have an inner conflict in which they fluctuate between loyalty to the mother-woman figure and an attraction to women as sexual objects. Loyalty to the first is linked to stability and integrity in family and social life, whereas the desire for the second represents disintegration of the individual and his role in society. The tension between these two views is seen in Willy, Biff, and Happy but is motivated uniquely in each of them. Willy's affair with the woman in Boston is partly a result of his loneliness but largely a way of boosting his ego. Motivated by a constant craving to be "well liked," he is happy to be "picked" by her. Happy's aggressive promiscuity is one overt aspect of his latent "jungle" life-style. He recognizes that his repeated, almost compulsive affairs with women related to higher executives at his work are an aspect of his "overdeveloped sense of competition" (p. 141). Biff, on the other hand, seems mostly to be pushed to feminine company by his father and brother, who see this as part of his being an admired star. In all three of them sexual attraction is depicted as morally deteriorating and contrary to their relationship to Linda as an idealized wife-mother figure: "They broke the mold when they made her" (p. 169). This inner contradiction is revealed differently in Willy's attitude towards her mending stockings, as an expression of his guilt feelings; in Happy's constant assurance that he longs for a meaningful relation with "Somebody with character; with resistance! Like Mom, y'know?" (p. 140); and in Biff's strong clinging to his mother, expressed as "I don't want my pal looking old" (p. 161) and opposed to his being "too rough with the girls" (p. 151).

The rhythm of the sequence of the two episodes focusing on sexual relations (the Boston woman, and the restaurant scene where the boys pick up two women) is also a formal means serving a thematic idea. The significance of the "Boston woman" is foreshadowed in Act I but only receives full dramatic revelation in the "Restaurant scene" in Act II, when it is reconstructed orally and visually in such a way as to show its significance in the wider context of Willy and Biff's relationship and their recognition of what is true and what is false in their lives. So, whereas in the

Boston scene it is the son who fails in social competition by flunking his test in mathematics, in the restaurant scene both father and son appear equally defeated in the economic and social struggle; and while in the Boston episode Biff, appalled by Willy's infidelity, realizes that his talkative, pretentious father is ineffectual (p. 207) and calls him a "phony little fake" (p. 208), in the restaurant scene Biff confesses to his father the pretensions and illusions of his own life too. Thus, sexual infidelity is related to the thematic focus of the play: the conflict between fantasy and reality.

The dramatic rhythm of *Death of a Salesman,* as made manifest in the development of character, takes place through a complex interplay between the function of *dramatis personae* and their interplay with the three levels of Willy's consciousness: first, on the level of ideality; second on the level of Willy's fantasies and dreams; and last, on the level of his perception of concrete reality. It is from these three levels of consciousness that the protagonist's three ego ideals—the absolute, the desiderative, and the attainable—emerge. Taken as a whole, Willy's three levels of consciousness dramatize his attitude to himself, to the "other" and to social reality.

II

The stage itself is a central element of the symbolic system of Miller's play. On the polyscenic set of *Death of a Salesman,* the dialectic processes taking place in the protagonist's mind are accompanied by shifts of location from one part of the stage to another.[8] Additionally, the set combines the elements of stage presentation with those of literary imagery that form symbolic clusters operating within the play's continuum of shifting consciousness between fantasy and reality. The dramatic presentation on stage is thus signalled, punctuated, and reinforced by recurrent visual and auditory effects. So, for example, the visual effects of foliage and trees, and the sound of the flute or of soft music, underscore Willy's rural longings; whereas pulsating music and loud sounds accompany Willy's erotic and savage "jungle" moods.[9]

A number of verbal references of symbolic significance recur throughout the text of Miller's play. These echo and enhance the play's rhythmic design. The significance that attaches itself to them derives from the associations they arouse in the protagonist's consciousness, where they are resolved into two principal symbolic clusters, connected with divergent attitudes that dominate Willy's imaginative life. The first cluster is connected with Willy's deep attachment to nature and nostalgia for the countryside, feelings whose ultimate point of origin is to be traced back to Willy's father. The major references that are included in this cluster are to trees, seeds, and "travel" in its broadest sense. The second cluster is associated with commerce and enterprise of the kind that is personified for Willy by his brother, Ben. The chief symbolic references of this cluster are to "jungle," Ben's watch, and diamonds.

An evident pattern emerges in the way in which the references to trees, wood, branches and leaves bind the domains of fantasy and reality in the play. They are clearly relevant to the ideal figure of Willy's father (a maker of flutes, a musical instrument of wood whose pastoral associations are immediate and altogether obvious), and to Willy's brother Ben (in whose vast tracts of Alaskan timberland Willy almost had a share).

Trees and leaves are the dominant stage effect when Willy's mind turns inward and toward the past, to a time when his longings for a rural existence were more nearly satisfied. As he casts his mind back to a time when his home stood in what was still a landscape setting, the large elm trees that had once grown on his property form an important part of his recollections. In the dramatic present, the elms are gone and all that remains of the rural Brooklyn he had known is his back yard, which by the play's end is the setting of Willy's last effort to reassert control over events by planning a garden in futile defiance of urban encroachment.

For Willy, being truly happy means working with tools—"all I'd need would be a little lumber and some peace of mind" (p. 151), he says, hoping for a better future. Trees are involved in his fantasies of Ben's success in the jungle and in the "timberland in Alaska" (p. 183). Trees color the imagery of Willy's expressions of his inner desperation and need for help, "the woods are burning" (pp. 152, 199). Trees and leaves are thereby involved rhythmically in the linguistic constructs of the play as well as in the visual setting of the stage: the memory of a hammock between the "big trees" (p. 143), of seeds in the garden, of working on the wood ceiling, and the lighting effect of the stage being *"covered with leaves"* (p. 142; see also pp. 151, 200). On the textual level, as well as on the stage, they become signs in the theatrical system indicating the rhythm between fantasy and reality.

Willy's enthusiasm for the outdoors and the countryside is also connected in his mind with the idea of travel and journeying. The idea of travel is inseparable from the images he has of the ideal figures from his past: that of his father driving his wagon and team of horses across the Western states; of Ben globetrotting between continents; and of Dave Singleman traveling in the smoker of the New York, New Haven and Hartford line. His own life, too, is inseparable from travel, and the maintenance of the family car is one of his major concerns. His car is essential to him for his livelihood, and it is also the instrument by which he chooses to bring an end to his life. It is the first thematically significant object to appear in the dramatic text of the play, when it is mentioned in a context that foreshadows the manner of Willy's death (p. 132).

The reference to nature is carried over to the second cluster of images bearing on the theme of commerce and enterprise, but appears now in the menacing guise of the "jungle," poles apart from the idyllic associations aroused by the cluster of rural symbols. Its explicit connection with the theme of enterprise and commerce, as well as its association with the attendant idea of aggressive and unscrupulous competition, is fully developed in the presence of all the principal *dramatis personae* in the scene of Ben's first apparition (pp. 154–60). The specific verbal context in which the reference first occurs is twice repeated almost verbatim by Ben ("... when I was seventeen I walked into the jungle, and when I was twenty-one I walked out. And by God I was rich": pp. 157, 159–60). On the first occasion that Ben speaks these words he does so at Willy's urging for the benefit of the boys. When he repeats them for the second time, it is at his departure and they are uttered for Willy's ears alone. What happens between the two utterances brings out the thematic significance of the passage as referring to the rule of the jungle that governs the sort of enterprise that Ben represents. And the event that drives this particular moral home is the sparring match between Ben and Biff, in which Ben departs from the rules of fair play and delivers himself of the precept, "Never fight fair with a stranger, boy. You'll never get out of the jungle that way" (p. 158).

By the time Ben's shade departs, Willy seems to have taken Ben's point, when he chimes in with great enthusiasm, "That's just the spirit I want to imbue them with! To walk into the jungle! I was right!" (p. 160). But the truth is that Willy was wrong. Ben's lesson is not about going into jungles, but *coming out* of them, alive and prosperous.

The "watch" and "diamond" references are associated through Ben with the "jungle" reference. Their connection with one another, and their symbolic bearing on commerce, become obvious once their association with the ideas of time and wealth is established, and we recall that these last are proverbially equated in the businessman's adage that time is money.

The watch and diamond references are merged, too, by a specific object in the play: the "watch fob with a diamond in it" that Ben had given to Willy, and Willy had in turn pawned a dozen years earlier to finance Biff's radio correspondence course (p. 160). Thus time and money, the two cherished commodities of business, are in Loman hands turned to loss rather than profit.

Death of a Salesman is rich in ironies on every level. This overall effect is immediately felt in the organization of the stage and the development of the characters, and evolves out of the conflict between dream and actuality that is the theme of Miller's play. In the case of the play's symbols, much of their ironic significance depends on the reversals of their evident or anticipated meaning when they are transposed from the mental domain of the protagonist's dreams and fantasies to objective reality, where events are determined by impersonal forces operating independently of his wishes and will.

III

On the level of plot, the rhythm of *Death of a Salesman* operates not only temporally, by a progression of dramatic action in causal sequence, but perhaps even to a greater extent spatially, as a consequence of the proximate and, at times, nearly simultaneous juxtaposition of real and imagined episodes that are presented on stage in order to be compared. The pattern that emerges from this juxtaposition is that of an alternative of what "is" and what "ought to be," between the reality of Willy Loman's situations in the past and present, and what he would have preferred them to have been. And to redress his grievances, the protagonist casts about in his memory for persons and events in order to weave agreeable fantasies around them that are surrogate fulfillments of his failed aspirations.

The dramatic progressions of Willy's shifts between dreams and reality are plotted structurally in terms of a rhythmic development whose general design spans the two acts of the play and whose principles can be discerned in the play's major subdivisions. These last, though not explicitly marked out scenes in the text of the play, are the effective equivalent of scenes, since they form identifiable "dramatic segments," as defined by Bernard Beckerman. According to Beckerman, the "substance" of such dramatic units consists of the action that takes place in them; between such activity-defined segments there are what he calls "linkages," by which each segment is tied to the one immediately preceding and following it.[10] In Miller's play, the substance of the acts, as well as the "scenes," consists of the particular dream or reality (and sometimes both) that is being enacted along the temporal vector that marks the path of Willy's career on stage. The linkages between these major units and their subdivisions are the creation of their spatial juxtaposition, on the basis of which the dramatic units are compared. Thus Willy's inner and outer worlds are enacted in scenes that are immediately juxtaposed, sometimes to the point of actually overlapping, and that mirror one another in a pattern of recurrence or reversal. The effect of all this is a spatio-temporal sequence that unfolds as an ironic interplay between fantasy and reality.

Willy Loman's attitudes toward the external world can be classified according to the degree in which they approach reality: *fantasy*, in which the protagonist concentrates on fulfilling unrealized wishes concerning the past and the future; *anticipation*, in which he prepares to cope with eventualities in the real world; and *action*, by which he attempts to come to grips with immediate, objective reality. As the plotting of the play progresses, Willy's fantasies gradually assert their sway over his anticipatory and active moods. This occurs in response to his frustration and failure to reinstate his control over his circumstances in the real world. Ultimately his fantasizing comes to dominate his conduct so completely that in his mind suicide becomes an achievement to be equated with success. His conflicts with himself and with the external world are dramatically manipulated on a variety of formal levels within which the rhythms of the plot are developed.

The rhythms of the plot of Miller's play may be analyzed in terms of plot units, as has been schematically set out at the end of this paper. The larger sweep of the dramatic progression is evident in each of the play's acts, in both of which the phases of exposition, complication, crisis, and resolution can be clearly discerned. Taken successively, the two acts follow the same pattern of alternation between fantasy and reality which is characteristic of the overall rhythmic organization of the plot. The first act is dominated by dreams and fantasies; these emerge in the second act under anticipatory and active guises, there to collide with objective reality and shatter. This general progression of dramatic events is supported by ironic juxtapositions that resolve themselves into a broader rhythm of tension and release.

The play starts out in the first act at a late point of attack, *in medias res,* with Willy attempting still to come to terms with reality but chiefly absorbed in recollections of the past. The exposition of the Loman family's past is principally accomplished through the dramatic presentation of the protagonist's fantasies. The exciting force that sets the action of the play into motion is the arrival of Biff, whose homecoming is the occasion for the arousal of Willy's guilt feelings and the onset of his deepening sense of personal failure and his growing realization of defeat. The interplay between the dramatic action of the real characters in the play and that of the episodes of the past which take place in Willy's imagination have the function of setting out and defining the complications in Willy's attitude towards himself and his environment. The enactment of events that take place within Willy's mind tends to suspend the dramatic action of the play until nearly the end of the first act, when the plot begins to gather momentum after the confrontation between the Loman parents and their sons.

The first act can be divided into six "scenes," whose rhythmic pattern is established by the principle of juxtaposition of the protagonist's dramatic present with his inner world. The last comprises a number of distinct attitudes of mind that fall into five general categories which have been defined for *dramatis personae* by Keir Elam, and called "subworlds" by him.[11] According to Elam, there are five possible categories of subworld: the *epistemic,* or the world of a dramatic character's knowledge; the *doxastic,* or the worlds of his beliefs; the *boulomaeic,* or the worlds of his hopes, wishes, and fears; the *oneiric,* or the worlds of his dreams, day-dreams, and fantasies; and the *deontic,* or the worlds of his "commands" (defined by Elam as "the states of affairs that he orders to be brought about").[12]

Willy Loman's boulomaeic and oneiric subworlds are expressed dramatically by means of "screen memories" of his inner world.[13] The scenes dramatizing Willy's inner world are juxtaposed with those in which his epistemic, doxastic, and deontic subworlds are enacted.

Between the first and the second acts, the relationships among Willy Loman's subworlds are altered in three principal respects. One such change is quantitative, and has to do with the relative amount of the text in each of the two acts that is devoted to dramatizations of the protagonist's fantasy world as opposed to the world of the "real" action of the play. Fully three-quarters of the text of the first act is given over to Willy's fantasy world—or, more specifically, to the enactment of his doxastic, boulomaeic, and oneiric subworlds. By contrast, a mere eighth of the second act consists of action taking place in the mind of the protagonist, whereas the overwhelming bulk of the same act is devoted to the presentation of Willy's deontic and epistemic subworlds, as he attempts to cope with his actual circumstances.

Another alteration of relationships may be observed in the rhythm of the shifts between the protagonist's inner world and actuality. These shifts in dramatic realm serve as the basis for my proposed division of the two acts of Miller's play into scenes, as set out at the end of this paper. Accordingly, the first act may be subdivided into six scenes, and the second act into twelve. The doubling of the number of scenes in the second half of the play is a function of the accelerated tempo of the protagonist's shifts of perspective, and the mounting disequilibrium in Willy's inner existence as well as the progressive weakening of his ability to distinguish between fantasy and reality.

And finally, as the action of the play progresses from the first to the second act, an alteration takes place in the direction of the shift between the protagonist's imaginary world and reality. In the first act the direction of change is from fantasy to reality; in the second act the direction is reversed.

From the outset of the first act, it is Willy's fantasy subworlds that dominate (i.e., his doxastic, boulomaeic, and oneiric subworlds), and the dramatic action consists largely of the enactment of memories that embody the protagonist's wishes and yearnings. By the end of the act, however, Willy's deontic subworld takes over, as he and his sons resolve to reassert themselves in the real world by undertaking practical courses of action—Willy by his decision to talk to Howard about improving his situation at work, Happy and Biff by their plan to ask Bill Oliver for a loan to start their own business. In the second act a reversal of direction takes place in which anticipation of change of fortune, and resolution to act, give way to fantasy. The direction of shift from reality to fantasy may be observed in the progression of the scenes of the second act, a synopsis of which I shall now undertake in terms of changing dramatic subworlds.

The dominant subworld in scenes 1 and 2 of the second act is deontic. In the first—the breakfast scene—Willy's plans of action in his own and his sons' behalf are revealed in his conversation with Linda. The deontic note struck in the first scene is sustained in the second, taking place in Howard's office, where Willy comes to practical grips with his situation by confronting his employer. Scene 3 dramatizes the effect on Willy of his defeat at the hands of Howard, which causes him to retreat into his boulomaeic and oneiric subworlds through his recollections of his family life in the past and his conversations with Ben; these memories subsume the protagonist's most profound desires and fantasies. In scene 4, set in Charley's office, the dominant mood is epistemic, as Willy obtains a clearer understanding of his real circumstances through his encounter with Charley and his son, Bernard. This consciousness deepens in scenes 5–7, the setting of which is Frank's Chop House. There, fresh from his humiliation and defeat, Willy is made to endure the revelation of the failure of his sons. The consequence is Willy's withdrawal into his fantasy subworlds, as he passes successively through deontic, boulomaeic, and oneiric states of mind. The progression of the enactment of Willy's consciousness is interrupted by scene 8, which is exceptional among the scenes of the second act, being entirely given over to a confrontation between Linda and her sons. However the theme is resumed in scenes 9–12, all of which take place in different parts of the

Act I

Dramatic progression	Scene	W's Mental realm	Locale of action	Characters on Stage	Protagonist's subworld
Exposition	1 (pp. 131–36)	(a)	Loman home	W, Linda	(epistemic-doxastic)
Complication	2 (pp. 136–42)	——	Loman home	Biff, Happy	——
	3 (pp. 142–51)	W(f)	Loman home	W, Biff, Happy, Linda, Charley	(doxastic-oneiric)
Crisis	4 (pp. 152–54)	W(a)	Loman home	W, Happy, Charley	(boulomaeic)
	5 (pp. 154–60)	W(f)	Loman home	W, Ben, Biff, Happy, Linda	(oneiric-boulomaeic)
Resolution	6 (pp. 160–72)	W(a)	Loman home	W, Linda Biff, Happy	(boulomaeic-deontic)

Act II

Dramatic progression	Scene	W's Mental realm	Locale of action	Characters on Stage	Protagonist's subworld
Exposition	1 (pp. 173–76)	W(a)	Loman home	W, Linda, Biff	(deontic)

Act II (*concluded*)

Dramatic progression	Scene	W's Mental realm	Locale of action	Characters on Stage	Protagonist's subworld
Complication	2 (pp. 177–83)	W(a)	Howard's Office	W, Howard	(deontic)
	3 (pp. 183–86)	W(f)	Howard's Office	W, Ben, Linda, Bernard, Charley, Woman	(boulemaeic-oneiric)
	4 (pp. 187–93)	W(a)	Charley's Office	W, Jenny, Bernard, Charley	(epistemic)
Crisis	5 (pp. 193–200)	W(a)	Frank's Chop House	Happy, Stanley, girls, Biff, W	(epistemic-deontic)
	6 (pp. 200–208)	W(f)	Frank's Chop House	W, Bernard, Woman, Biff	(boulomaeic-deontic)
	7 (p. 209)	W(a)	Frank's Chop House	W, Stanley	(boulomaeic)
Resolution	8 (pp. 210–12)	——	Loman home	Linda, Biff, Happy	——
	9 (pp. 212–13)	W(f)	Loman home	W, Ben	(oneiric-boulomaeic)
	10 (pp. 213–18)	W(a)	Loman home	Biff, Happy, Linda, W	(epistemic-boulomaeic)
	11 (pp. 218–19)	W(f)	Loman home	W, Ben	(oneiric-boulomaeic)
	12 (p. 220)	W(a)	——	——	(deontic)

Note: W = Willy: (a) = actuality, and (f) = fantasy

Loman home, the setting of Willy's final withdrawal into his private world. In these closing scenes of the play Willy is torn between his comprehension of his actual situation (specifically in regard to his relationship with his sons and Linda, as presented in scene 10) and his retreat into his fantasy subworlds (scenes 9 and 10).

Stated in the most general terms, therefore, in the second act of Miller's play the direction of movement of the rhythmic shifts of the protagonist's consciousness through the various subworlds is from the deontic to the doxastic and boulomaeic, by way of epistemic. There is additionally an ironic undercurrent to the overt pattern of the shifts in the protagonist's mental attitudes. To the very end Willy persists in regarding his wishes and fantasies as representing attainable goals in the real world. Thus when he takes his life he does so in the belief that his action will obtain the money from his life-insurance policy for Biff (Willy's "diamond" for his son), and that the crowd of mourners that his funeral will attract will vindicate his apparent failure in life. These hopes are treated by him as though they are deontic, but in the Requiem at the end of the play they are shown up to be doxastic and boulomaeic.

The focus of the unifying rhythm of *Death of a Salesman* is the theme of the loss of control by the protagonist over the world in which he lives. The various elements that go to make up Miller's play are dramatically presented primarily from inside the protagonist's consciousness, whose shifting perspectives establish the rhythmic progression of the work. Moreover the progression of the play's dramatic rhythm ironically reveals the static nature of the subject to which this essentially dynamic principle is being applied. The variety and mobility taking place between dream and reality—the fixed poles of Willy's shifts of consciousness—are exposed as being equally illusory and meaningless; so that these fundamentally antithetical realms converge to become identical. As the rhythm of the play's dramatic progression unfolds, it reveals Willy's dream (or nightmare, rather) to be the protagonist's single and abiding reality.

NOTES

[1] All references to *Death of a Salesman* in this paper are from *Arthur Miller's Collected Plays*, Volume I (New York, 1965), pp. 129–222.
[2] See Helen Wickham Koon's Introduction to *Twentieth Century Interpretations of* Death of a Salesman (Englewood Cliffs, NJ, 1983), p. 13.
[3] Paul M. Levitt, *A Structural Approach to the Analysis of Drama* (The Hague and Paris, 1971); Kathleen George, *Rhythm in Drama* (Pittsburgh, 1980). Levitt regards rhythm in theater to be the creation of two "change producing elements" which he identifies as "recurrence" and "reversal": recurrences take place in such features as the relationships between characters, and in the repetition of phrases, words, symbols, and motifs; reversals are the result of abrupt changes in the circumstances and situations of the plot; Kathleen George, in her summary of critical opinion concerning rhythm in drama, observes that dramatic rhythm resides essentially in the "alternation between opposites, generally producing a pattern of tension and relaxation" connected with the content of a play and felt by the audience on the level of expectations and their fulfillments; see her Introduction, *Rhythm in Drama*, pp. 13–16, esp. p. 9.
[4] *Arthur Miller, Dramatist* (New York, 1967), p. 23.
[5] In considering the difference between Charley and Willy, Arthur Miller has observed that, unlike Willy

Loman, "Charley is not a fanatic . . . he has learned to live without that frenzy, that ecstasy of spirit which Willy chases to his end"; Miller, Introduction, *Collected Plays,* p. 37.

[6] Elizabeth Ann Bettenhausen regards Biff and Happy to be extensions of two different aspects of Willy: "In a sense the two sons simply continue the two sides of Willy: Biff, seeing the fragility and even the illusion of the vicarious identity which depends on being well liked in the business world, chooses to accept the challenge of a different destiny. Happy, on the other hand, is captivated by the challenge of the dream and bound to the possibility of success"; "Forgiving the Idiot in the House: Existential Anxiety in Plays by Arthur Miller and its Implications for Christian Ethics," unpublished Ph.D. dissertation, the University of Iowa, 1972, p. 121.

[7] Cf. Sheila Huftel, *Arthur Miller: The Burning Glass* (New York, 1965), p. 108, where she observes that Biff "lives heroic in Willy's mind."

[8] About the rhythmic function of the polyscenic stage, see *Rhythm in Drama,* p. 133. Concerning its role in Miller's play, see: Edward Murray, op. cit., and Dennis Welland, *Arthur Miller* (Edinburgh and London, 1961), p. 63.

[9] Cf. Helen Marie McMahon, "Arthur Miller's Common Man: The Problem of the Realistic and the Mythic," unpublished Ph.D. dissertation, Purdue University, 1972, pp. 42–45; Enoch Brater, "Miller's Realism and *Death of a Salesman,*" in *Arthur Miller,* ed., R. A. Martin (New York, 1982), pp. 115–26, and esp. 118–22; Brian Parker, "Point of View in Arthur Miller's *Death of a Salesman,*" in *Twentieth Century Interpretations,* pp. 41–55.

[10] Bernard Beckerman, *Dynamics of Drama: Theory and Method* (New York, 1970), p. 42. On the "triggers" to the linkages between the scenes of Miller's play, see Franklin Bascom Ashley, "The Theme of Guilt and Responsibility in the Plays of Arthur Miller," unpublished Ph.D. dissertation, the University of South Carolina, 1970.

[11] Keir Elam, *The Semiotics of Theatre and Drama* (London, 1980), esp. p. 114: "When characters or spectators hypothesize a state of affairs in WD [i.e., the dramatic world] whether it proves true or false, one can talk of the *subworlds* projected on to it."

[12] Ibid., p. 115.

[13] "Screen memories" are visual recollections taking a "cinematic" form. See, Otto Fenichel, *The Psychoanalytic Theory of Neurosis* (New York, 1945), pp. 145, 149, 327, 341, 529.

Kay Stanton

WOMEN AND THE AMERICAN DREAM OF *DEATH OF A SALESMAN*

Arthur Miller's stated intention for *Death of a Salesman* was to create a "tragedy of the common man."[1] Although commentators argue over the meaning of "tragedy" in this phrase,[2] the word "man" has been taken as sexually specific rather than as generic in most responses to the play. Undoubtedly, the play is heavily masculine. Willy Loman is the tragic protagonist, and the effects of his tragic flaws are clearly engraved upon his sons. The roots of Willy's tragedy seem to be in his lack of attention from his father and his perceived inadequacy to his brother, Ben. All conflicts seem to be male-male—Willy versus Biff, Willy versus Howard, Willy versus Charley—so it has been easy for productions, audiences, and commentators to overlook, patronize, or devalue the significance of women in the play.[3] The tragedy of Willy Loman, however, is also the tragedy of American society's pursuit of the American Dream, which the play both defines and criticizes. Careful analysis reveals that the American Dream as presented in *Death of a Salesman* is male-oriented, but it requires unacknowledged dependence upon women as well as women's subjugation and exploitation.

The masculine mythos of the American Dream as personified in Willy Loman has three competing dimensions: the Green World, the Business World, and the Home. All three have ascendant male figure heads and submerged female presences. The Green World is the "outdoors" realm of trees, animals, handcrafting, planting, and hunting, and it takes both pastoral and savage forms. The pastoral aspect is associated with ancestral flute music and Willy's yearnings for his father and, in the next generation, with Biff's enjoyment of farm and ranch work, that which provokes Happy to call Biff "a poet," "an idealist."[4] The savage element is seen in Willy's beliefs about Ben.[5] Whereas Father Loman was a creative figure, moving in harmony with nature by making and disseminating music, Ben is an exploiter and despoiler of nature. In both pastoral and savage aspects, the Green

---

From *Feminist Rereadings of Modern American Drama*, edited by Jane Schlueter (Rutherford, NJ: Fairleigh Dickinson University Press, 1989), pp. 67–102.

World represents freedom and self-reliance and is a place to test and demonstrate one's masculinity. To Willy, "A man who can't handle tools is not a man" (44), and Biff tells Happy that "Men built like we are should be working out in the open" (23). As Ben is said to have walked into the jungle when he was seventeen and walked out when he was twenty-one, rich, the Green World was the means through which he entered manhood. What is submerged in both aspects is the femininity of nature and the dependence of the masculine on it. Biff states, "There's nothing more inspiring or—beautiful than the sight of a mare and a new colt" (22), and the jungle of Ben is a feminine symbol ("One must go in to fetch a diamond out" [134]), but the feminine is the raw material upon which the male asserts himself. Biff tells Happy that they should "Raise cattle, use our muscles" (23), and the jungle must yield its riches to Ben's mastery. Ben's superior masculinity is also proved by his having seven sons, but his wife is only mentioned as the communicant of the news of his death. Yet she is both producer-sustainer and survivor of life. Thus the female is the necessary element in the production of masculinity, but her role must be severely circumscribed.

The Loman family history can be pieced together through Willy's flashback conversation with Ben[6] (partly conflated with his conversation with Charley) and his present conversation with Howard. Apparently, Father Loman was a travelling maker and seller of flutes who went off to seek adventure in Alaska and deserted Mother, leaving her with two boys to raise alone. Then Ben ran off when he was seventeen and Willy was not quite four years old. Thus Willy and Mother were left alone together. The desertion by his father left Willy feeling "kind of temporary" (51) about himself and provoked Ben to imitate and surpass what his father had done. Both sons mythologize the father: to Willy he was "an adventurous man" with "quite a little streak of self-reliance" (81); to Ben he was "a very great and a very wild-hearted man" who with "one gadget" (the flute) supposedly "made more in a week" than a man like Willy "could make in a lifetime" (49). Both trivialize the role of their mother. Ben calls her a "Fine specimen of a lady" and the "old girl" (46) and assumes she would be living with lesser son Willy. But she is the woman who bore and raised Ben, whom he deserted and made no attempt to contact, not even knowing that she had "died a long time ago" (46). Willy's only other stated information about Mother Loman is his memory of being "in Mamma's lap" listening to "some kind of high music" coming from "a man with a big beard" (48). The mother thus provided the position of comfort from which to attend to the father. Mother is never mentioned again, although hers would be an interesting story. How did she support and raise the four-year-old Willy? Willy seems to have had no further communication from his father, which implies that Father Loman never sent money.[7] Mother must have had "quite a little streak of self-reliance" also.

Willy entreats Ben to tell his boys about their grandfather, so they can learn "the kind of stock they spring from" (48).[8] Mother Loman and her stock and Linda and hers seem to have had no bearing on the production of the boys. An Edenic birth myth is implied, with all Loman men springing directly from their father's side, with no commingling with a female.

In both Ben and Willy, the first desire of manhood is reunion with the father. When Ben ran off, it was "to find father in Alaska." Willy's questions about whether Ben found him and where he is are not answered directly. Ben states that he had had a "very faulty view of geography"; discovering that he was headed due south, he ended up in Africa rather than Alaska. Thus Ben avoids saying whether he knows anything about Father by returning attention to himself. But what he does reveal inadvertently is that, in trying to run toward his father, he actually ran further away in the opposite direction. He discovered his mistake "after a few days" (48), so he could have changed direction but did not. Instead of joining his father, he obviously decided to beat him.

Whereas Ben follows his father's path by running off for adventure, Willy follows it by becoming a travelling salesman. When Willy was "eighteen, nineteen," only slightly older than Ben had been at his departure, he was "already on the road" as a salesman. Yet, unsure "whether selling had a future" for him, Willy at that age "had a yearning to go to Alaska," to "settle in the North with the old man" (80–81) and to be with his older brother. Mother was most likely still alive at this point, and Willy felt that he must break from her to establish his manhood, as he believes his father and brother had done. But, less independent than they were, Willy wishes for a family connection that includes only the three male members, a rebuilding of the family *without* Mother. Willy continually attempts to find or build an all-male realm of patriarchal-fraternal community.[9] This yearning provides the basis for his refrain of the "liked" and "well liked," which are set apart from the "loved." Willy probably had decided that Ben, as first son, had been "well liked" by their father, and he was only "liked," if regarded with affection at all. Willy would have been loved by his mother, but because that love had not been earned or seized but given freely, it did not have the same value as being "well liked" by his father. Linda, as Willy's wife, seems to have picked up where Mother left off, replacing her. Linda sings Willy to sleep with lullabies and "mothers" him in countless ways—and she is made to seem responsible for Willy's rejection of Ben's proposition to go with him to Alaska.[10] But Linda is obviously being made the scapegoat in this episode. Ben's offer is not for the two brothers to work together: Ben merely proposes a job in Alaska, where he had "bought timberland" and needs "a man to look after things" for him because he is heading back to Africa. Even without Ben, Willy finds the offer tempting in terms of pastoral male community: "God, timberland! Me and my boys in those grand outdoors!" (85). Ben interprets it more aggressively: "Screw on your fists and you can fight for a fortune up there."[11] Linda's strongest objection is "why must everybody conquer the world?" (85)—she sees no value in cut-throat competition—but her supporting points are Willy's own statements about his career fed back to him. Willy refuses the offer after Linda makes reference to Dave Singleman.

When the adolescent Willy had "almost decided to go" to find his father in Alaska, he met Dave Singleman, an eighty-four-year-old salesman who had "drummed merchandise in thirty-one states" and who could now simply go into his hotel room, call the buyers, and make his living in his green velvet slippers. Willy saw that and "realized that selling was the greatest career a man could want" (81). Obviously, Willy found in Dave Singleman a substitute father figure. Singleman had explored and imposed his will (through selling) upon a vast territory, as Father Loman had, but Dave Singleman had managed it in a civilized and comfortable way: in a train rather than a wagon, a hotel room rather than around a fire, and with the Green World transformed into the ease of the green velvet slippers, which he wore even in his death in the smoker of a train. The myth of Dave Singleman is equally as strong for Willy as the myth of his father, imaging as it does for him the perfect life and death, as Dave Singleman died the "death of a salesman," with "hundreds of salesmen and buyers" at his funeral and sadness "on a lotta trains for months after that" (81). Singleman's name implies his lack of dependence on women, and he demonstrates to Willy that a life of material comfort without pioneer ruggedness can still be manly. The realm of comfort had probably been associated in Willy's mind with his mother. Through Dave Singleman's model, Willy realizes that it is possible to establish himself as "well liked" in an all-male community outside of and larger than the male immediate family. This community is the Business World, which provides more stability and comfort and more variety of and competition among consumer goods than those handcrafted in the vast out-doors. In the face of both temptations to choose the Green World, Willy chooses the Business World, the realm of his surrogate father, Dave Singleman.

The Business World has the potential to swallow up the achievements of the Green World: Willy tells Ben that "The whole wealth of Alaska passes over the lunch table at the Commodore Hotel, and that's the wonder, the wonder of this country, that a man can end with diamonds here on the basis of being liked!" (86). The myth of the American Business World provides Willy with the fantasy means of beating his father and his brother. But the complexity of the Business World also defeats the simplicity of the Green World. Ben proudly claims to have had many enterprises and never kept books, but such practices are impossible in the Business World. Decision-making and increased competition take the place of handcrafting and manual exploitation of resources. Yet women are the submerged element in this realm, too. As the male realm moves indoors, it brings in the female to attend to the details of daily maintenance considered too trivial for male attention—typing letters, keeping records, collecting evidence, and, perhaps the most important function, screening out lesser men. Instead of testing himself directly on feminine nature, a man in the Business World must test himself by making an important impression on the female secretary-receptionist before meeting with the male decision-maker. Thus the female provides access to the patriarchal male authority. This element is seen clearly in Biff's attempt to make a date with Bill Oliver's secretary to gain access to him, after waiting five hours unsuccessfully, and in The Woman's statement that Willy has "ruined" her because, after their sexual liaison, she now sends him directly to the buyers, without waiting at her desk. Woman as trivialized Earth Mother in the Green World becomes Woman as trivialized Bitch-Goddess Success in the Business World.

Women in the Business World are marked as whores simply because they are there, perhaps because of their function as access givers, although the reconstitution of the submerged shows them to be otherwise. As Willy, deeply and loudly involved in one of his flashbacks, approaches Charley's office to borrow money, Jenny, Charley's secretary, tells Bernard that Willy is arguing with nobody and that she has a lot of typing to do and cannot deal with Willy any more. She is an insightful, kind, put-upon, hard-working woman. When Willy sees her, he says, "How're ya? Workin'? Or still honest?", implying that her income is made through prostitution. To her polite reply, "Fine. How've you been feeling?", Willy again turns to sexual innuendo: "Not much any more, Jenny. Ha, ha!" (90–91).

Assertion of success for Biff, and especially for Happy, is also bound up with sexual exploitation of women. In their first appearance, they alternate between discussing their father and their own past and current lives, always coming to an association with women. When they recall their "dreams and plans" of the past, an immediate connection is made with "About five hundred women" who "would like to know what was said in this room." They hark back crudely to Happy's "first time," with "big Betsy something," a woman "on Bushwick Avenue," "With the collie dog!": "there was a pig!"[12] Happy states that he "got less bashful" with women and Biff "got more so"; when he questions what happened to Biff's "old confidence" (20–21), Biff returns the discussion to their father. Biff's self-confidence rests on sexual confidence; its diminishment is tied to his father.[13] For Happy, success is measured using women as markers, as he moves up from the initial "pig" with a dog to "gorgeous creatures" that he can get "any time I want" (24–25)—but to him they are still "creatures," not human beings like himself. Although Biff and Happy agree that they each should marry, find "a girl—steady, somebody with substance," "Somebody ... with resistance! Like Mom" (25), Happy delights in turning other men's "Lindas" into his private objects of sport. He attributes his "overdeveloped sense of competition" (25) to his habit of "ruining," deflowering, the fiancées of the executives at the store where he works, then attending their weddings to savor his secret triumph publicly. Because he cannot accept his low status in the Business World, he must take what he interprets to be the possessions of his superiors—their women—robbing them of their supposed only value, the gold of their virtue and jewels of their chastity, and delivering the damaged goods for his superiors to pay for over a lifetime of financial support.

Happy uses women as Ben used the jungle and timberlands, and he carves out this territory for himself as Ben had. Just as Ben sought adventure like his father but found it in another direction, Happy sought the self-confidence of the older brother Biff and found sexual confidence, and it is now where he has superiority over his brother. Although they both hope to have a fraternal life together—male bonding with limited, sex-defined participation of women—they have competing versions. Biff, more attracted to the Green World, wants to buy a ranch that they both can work, and Happy plans for them to go into business together, share an apartment, and for himself to oversee Biff's having "any babe you want" (26). Later, in the restaurant, when Biff tries to tell Happy about his attempted meeting with Bill Oliver, to put forth Happy's own plan for going into business together, Happy turns Biff's attention to the "strudel" he has been attempting to pick up,[14] insisting that Biff demonstrate his "old confidence" (21) before he speaks of the Oliver meeting. Happy wishes to establish a safety net of sexual confidence to protect them against news of failure that he may anticipate and fear, and he perhaps wants unconsciously to show off his "success" to contrast Biff's probable failure. Magnanimous Happy will give this choice female morsel to Biff if he will only say he wants her—assuming in advance that she has no choice but to acquiesce.

During his assault on the "strudel," the "Girl" in the restaurant (later named Miss Forsythe), Happy quickly defines himself as a salesman and asks, "You don't happen to sell, do you?", with a double entendre on prostitution. Her answer is "No, I don't sell"; she is a model whose picture has been on several magazine covers. But Happy continues to insist to Biff that "She's on call" (101–2). At Happy's entreaty, she rounds up a friend, Letta, who is not a prostitute either.[15] Letta is to begin jury duty the next day, so we may assume that she is a responsible citizen without an arrest record, one qualified to hear evidence and evaluate testimony. When she asks whether Biff or Happy has ever been on a jury, Biff answers, "No, but I have been in front of them!" (114). This is supposedly a joke, but it later proves to be true when we learn that Biff had served three months in jail for theft. Woman as nurturer and care-giver was the submerged element in the Green World; Woman as judge and determiner of truth and value is the submerged element in the Business World.

Yet men in the Business World both need and despise the presence and participation of women, who are continually regarded as whores. Stanley, the waiter in the restaurant, calls the two women, whom he had never seen before, "chippies," presumably because they left with Biff and Happy. The double standard in full force, women are allowed no sexual adventurism: one real or supposed sexual experience and they are "ruined" forever by male standards.[16] Happy makes women like Miss Forsythe and Letta the scapegoats for his inability to marry: it is a "shame" that "a beautiful girl like that" (Miss Forsythe) can be "had" by him. He cannot marry because "There's not a good woman in a thousand" (103). This slander covers Happy's submerged fear that if he tries to marry a woman, another man might do as he does and "ruin" her. He cannot invest himself in one woman because he fears competing men who might rob him of his woman's supposed only value, the chastity of virginity and sexual fidelity.

In his initial conversation with Biff in the play, Happy himself makes a connection between his taking of women and taking of money: "Manufacturers offer me a hundred-dollar bill now and then to throw an order their way. You know how honest I am, but it's like this girl, see. I hate myself for it. Because I don't want the girl, and, still, I take it and—I love it!" (25). It is Happy, not any woman in the play, who is a prostitute. He is not only more sexually promiscuous than any of the women, but he also takes money under unsavory circumstances. Thus he projects his own whorishness onto women in the play's clearest character depiction of male-female Business World dealings. As Woman is present in the public world of business, her ultimate function is to absorb the projection of what the men cannot acknowledge in themselves.

Just as the Green World overlaps with and is transformed into the Business World, so the Business World overlaps with and transforms the Home, which also maintains remnants of the Green World. The Home is the only realm where Willy can be the father, the patriarchal authority, so he invests it with sanctity.[17] Much is made of the physical details of the Loman home in the opening stage directions. The home is *"small, fragile seeming,"* against a *"solid vault of apartment houses."* The house is symbolic of Willy, the apartment houses representative of the big uncaring society that has "boxed in" the little man. An *"air of the dream"* is said to cling to the Loman home, *"a dream arising out of reality."* We are given a few particulars of the reality: *"The kitchen at center seems actual enough,"* with its table, chairs, and the refrigerator, the palpability of which is underlined later through discussion of its repair needs. Other "real" elements are the brass bedstead and straight bedroom chair and *"a silver athletic trophy"* (11). The set reflects Willy's mind, and these elements are most real in life to him. The kitchen and bedroom are the traditional areas of Woman and Linda, and the trophy is the one tangible piece of evidence of Willy's son Biff's "success."

The house evidently also represents the myth of the man's Home being his castle—or here, castle in the air, the *"air of the dream"* (11) clinging to the Home. Willy's failure to get love from his father and brother in the Green World and his failures in the Business World can be obfuscated in the Home, where he is what he defines himself to be. In his interaction with his wife, Linda, Willy habitually patronizes, demeans, and expresses irritation at her; anything he says, no matter how trivial or self-contradictory, is made to seem more important than anything she says. Yet in one of his very few compliments to her, he says, "You're my foundation and my support, Linda" (18). His praise of her is not only placed wholly in the context of himself, but it also partakes of architectural imagery, defining Linda's place in the Home. She is the foundation and support of the Home, the "real" element that Willy can extrapolate from and return to as he constructs his fantasy life.[18]

The Loman men are all less than they hold themselves to be, but Linda is more than she is credited to be.[19] She is indeed the foundation that has allowed the Loman men to build themselves up, if only in dreams, and she is the support that enables them to continue despite their failures. Linda is the one element holding the facade of the family together. Yet even Miller, her creator, seems not to have fully understood her character.[20] Linda is described in the opening stage directions as follows: *"Most often jovial, she has developed an iron repression of her exceptions to Willy's behavior—she more than loves him, she admires him, as though his mercurial nature, his temper, his massive dreams and little cruelties, served her only as sharp reminders of the turbulent longings . . . which she shares but lacks the temperament to utter and follow to their end"* (12). She thus seems inferior to Willy; yet she demonstrates a level of education superior to his in terms of grammatical and mathematical ability, and she is definitely more gifted in diplomatic and psychological acumen. In her management of Willy, she embodies the American Dream ideal of the model post–World War II wife, infinitely supportive of her man. She makes no mistakes, has no flaws in wifely perfection. But the perfect American wife is not enough for American Dreamers like Willy. He has been unfaithful to her, and he rudely interrupts and silences her, even when she is merely expressing support for him. She can be the foundation of the house; he must rebuild the facade.

If the Loman house represents the Loman family, with Linda as the steady foundation and support, the facade is constructed with stolen goods. The enemy apartment buildings that so anger Willy have provided the materials that he and his sons used in such projects as rebuilding the front stoop. Linda knows that they need not have been "boxed in" by the apartment buildings; she says, "We should've bought the land next door" (17). Possibly she had suggested the idea at the appropriate time but was ignored. But Willy prefers to transfer the blame for the diminishment of his Green World: "They should've had a law against apartment houses. Remember those two beautiful elm trees out there? . . . They should've arrested the builder for cutting those down" (17). Of course, there is a law against stealing property, which Willy thought nothing of disobeying when he encouraged the boys to steal from the construction site, calling them "fearless characters" (50). Laws are for lesser men to follow, not the Loman men. In the realm of the Home, Willy and his sons are associated with rebuilding through theft, and Linda is associated with cleaning, mending, and repair.

In Willy's flashback sequences, Linda habitually appears with the laundry, suggesting that it is her responsibility to clean up the males' dirtiness, on all levels. In both past and present, she is shown mending, not only her own stockings but also Willy's jacket. Often when Linda speaks, she discusses repairs, which she oversees; she must mend the male machinery. Willy is "sold" by other salesmen or advertisements on the quality of products and fails to recognize that even the "best" breaks down from daily wear and tear—including Willy himself. Although Linda's functions of cleaning, mending, and overseeing repairs are traditionally "feminine," they are significant because they are the ones maintained when other traditionally "feminine" elements are appropriated by Willy. It is not Linda but Willy who asserts the importance of physical attractiveness, who prefers a fantasy life of glamor to the reality of daily toil, who suffers from the "empty nest syndrome," and who insists on having the most significant role in child-rearing.

Willy works hard at preventing Linda from having any substantive impact on shaping the boys' characters; he tries continually to make them his alone, just as he had implied that they had sprung from his "stock" alone. After thanking God for Adonis-like looks in his sons, Willy confesses to Linda that he himself is "not noticed," "fat," "foolish to look at," and had been called a "walrus" (37).[21] Evidently, the physical attractiveness, strength, and resilience of the boys derive from Linda rather than Willy, but "God," not she, is given credit. Although Linda is the continual presence in the boys' lives at home, as Mother Loman had been for Willy, Willy undermines Linda's authority when he returns from the road. In a flashback sequence, Linda disapproves of various manifestations of Biff's bad behavior and runs from the scene almost in tears after Willy refuses to support her. She represents human dignity and values: cooperative, moral, humane behavior as opposed to lawless assertion of self over all others through assumed superiority. Just as Woman was unacknowledged creator-sustainer of life in the Green World and determiner of value in the Business World, in the Home, Woman, through Linda as submerged element, is the measure of human dignity and the accountant of worth.

Linda is the foundation and support not only of the Loman Home and Willy himself but also of the plea for sympathy for Willy of the play itself. She is used to establish Willy's significance as a human being to the boys and to the audience. In her most famous speech, she asserts that, although not a "great man," not rich or famous, and "not the finest character that ever lived," Willy is "a human being, and a terrible thing is happening to him. So attention must be paid. . . . Attention, attention must be finally paid to such a person" (56). Linda thus articulates his value and notes the real worth beneath the sham presentation. But the boys have been taught too well by Willy to disregard her message. When she reveals that the company had taken Willy's salary away five weeks before, and Biff calls those responsible "ungrateful bastards" (57), she states that they are no worse than his sons. The male world is ungrateful, unappreciative of such contributions as Willy made; only Linda understands and values them. Whenever she attempts to bring Biff and Happy to consideration for their father, they habitually shift blame away from themselves, pretend there is no problem, and/or change the subject and start bickering between themselves on their competing ideas and ideals. Just as Willy leaves the repair of household appliances to Linda, the boys leave the repair of their broken-down father to her.

The Loman men do see Linda as a validator of value, but they objectify virtue in her and assume that, if they have a woman like her, they will possess virtue and not need to develop it on their own. Both Biff and Happy wish to marry a girl just like the girl who married dear old Dad, and they believe such possession will immediately transform their lives and bring them to maturity. They, like their father, want to subtract value from a woman to add to their own; none of the Loman men is able to keep an accurate account of himself. In the Loman Home, only Linda understands what has value, what things cost, and how much must be paid to maintain and repair the Home life. Her other function, therefore, is computing the family finances, doing the family math. She must tactfully bring Willy to face the truth of his commissions from his inflated exaggerations of success to maximize such resources as there are, and Willy resents her for returning him to the foundation of himself as lesser money-earner from his dreams of wealth. As representative and accountant of worth, she must be trivialized and devalued, as must math.

As noted above, besides Linda and her spheres, the only other real element to Willy in the Loman Home is Biff's athletic trophy. Linda's significance in the Home is suppressed largely through the elevation of sports. The Loman men's idolatry of aggressive male-male competition relegates women into being the devalued objects and instruments of sports. Happy states that the "only trouble" with his promiscuity with women is that "it gets like bowling or something. I just keep knockin' them over and it doesn't mean anything" (25). Similarly, The Woman in the Boston hotel room, disabused of the idea that she means anything to Willy, interprets herself as his football. As instruments of sports, women are the means for starting the competitive game, the object they fight over, and the possession that marks the winners and assures them of being "well liked."

The worst mistake that Willy makes with his sons is in his foisting upon them the notion that sports success guarantees financial success. The adult Happy feels superior because he can "outbox, outrun, and outlift anybody in that store," so he cannot bear to "take orders from those common, petty sons-of-bitches" (24). He believes that the strength of his masculinity should overcome all competitors, although selling merchandise has little to do with displays of physical prowess. The adult Biff also finds holding a job difficult because of his self-image of athletic superiority. This is the "spirit" that Willy successfully manages to "imbue them with" (52), the spirit that he associates with Ben. Not only does Ben assert that making a fortune depends on screwing on one's fists, but he also provides a demonstration by challenging Biff, tripping him, and aiming an umbrella's point at his eyes in phallic threat, saying "Never fight fair with a stranger, boy. You'll never get out of the jungle that way" (49). Biff and Ben are family members, not "strangers," but Ben's aura is partly maintained by establishing distance between himself and other men: no man is allowed to seem his peer or comrade. This "overdeveloped sense of competition" that Willy cultivates in his boys, which can only be satisfied by being "number-one man," puts the boys in competition with each other (seen most clearly in their dream of selling sporting goods by heading competing teams) and ultimately in competition with their father.

Sports in the play partakes of Green World elements by providing an arena in which to test and demonstrate masculinity in its most elemental form. When Charley appears in his golf pants in one of Willy's flashbacks of Ben, Willy says, "Great athlete! Between him and his son Bernard they can't hammer a nail!" (51). Charley had been "man enough" to father Bernard, so he can still be a sports participant; similarly, the adult Bernard, father of two boys, is shown with tennis rackets. But golf and tennis are genteel, civilized sports; real men shine in boxing (shown in Willy's gift to the boys of a punching bag) and, especially, football. Because football is played outdoors on a green field and involves seizing territory in pursuit and manipulation of a valued object, it recaptures the savage Green World of Ben in the jungle with the diamonds. Because football is a male team sport that provides opportunity for an individual to "make an impression," "create per-sonal interest," and be "well liked" (33), it epitomizes the Business World. The football star, Biff in high school, brings to the Home a trophy as validation of value, and feminine support comes in having "a crowd of girls behind him" (32) and in having "the girls pay for you" (28). For Willy, therefore, football becomes the ideal means of synthesizing the realms of Green World, Business World, and Home into his desired male community. As such a synthesis, football assumes mythic proportions; on the day of the Ebbets Field game, Biff appears "Like a young god. Hercules—something like that. . . . A star like that, magnificent, can never really fade away!" (68).

This fantasy synthesis, however, does not pass the test of reality. The values of sports fail to overcome the combined challenge of the feminine and math. Just as the Loman house is partly constructed with stolen materials, so Biff's success in high school is partly established through theft of knowledge, especially of math, from Bernard. Like Linda and the suppressed feminine elements of the Green World and Business World, Bernard in the sports synthesis is a demeaned and exploited presence. Because he "loves" Biff, without feeling a need to compete with him, Bernard is "anemic" (32), emasculated, made feminine by the hypermasculine standards of sports.

Through their belief in the justified predominance of male-male competition over feminine measurement of value, the Loman men can rationalize, even sanctify, theft. Willy steals from Linda the respect of parenting and steals through The Woman a higher place in the Business World than he deserves. Happy steals the women of his superiors to avoid competition in the prescribed arena and to inflate his sense of self-worth. Thus both younger sons, Willy and Happy, compete primarily through Woman as object, but older son Biff, like older son Ben, competes more directly with the male, making defeated men like women through emasculation.

Biff's theft of answers from Bernard, who loves him, is of a piece with his theft of a football from the locker room (indirectly from the coach) and the carton of basketballs and gold fountain pen from Bill Oliver. All involve theft of masculinity from a trusting and approving male authority figure. The confused Loman male sense of mathematics is such that one can only be something if everyone else is nothing. One must add to himself by seizing from others and never subtract from himself through giving to others; giving is what women and lesser men must do. Therefore, one becomes the most valuable by taking that which signifies value from all others, male and female. Female value in this system is relegated to support and sexual functions, and male value resides in the phallus. But one cannot have all and be number-one man unless one ultimately castrates the father. Each of Biff's thefts is a preparation for and rehearsal of the theft of his father's phallus.[22]

Sports, then, only seems to be the perfect synthesis of the three realms and thus of the patriarchal-fraternal community that Willy seeks continually. Pushed to its inevitable conclusion, the sports mythos demonstrates that a paternal-fraternal community cannot exist in its forum. Willy wants to celebrate an ideal of brotherhood for lesser men (who are actually like himself) to follow, while he would be the patriarchal authority, idolized by all, especially Biff. Yet when Willy is rational, he believes that although Biff has the potential to be number-one man he himself does not. Biff cannot be both more than Willy and less than Willy: there is a glaring contradiction in logic—it does not add up. In fulfilling his expected potential, Biff would have to grow up, to surpass Willy, to recognize that his father is less than himself. For the "young god" to become an adult god, he would have to dethrone, "castrate," the "fake" god, Willy.

Even before the Boston incident, Willy was dangerously close to being "found out" as less than his stolen, self-constructed image in the boys' eyes.[23] He had promised to take the boys on a business trip; if he had done so, they would have seen that he was a "fake," that the waves did not part for him. If he had not taken them, he would have been a "liar." If Biff had not learned of The Woman, Willy would have had to confront the math teacher and probably fail to get the extra points for Biff. But these crises of faith in the father are forestalled because Biff witnesses him with The Woman.

When Willy and Biff meet in Boston, both have failed: Biff has failed math, and Willy has failed marital fidelity. These failures are accompanied by masculine dream-value system failures: Willy has failed to uphold the family as the sacred cornerstone of success, and Biff has failed to be universally well liked by lesser men. In present time, each blames the other for his failure, but The Woman is made the foundation of the failed relationship between father and son.[24] Although the Loman men contrast Linda as "somebody with resistance" with the women of the Business World, who can be "had,"[25] The Woman epitomizes those women, and she overlaps with and parallels Linda.

Willy continually links Linda and The Woman unconsciously. Linda's attempted ego-inflating praise of Willy in a flashback as the "handsomest man in the world" (37) to her (after he had confessed feeling foolish to look at) brings on a flashback within a flashback in the laughter and then the first appearance of The Woman. Although in context the laughter signifies The Woman's enjoyment of Willy's company, the dramatic effect is that she is laughing at him rather than with him. As he comes out of the flashback within flashback to the flashback, Linda's laughter blends with that of The Woman. The Woman's laugh returns when evidence of Biff's bad behavior, provided by Linda and Bernard, haunts Willy's flashback, testifying that Willy raised Biff by the wrong standards—his rather than Linda's.

The Woman is not even dignified by a name in the list of characters and speech headings, although her name may be Miss Francis. By being simply The Woman, she figures as a temptress, a femme fatale, and this impression is reinforced by her laughter, the music accompanying her appearances, and her appearance in a black slip. Yet her description in the stage directions is at odds with this impression. She is *"quite proper-looking, Willy's age"* (38). Furthermore, she is far from being a prostitute—she is a business contact of Willy's, someone (probably a secretary-receptionist) with the power to choose whom the buyers will see—and she lives with her sisters. Her payment for sex with Willy is silk stockings. She needs silk stockings to wear to work and can probably ill afford them on her salary. Yet the stockings also become an important symbol. When she mentions the promised stockings, Biff understands his father's relationship with her, and when Linda mends her own stockings, it reminds Willy of his guilt. Thus Linda and The Woman are bound together by the stockings, which reinforce their other connections: they are good-humored women of about the same age who both genuinely like Willy.[26] The essential difference between them is that one has chosen to marry and work inside the Home, and the other has chosen not to marry and to work in the Business World. Linda herself is like a mended stocking, torn and tattered by Willy but still serviceable through the strengthening of her own moral fiber. The Woman is a "new" silk stocking, new territory on which Willy can test himself. Both are made to be objects, but both also witness the failures of masculine values.

Contrary to surface appearance, then, there are not two kinds of women in the play, good and bad. All of the women are conflated in the idea of Woman: all share more similarities than differences, particularly in their knowing, and having the potential to reveal, masculine inadequacy, although generally they have been socialized not to insult a man by revealing their knowledge to his face. The Loman men all agree that the truth of masculine inadequacy or failure must be kept from women, because if women do not know, men can maintain their pretenses among other men and to themselves. What most upsets Biff about his father's flashback ravings is that "Mom's hearing that!" (27), and Happy habitually lies about himself and other men to women. When Willy borrows money from Charley, it is to pretend to Linda that it is his salary—but Linda knows about the loans. Willy tries to force Biff into a fabricated version of the meeting with Bill Oliver, supposedly so he can have good news to bring to Linda—but it is he, not Linda, who craves good news from Biff. Linda also knows and tells her sons that Willy has been trying to commit suicide. Like Letta, she is associated with collection and evaluation of evidence. Not only does Linda find the rubber gas hose (during her repairs), but she knows of other suicide attempts that Willy has made with the car. As she begins to tell the story of the witness, she says, "It seems there's a woman," and Biff quickly responds, "What woman?" (58–59), obviously assuming that Linda means The Woman in Boston. Linda not only overlaps the function of Mother Loman, but she and the insurance company's woman witness are alike in knowing about Willy's suicide attempts; the woman witness is linked to The Woman in Biff's mind; Willy treats Jenny as he probably had treated The Woman; and, in the restaurant, Miss Forsythe and Letta provoke Willy's memory of The Woman, as had Linda. The synthesis that Willy seeks among the Green World, Business World, and Home is achieved not by male community but collectively through the women, who independently rise from their positions as submerged elements to join in a circle of femininity and summation of value that closes in, without acknowledgment, on the truth of the Loman men.

The emergence of suppressed Woman occurs in the midst of an intended paternal-fraternal celebration of triumph in the restaurant.[27] Linda was not invited;

the savoring of success was for the men only. Willy was to have wrested a New York job for himself from his symbolic "son" Howard, and Biff was to have convinced his symbolic "father" Bill Oliver to invest in Happy's idea of the Loman Brothers sporting goods teams. But the dreams of success for the day failed to become realized. Howard, delighting in being a "father" himself (evidenced by his pride over his son's performance on the wire recorder)[28] is not impressed by Willy's assertion of fatherhood (his supposed fraternal relationship with Howard's father and his exaggerated claims to have "named" Howard) and in fact fires Willy for failing to "pull his own weight" (80). Biff fails also, not even making an impression on the secretary, let alone Bill Oliver, who sees him only momentarily and does not remember him. Enraged at being treated like a lesser man, Biff re-enters Oliver's office and steals his gold fountain pen, completing the castration of the symbolic father from whom he had stolen basketballs years before. Thus, once again, as in Boston, Willy has failed as father and Biff has failed as son. The restaurant scene recapitulates as well as calls forth the Boston scene as the double failures unfold, but now a transfer of phallic power takes place. Willy seems unable to face his failure to his family until he sees his sons grow into the same action. As Willy "betrayed" the family with The Woman, so Biff and Happy "betray" him by deserting him in the restaurant and leaving with Miss Forsythe and Letta.

In an early line in Willy's culminating flashback—"Willy, Willy, are you going to get up, get up, get up, get up?" (114)—The Woman's iteration of "get up" implies not only getting up to answer the knocking at the door but also getting up the ladder of success and, perhaps, erection. Sexual performance is one realm where a man cannot be a fake—the woman knows if he fails. Woman is the means not only of phallic inflation but also of phallic deflation, both by satisfying his need of her and by her potential for intimidation to impotence. Yet The Woman, like Linda and the women in the restaurant, complies by providing the man with what he desires, the necessary boost in self-confidence. Although her baby-talk manner of speech is meant to make her seem otherwise, The Woman has a sense of responsibility about her job and the intelligence to sense masculine feelings of inadequacy and say the "proper" things to dispel them, even if her own humiliation results. But she also grants herself the freedom of taking sexual initiative: "You didn't make me, Willy. I picked you" (38). And she unabashedly enjoys sex: "Come on inside, drummer boy. It's silly to be dressing in the middle of the night" (116). This implies that she has not yet been satisfied by Willy, and perhaps the laughter so often associated with her also represents his fear that she will laugh at his inadequacy/impotence, which he must overcome by diminishing her.

The Woman insists that Willy acknowledge the knocking, which literally is Biff knocking at the door and symbolically is Willy's own conscience knocking, which he tries to deny. Before Willy opens the hotel room door, he hides The Woman in the bathroom, associating her with "plumbing" and bodily functions. But The Woman becomes the means of destroying the masculine mythos by coming out of the bathroom.

When Willy lets Biff into the room, Biff confesses his math failure. Willy is shocked and tries to displace blame onto Bernard. But Bernard has not failed in loving submission to Biff—although he "stole" from Bernard, Biff only "got a sixty-one" (118). The numbers, so denigrated before, are extremely important now, and Biff needs Willy to get him the extra four points. If they had left then, Willy's failure would have remained secret, but his authority would have to be tested against that of another patriarchal figure. Biff, however, goes on to rationalize his failure. This unimportant math class comes right before all-important sports, so he "didn't go enough" (118), avoiding submission to its alternative value system. Then, too, he is not "well liked" by the teacher; Mr. Birnbaum "hates" Biff for doing a comical imitation of him in front of the class. Biff steals the teacher's self-esteem by imitating him and showing him as a lesser man. Thus, although Biff failed, he succeeds in displacing another male authority figure. Biff increases his own esteem of his classmates by decreasing their esteem for the teacher, and he repeats his imitation for his father's approval. Willy pauses to savor Biff's triumph over male authority and to share male communion by laughing at a supposed lesser man who holds Biff's fate in his hands. But just as Mr. Birnbaum had walked into the midst of Biff's ridicule, so does The Woman intrude into its repetition by joining in their laughter and coming out of the bathroom.

Undoubtedly, most readers and audience members feel tension as Biff and Willy talk, knowing that The Woman is hidden in the bathroom, and they are upset when she makes her presence known. The scene is set up in such a way as to protect the males and to put the blame entirely on her. If only she had kept her mouth shut! If only she had stayed in the bathroom where she belonged! But she does not; she insists on being part of the fun, of sharing in the male-defined game. When she enters, she not only laughs, but she also lisps her lines, imitating Biff's imitation of Mr. Birnbaum—but a woman must not be allowed to share in male camaraderie or to ridicule a lesser man.

To dispel Biff's shock at her presence, Willy begins his *"striving for the ordinary"*. He names her, probably giving her real name, but promoting her: "This is Miss Francis, Biff, she's a buyer" (119). Her promotion is in a sense true—she *has* been a buyer of what Willy is selling—himself as a likeable commodity.[29] She had also bought into the idea that she was a human being to him. But when she sees herself treated as an embarrassment, merchandise no longer desired, she insists at least on the material terms of agreement. Willy tries to force her out into the hall without her clothes, but she demands her promised stockings. Willy tries to deny, but she is armed with numbers: "You had two boxes of size nine sheers for me, and I want them!" (119). And Willy finally produces them for her.

What seems to make "Miss Francis" a "bad" woman is that she refuses to be walked on the way Linda is, that she dares to insist on being recognized and dealt with according to the terms of the contract, and that she understands and resents being humiliated. After she identifies herself as the football that has been kicked around in the male game, she takes her clothes and leaves. The Woman literally has been undressed and Willy literally has been dressed, but Biff has symbolically witnessed Willy defrocked of the patriarchal mantle and has encountered the deflated phallic reality of his father. Through the stockings, Biff has seen the sanctity of family life reduced to an exchangeable commodity: "You—you gave her Mama's stockings!" (121), he says, as he bursts into tears and gives up on his life in terms of Business World success. For once he seems to identify with Linda; if she as wife-mother can be reduced to an object of exchange by his father, so can he as son. Biff accuses his father of being a "liar" and a "fake" (121) and departs.

The projection of the undressed state onto The Woman, however, has left the resolution of the phallic conflict between father and son unresolved until the double masculine failures repeat themselves. In real time, Biff is now armed with two stolen phalluses: Bill Oliver's gold pen, representing the symbolic paternal power of the Business World, and the rubber gas hose, Willy's self-destructive phallus in the Home. Without either of them consciously recognizing it, Willy is "emasculated," put into the position of The Woman, as Biff deserts Willy, leaving his father "babbling in a toilet."[30]

Just as The Woman was the scapegoat for Willy's desertion and failure of the family, so Miss Forsythe and Letta are the scapegoats for his sons' desertion and failure of him. But as masculine failure had been the means of bringing The Woman out of the bathroom of the Business World, so it brings Linda out of her limited position of foundation and support in the Home. Significantly, Linda is at her most assertive and ominous after the incident with The Woman. She flings down the boys' proffered bribe of flowers, presented by Happy as he displaced blame onto women for his and Biff's desertion of their father. But in her wrath, Linda is a superior match for both boys. They cannot cover up or smooth over the truth in her presence, although they sheepishly continue to try. Linda can be threatening not in her own right, but for Willy. Her reaction in this scene is perhaps what could be expected from a woman whose husband had been unfaithful. Yet her devotion to Willy is such that we believe she would not have come at *him* that way. Although Linda has bought into the system enough to condemn the women as "lousy rotten whores!" (124), she blames her sons more for going to them. She attempts to throw the boys out of the house and stops herself from picking up the scattered flowers, ordering them, for once: "Pick up this stuff, I'm not your maid any more." Linda finally declares her independence from her role, recognizing that she is better than they are.[31] For both Linda and The Woman, male failures have provoked female sense of injustice and realization of victimization. Happy turns his back on Linda's order, refusing to acquiesce to feminine dominance, but Biff gets on his knees and picks up the flowers, as he understands that he is a failure as a man. Willy has been put into the position of the humiliated and abandoned one, like The Woman, the football kicked around in the competition. Linda achieves this position through empathy with him but rises above it into female control, short-lived as it is: women can take charge when the men are defeated by one another. When Linda accuses Biff, "You! You didn't even go in to see if he was all right!" (124), she is condemning him partly for shunning all of her influence, the nurturing and tending, the human compassion. But Biff insists on seeing Willy now, over Linda's objections. Because he has become as bad as Willy in betraying Linda, he and Willy can understand each other.

Recognition of his own and Biff's failures in both the Business World and Home makes Willy revert to the Green World as he attempts to reclaim his lost masculinity after the disaster in the restaurant. "The woods are burning!" (107), as he has previously noted, so he must buy some seeds, because "Nothing's planted. I don't have a thing in the ground" (122). His action will be futile in his yard, the remnant of the Green World remaining in the Home realm, because, as Linda knows, "not enough sun gets back there. Nothing'll grow any more" (72). The Green World has become a sunless/sonless void through male depletion of it, but Willy must continue to assert his masculinity on it, imposing the hoe, as Green World phallic symbol, on Mother Earth. In planting his seed, he attempts to renew Biff's conception—his own of Biff and Biff's of him, to start over as new father and new son on a pastoral basis.

The three realms of Green World, Business World, and Home, however, cannot be separated in Willy's mind, and, as he plants, he considers with a hallucinated Ben his suicide plan—he is actually digging his own grave. His previous suicide plans recapitulate his past and have submerged feminine elements. In the first attempt, femininely witnessed, he was driving down the road, went off track into a little bridge, and was saved only by "the shallowness of the water" (59). The road is symbolically connected with being "on the road" of the Business World, the bridge is perhaps sex as a connection out of his loneliness that he got off track into, and the shallowness of water the prescribed shallow but supportive function of Woman that "saved him." The second plan, associated with the Home, involves the phallic rubber hose, but the success of that attempt rests on the "new little nipple" (59), a feminine symbol, on the gas pipe. The third plan is formulated in "pastoral" aspect and approved of in "savage" aspect in the Green World, and it uses elements of the Business World and Home realms as well, thus becoming a replacement for the failed synthesis of the three realms in the sports forum. The suicide will be feminine in being a return to the womb, the pre-competitive sanctum. But as such, it will be another scapegoat for masculine failure.

The suicide plan provides Willy with the fantasy means of reestablishing a fraternal relationship with Ben. Although he had "missed the boat" of Ben's success, Willy can catch the "boat" of death to join the recently dead Ben and, through him, their dead father. In this proposed paternal-fraternal community, Woman is again made the foundation. Willy asserts to the hallucination of Ben that the proposition is "terrific" because "the woman has suffered" (126). But what his understanding of Linda's (and through his ambiguous phrasing, The Woman's) suffering is not revealed. Apparently she has suffered because he has failed to live up to his own standard, not that he has ever seriously considered hers: "A man can't go out the way he came in, Ben, a man has got to add up to something" (125). Thus, the suicide synthesis, like the sports synthesis, involves a confused fantasy appropriation of math. Rather than continuing to live while "ringing up a zero" (126), Willy wants to turn himself into money through death as he perceives Ben had. His plan is a "twenty-thousand-dollar proposition" that is "Guaranteed, gilt-edged" (126). The money, which he will try to steal from the insurance company by making his death seem accidental, will be Willy's gold. Gold had been the value symbol associated with Business World success through Bill Oliver's gold fountain pen and with sports success as Biff in the legendary Ebbets Field game had appeared "in gold." But the death is also imaged as a "diamond, shining in the dark, hard and rough, that I can pick up and touch with my hand" (126). While he puts his seed into the earth, he wants to get something out, the diamonds that his brother found but that he had missed, the value to be appropriated from the Green World as he simultaneously adds and subtracts. A diamond is "Not like—like an appointment!" (126) that is soft in contrast to the manly hardness of the diamond. The death would be tangible in the money, but Willy quickly jumps to another appointment: the funeral, which he envisions will be "massive," attended by "all the old-timers" from four states, because, as Biff never realized in thinking him "nothing," "I am known!" (126). The suicide plan thus becomes the perfect merging of Green World, Business World, and Home, as he, like Ben, will go into the dark jungle of the unknown and come out rich; will, like Dave Singleman, have the death of a salesman in a grand funeral and secure the hero-worship of Biff in the legacy of controlling Biff's future. In forming this synthesis, Woman is exploited once more. Although the plan had begun in relation to Linda, because "the woman has suffered," she has been left out of the grand male scheme again because the money will go to Biff, not her, so that Willy can "amount to something" by masculine standards by regaining the phallus and looking "big" in Biff's eyes.

Although the gold of the gilt-edged insurance policy and the diamond of suicide are presented in masculine terms, they too have submerged feminine significance, because gold and diamond are the elements of a wedding ring. Rather than interpreting gold and diamond as objects to be stolen, Willy could recognize that he already has them in Linda, could understand that value can be achieved rather than objectified and seized, if he submits himself to Linda's system of worth. In her system, big or little, inflated or deflated, are irrelevant to having compassion and dignity and sharing love. But Ben is the primary rival to that vision; he and the suicide plan ultimately represent infidelity to a true marriage with Linda.

Willy is preparing himself to enter the dark, yet he really wants to "get back to all the great times" that "Used to be so full of light and comradeship" (127). One of his main problems is that he yearns for the boys' adolescence that provided him with his own, out of which he and the boys have never quite grown. But the joy of their fraternal adolescence died in their struggle for phallic patriarchal power, and now Biff enters to take the hoe, the last remaining phallic symbol, away from Willy and to assert paternal authority by demanding that Willy return to the Home to "tell Mom" of their failures as father and son. As·Willy has been trying to re-establish roots in a pastoral Green World, Biff has determined to uproot himself by leaving permanently for his pastoral Green World.

The confrontation scene between Willy and Biff begins in the Green World remnant, the yard, but it must be played out in the Home, in front of Happy as lesser man, and especially Linda. When they enter, Linda withdraws into her support function for both of them, gently asking Willy, "Did you plant, dear?" (128), and allowing Biff the "public" credit for her idea, in fact demand, that Biff leave the Home forever. But Biff cannot leave without wanting Willy to shake his hand, thereby acknowledging his defeat and Biff as the winner. Neither Biff nor Willy is ready for it to be over until one has asserted authority over the other, so they begin a contest of competing reasons for Biff's failure: blaming it on Willy or attributing it to Biff's spite. Willy repeatedly turns to Linda to ratify his version, spite. Yet what Willy wants here is for Biff to maintain the masculine system of conspiracy, which involves protecting Woman (and themselves) from the truth of male failure. If he can make Biff submit to this version, Willy will both triumph over Biff and be safe in Linda's eyes. Although Biff repeatedly denies attributing blame to his father, Willy is too agitated to hear Biff's response. Instead, he accuses Biff of "trying to put a knife in me" (130)—using phallic weaponry against him. Then Biff rises to the challenge, not with a knife but with the rubber hose.

Just before he shows the hose, Biff says, "All right, phony! Then let's lay it on the line." The implication, especially through the word "phony," is that Biff will reveal Willy's infidelity in front of Linda and Happy, conflating infidelity with the suicide attempts. But both Linda and Happy already know about the hose and try to prevent Biff from disclosing that they know. It is like presenting the naked phallus in public: indecent exposure. Willy pretends not to recognize the hose, but it is the revelation of Willy's rising ("What is this supposed to do, make a hero out of you?") and falling ("This is supposed to make me sorry for you?") phallus. But even this is not enough; Biff perseveres that Willy is "going to hear the truth—what you are and what I am!" When Happy interrupts, Biff begins with him: "You big blow, are you the assistant buyer?", asserting that Happy is "full of it! We all are! And I'm through with it" (130–31). This affirmation, along with Biff's statement a few lines earlier that "We never told the truth for ten minutes in this house!" (131), implies that Linda is included, but not if we remember that she has never been given the status of being one of them. She alone has told the truth of what Willy is, what the boys are, and of Willy's suicide plans (albeit to the boys but not Willy). Again she is discounted, but with her value appropriated yet unacknowledged.

Now that Willy's phallic flaws have been made public, Biff must confess his own: "I stole myself out of every good job since high school!"—and he had spent time in jail for theft. Although Biff had earlier absolved Willy from blame, he places it now: Biff "never got anywhere" because Willy "blew me so full of hot air I could never stand taking orders from anybody! That's whose fault it is!" The tumescent image here connects with his calling Happy a "big blow" (131), and both reveal Biff's recognition of the artificially inflated phalluses of all the Loman men; he tries to make himself and them face their own deflated condition.[32] Willy's response is "Then hang yourself! For spite, hang yourself!" Thus Biff's confession of failure leads Willy unconsciously to the same conclusion as his own of suicide. But Biff answers that "Nobody's hanging himself" (131–32). He has finally learned that acknowledging limitations does not lead necessarily to self-annihilation but to choosing alternate paths—for him, acceptance of the pastoral Green World and rejection of the Business World.

Biff's castration of the Business World in his theft of the gold pen has resulted in his recognizing the pointlessness of stealing other men's phallic power to "become what I don't want to be" (132)[33] and his accepting the Green World as the appropriate realm for his truest inclinations. But because the Green World also involves asserting manhood, Biff still cannot be free to enter that realm until he completes his "castration" of Willy by imposing his new-found truth. He now turns, significantly, to the "real math" of value computation to do so, asserting to Willy that "I'm a dime a dozen, and so are you!", that Willy is only a "hard-working drummer" and Biff himself, on any turf, is "one dollar an hour." Furthermore, Biff is "not bringing home any prizes any more" (132), and Willy is not to expect them. Once he has defined himself as "nothing," Biff can and does cry. We have only seen him cry once before, in the hotel room, and these tears connect these two incidents. They culminate in the conclusion of the conflict, which had been delayed by sustaining the masculine myth between them. But this resolution has taken place on the grounds of relating represented by Linda: the emotional, compassionate way of interaction. Willy turns to Linda for an explanation of Biff's tears, recognizing that she can understand better. Biff has finally learned to love himself and Willy for what they are, pretensions stripped away—what Linda has been advocating and has demonstrated throughout, without recognition.

Biff asks to be let go, for Willy to "take that phony dream and burn it before something happens" (133). But he cannot carry through and re-establish a relationship on compassionate terms; he can only escape: "I'll go in the morning." And once again, Linda is made to do the difficult part: "Put him—put him to bed" (133).

At first it seems strange that Willy, who has gotten what he wanted—the return of Biff's love—still intends to commit suicide. He is enraptured because Biff has become a boy again; they have gone back to the day when Biff confronted him in the hotel room, and it has been "made right," with Biff acknowledging Willy as the one in control and with the power to "take and burn that phony dream." But neither Biff nor Willy follows through. Neither can handle a relationship that is based on "feminine" compassion and mutual self-recognition. Yet Willy is pleased because he now believes that Biff will accept the money; perhaps he has an idea that his suicide will burn away the phoniness from the dream but leave the dream intact.

Linda alone feels the danger and asks Willy to come to bed. But Willy must seize and make the most of this moment of glory, take the ball and run with it, listening to Ben again. Willy makes the same mistake that he has always made: not appreciating real moments of value as they happen because they have always got to be topped with bigger dreams for the future. That prevented his full enjoyment of the boys' youth, and that prevents him from living on. He can only think to top this moment by leaving Biff twenty thousand dollars. If Biff has done a great thing in crying to Willy, sacrificing his self-image to his father, Willy must sacrifice his life for Biff, still competing with him. Happy appropriately asks for recognition now, behaving as if he had been the source of the trouble, maintaining that he is going to be the perfect son, replacing Biff, staying and living out the dream. But Willy cannot even acknowledge his younger son as he pays increasing attention to his older brother. Therefore, Linda must give Happy the comfort he needs.

As Biff and Happy go to bed, only Linda remains as a living interactive presence for Willy. In his last moments on stage, he alternates between attending to the real voice of Linda and the fantasized voice of Ben. Linda continually entreats him to follow her, and she is put into direct competition with his desire to follow Ben. Willy cannot acknowledge the superiority of the feminine value system to his own, so he must choose Ben. Ben's way is presented erotically—"One must go in to fetch a diamond out" (134)—one must enter sexually, impose the phallus, to get a diamond—son—out. Linda's "I want you upstairs" (134) is both a command and, perhaps, a sexual invitation, to counter the sexuality of Ben's offer. But Willy cannot satisfy Linda on her terms. When Linda says, "I think this is the only way, Willy," meaning that Biff should leave, Willy conflates it with the suicide plan: "Sure, it's the best thing." And Ben agrees: "Best thing!" (134). Here is the only point where all three agree, but two are agreeing to a plan between them, to a dream in which Woman is left out, not to the basis of the real experience just past.

Willy is finally left alone with Ben, as he wishes. The male-male connection can now be savored only by males, with no female commentary. He shares with Ben his wonder that Biff loves him and always has. But instead of being content with love, Willy must inflate it to worship which he seeks to provoke in Biff by his suicide that Ben now urges him toward, promising, "It's dark there, but full of diamonds." When Linda calls, his reply, "Coming!" (135), answers Ben more than her.

Before following Ben, Willy *"elegiacally"* relives the preparation for the Ebbets Field game, the day of Biff's stardom, when Willy was the authority figure. After much advice, he says, "There's all kinds of important people in the stands" (135) and suddenly recognizes his aloneness in the male-defined game. Willy starts asking for Ben, but instead Linda calls again. She has repeatedly offered acceptance on the terms of love for being what he is, average, and Biff has just offered the same, but Willy must make one more grandstand play. Yet it is obvious that accepting love, the feminine way, frightens him. Responding to Linda's call, he tries to quiet her, but his "sh!" unleashes *"sounds, faces, voices"* (136) that swarm in upon him, and he tries to "sh" them too. They are probably the voices of truth represented by Woman, the contradictions and failures in his world view. In the midst of his "sh"-ing, the ancestral flute music of his father stops him, rising in intensity *"to an unbearable scream"* (136). The music of male harmonic blending is now the only thing he hears, although Linda, and even Biff following her lead, calls out again. But the music draws Willy to the car, another symbol of masculine unity in the play, and Willy, the car, and the music all crash, *"in a frenzy of sound, which becomes the soft pulsation of a single cello string,"* which further develops into *"a dead march"* (136). Willy has crashed the car and killed himself, driven to the beat of the male song.

The scene dissolves into a dumb show of preparation for the funeral, with the *"leaves of day"* appearing *"over everything"* (136), suggesting Willy's final rest in the pastoral dream that was just as much death for him as were the other dreams. But as the Requiem begins, Charley notes that "It's getting dark, Linda" (137). Willy is finally put to rest in the darkness that he had sought, the void that the competing realms made of Woman, and he exists now only in the competing summations of his value presented by Linda, Charley, Biff, and Happy.

Critics have often been puzzled at Linda's speech of incomprehension at the grave, because she knew Willy was trying to kill himself.[34] But what she cannot understand is why. The reason is partly that Willy could not accept no longer being a boy or having a hope of boyhood in his sons—that the dreams could not be realized. Linda is always patronized for not understanding Willy's "massive dreams," but she comprehended the dreams well enough. Willy Loman's "massive dreams" were little more than adolescent male dreams of *being massive*. What Linda cannot understand is why those dreams of inflated masculinity are more important than family love, compassion, and respect—why real virtues are seen to have no honor and the "little man" cannot accept his dignity.

As the male characters present their competing versions of who Willy was and what he represents, it becomes evident that they understand him less than Linda does. Each identifies himself with Willy, making a male synthesis to contrast and outdo Linda. Biff relates to the camaraderie and construction, the "nice days" such as "Sundays, making the stoop." Forgetting that the stoop was constructed from stolen materials, Biff muses fondly, "there's more of him in that front stoop than in all the sales he ever made." Linda's reply may be meant as a punning sexual tribute: "He was so wonderful with his hands."[35] But then Biff says his famous lines, "He had the wrong dreams. All, all, wrong." Happy responds angrily, but Biff continues, "He never knew who he was," speaking as much about himself as Willy. Charley begins his "Nobody dast blame this man" speech partly to break up a pending fight between the boys. Oddly, in saying what a salesman is, Charley has to specify what he is not, including "He don't put a bolt to a nut"—which Willy actually did, albeit not as a salesman. Charley also is talking partly about himself: he has been the one unaccustomed to using the tools of reconstruction. Furthermore, it is Charley, the unsentimental, non-dreaming realist, who now says, "A salesman is got to dream, boy. It comes with the territory," thus combining his reality with acceptance of Willy's dream. This speech does little to reconcile Biff and Happy, who ignore it and continue their rivalry. Once again, Biff suggests his fraternal dream—that Happy go with him—but Happy says, "I'm not licked that easily" and refers once more to his fraternal dream, "The Loman Brothers!" Happy reaffirms the part of Willy that he identifies with: "the only dream you can have—to come out number-one man" (138–39). He plans to show Biff and everybody else that Willy Loman did not die in vain.

What Willy did die for if not in vain is not clear in any of the characters' minds, particularly not in Happy's, because not much earlier he had denied that Willy had any "right" to kill himself. Happy's speech is meant to be received by the audience as pathetic, and it is. For one, it defines the only dream possible as coming out "number-one man," women excluded, other men trampled beneath. Biff has now rejected it and turns to his mother. But Linda sends the men on their way, so that she, the only one who truly loved Willy, can be alone with him, and the flute music plays through her speech.

Alone at his grave, Linda asks Willy to forgive her for not being able to cry. Her loyalty and dedication to Willy are such that she wishes to do the expected, appropriate, female supportive behavior even when Willy is no longer there to require it. The two notes sounded alternatively throughout the speech are that she cannot cry and she cannot understand it. Thus part of what she cannot understand is why she cannot cry. On the one hand, Willy's death seems like just another of his absences, when she carries on, managing the bills, etc., as always. She has made the last payment on the house today, and "there'll be nobody home," considering herself, as Willy had, to be nobody. But suddenly a sob rises as she says, "We're free and clear." The idea of freedom releases her to sob more fully: "We're free ... We're free" (139). What she cannot yet sort out, perhaps, is that she could not cry for Willy because of her unconscious sense of his oppression of her and her sons. She will no longer have to bend under the burden of the masculine ego. Biff is free of the patriarch now, and so is she: free and crying in the emotional intensity that her freedom releases.

Although mystified to seem otherwise, the male American Dream of *Death of a Salesman* is, as the play shows, unbalanced, immature, illogical, lying, thieving, self-contradictory, and self-destructive. Only Willy literally kills himself, but the Dream's celebration of the masculine mythos is inherently self-destructive in its need to obliterate other men or be obliterated, to castrate or be castrated.[36] It prefers to destroy itself rather than to acknowledge the female as equal or to submit to a realistic and balanced feminine value system. This tragedy of the common *man* also wreaks the suffering of the common *woman*, who has trustingly helped the man to maintain and repair the Dream and has helplessly watched him destroy it and render her sacrifices meaningless. One could argue that Linda as common woman possesses more tragic nobility than Willy.[37] Her only flaw was in harnessing all of her talents and energies to support the self-destructive American masculine mythos that requires Woman's subjugation and exploitation. Yet, at the end of the play, Linda lives—and even, for once, gets the last word. Biff, under her unacknowledged influence, now even shows her some tenderness as they leave the stage. But Happy exists last, alone, with the male music of the flute remaining, reminding us of the perpetuation of the Dream.

Thus the audience and readers are left with a choice between Happy and Linda, as Willy had had a choice between Ben and Linda. We can continue to side with the immature masculine mythos in degrading and ignoring Woman while making her the scapegoat for failures in American male-dominated society, or we can free Woman to rise from her oppression by choosing with her the appreciation of love and compassion, the recognition of the values of human dignity, and the worthwhile contributions of men *and* women.

NOTES

[1] See Arthur Miller, "Tragedy and the Common Man" [1949], in *The Theater Essays of Arthur Miller*, ed. Robert A. Martin (New York: Viking Press, 1978), pp. 3–7, and "Introduction" to Arthur Miller, *Collected Plays* (New York: Viking Press, 1957), pp. 3–55, especially pp. 31–36.

[2] Much of the criticism on the play involves the question of whether it can properly be called a tragedy. For a summary of the various positions, as well as for a distillation of analysis of the work as social drama and for discussion of its place in theater history, see Helene Wickham Koon, "Introduction" to *Twentieth Century Interpretations of* Death of a Salesman, ed. Helene Wickham Koon (Englewood Cliffs, N.J.: Prentice-Hall, 1983), pp. 1–14.

[3] Note the example of "Private Conversations" (produced, directed, and photographed by Christian Blackwood), the 1985 PBS documentary in the *American Masters* series that was a commentary on the filming of the televised version of the 1984 Broadway production of *Death of a Salesman*, starring Dustin Hoffman. In it, the male lead actors, director, Miller, and even male guests made pronouncements on the play, but no comments from Kate Reid, who played Linda, were included, although Dustin Hoffman's flirting with a female stagehand and his remark about the physical endowments of Kathy Rossetter as The Woman were.

[4] Arthur Miller, *Death of a Salesman* (New York: Viking Press, 1949), p. 23. Subsequent references are cited parenthetically by page number within the text.

[5] Although some mention that Ben has achieved mythic stature in Willy's mind, I seem to be alone among critics in believing, and finding Linda capable of believing, that Ben was just as much of a "fake" as Willy; lying and exaggerations of success do seem to be typical traits in Loman men. Ben keeps his two visits short and gives supposedly profound but actually vague explanations of his wealth. Although he offers Willy a job, he surely knows that there is no danger of Willy's accepting it. His gift of a diamond watch fob to Willy hardly constitutes proof of his success in diamond mines, because he could have simply bought or stolen one to dazzle Willy. If Ben were as rich as he claims to be, he could have made some provision for his only brother in his will (if only to impress him further), even if he did have seven sons. But what Ben really was matters less to Willy than what he believed Ben to be.

[6] I use the word "flashback" for convenience; Miller, in "Introduction" to *Collected Plays*, maintains that "There are no flashbacks in this play but only a mobile concurrency of past and present" (p. 26).

[7] My interpretation here is directly opposite to that of Lois Gordon, *"Death of a Salesman: An Appreciation,"* in *The Forties: Fiction, Poetry, Drama*, ed. Warren French (Deland, Fla.: Everett/Edwards, 1969), who states that "The first generation (Willy's father) has been forced, in order to make a living, to break up the family" (p. 278).

[8] Barclay W. Bates, "The Lost Past in *Death of a Salesman*," *Modern Drama* 11 (Fall 1968): 164–72, suggests that Willy tries to function as the "dutiful patriarchal male intent upon transmitting complex legacies from his forbears to his progeny" (p. 164).

[9] Willy's dream of a male patriarchal-fraternal community corresponds to the American Dream of the United States as male-dominated capitalist (patriarchal)/democratic (fraternal) nation.

[10] Many critics blame this incident on Linda. For example, Barry Edward Gross, "Peddler and Pioneer in *Death of a Salesman*," *Modern Drama* 7 (February 1965): 405–10, says, "Linda discourages him from accepting the one opportunity which would allow him to fulfill his pioneer yearnings ... [she] frustrates the pioneer in Willy because she fears it.... What Linda does not understand is that Willy was brought up in a tradition in which one had worlds to conquer and that the attempt to conquer them was the mark of a man" (pp. 407–8).

[11] Paul Blumberg, "Sociology and Social Literature: Work Alienation in the Plays of Arthur Miller,"

American Quarterly 21 (1969): 291–310, determines that, in sociological terms, Ben represents the nineteenth-century robber baron, "hard, unscrupulous, firm, self-reliant, full of . . . self-confident energy," whereas Willy represents "the new, salaried, pathetically other-directed middle class" (p. 300).

[12] Note the Green World implications in the animal images, and in the nature association and sexual pun of the "Bushwick" location, of this woman.

[13] Both Richard J. Foster, "Confusion and Tragedy: The Failure of Miller's Salesman," in *Two Modern American Tragedies: Reviews and Criticism of* Death of a Salesman *and* A Streetcar Named Desire, ed. John D. Hurrell (New York: Charles Scribner's, 1961), pp. 82–88, and Joseph A. Hynes, "Attention Must Be Paid. . . ." *College English* 23 (April 1962): 574–78, reprinted in *Arthur Miller, Death of a Salesman: Text and Criticism,* ed. Gerald Weales (New York: Viking Press, 1967), pp. 280–89, note inconsistencies in the play, particularly in the character of Biff, but neither, nor any other critic I have read, detects what is to me a troubling contradiction. When were Biff and Happy together conducting those seductions of "About five hundred women"—before or after the incident in Boston? If Biff, brimming with sexual confidence, had already had several successful experiences and had supervised Happy's initiation *before* he had gone to Boston, he surely would not have been so shocked and devastated at learning of his father's affair. He conceivably could have begun and brought Happy into a rampage of promiscuous sex as a reaction to Willy's adultery, but that interpretation seems to be at odds with Happy's mention here of Biff's mysterious change in character toward bashfulness and loss of "confidence."

[14] By calling this woman a "strudel," Happy continues in his habit of self-centered definition of women by projection: when he went to his first woman to satisfy *his* "natural" but "animal" urges, *she* was framed in natural, animal images; here, as he is in a restaurant, Miss Forsythe is an item on *his* menu—a delicacy to be ordered, "bought," devoured, and digested to provide him with sustenance.

[15] Thomas E. Porter, *Myth and Modern American Drama* (Detroit: Wayne State University Press, 1969), like many critics, calls these women "prostitutes" (p. 143). Eric Bentley, *In Search of Theatre* (New York: Knopf, 1953), asks, "Has [Miller] given us a suitable language for his tarts (in the whoring sequence)?" (p. 87), without thinking to question whether the language of the women might be right and the unreliable Happy's assumptions about them wrong.

[16] Note that male and female interpretations of female "ruin" do not correspond: The Woman sees her "ruin" not in being "used goods" but in allowing her job performance to be affected by a sexual relationship.

[17] In Arthur Miller, "The Family in Modern Drama" [1956], in *Theater Essays,* ed. Martin, pp. 69–85, Miller postulates that all plays considered "great" or even "serious" examine this problem: "How may a man make of the outside world a home? How and in what ways must he struggle, what must he strive to change and overcome within himself and outside himself if he is to find the safety, the surroundings of love, the ease of soul, the sense of identity and honor which, evidently, all men have connected in their memories with the idea of family?" (p. 73).

[18] Whereas I see Linda as the foundation of what is good in Willy as opposed to his "massive dreams," in which he separates himself from association with her, many critics make Linda the foundation for Willy's problems. For example, Guerin Bliquez, "Linda's Role in *Death of a Salesman," Modern Drama* 10 (February 1968): 383–86, states that "Linda's facility for prodding Willy to his doom is what gives the play its direction and its impetus" and projects onto Linda the play's thematic "cash-payment fixation" (p. 383). Karl Harshbarger, *The Burning Jungle: An Analysis of Arthur Miller's* Death of a Salesman (Boston: University Press of America, 1980), misappropriates "feminism" to advance his theory that Linda, beneath her "show of the 'perfect' wife," is "attempting to destroy her husband" (p. 7). He twists her statements of support of Willy into attacks (pp. 8–21) and even accuses her of an incestuous desire for Biff (p. 28).

[19] Critics often give Linda even less credit than does her family. Henry Popkin, "Arthur Miller: The Strange Encounter," *Sewanee Review* 67 (1960): 34–60, calls Linda "not in the least sexually interesting" (p. 56), forgetting Willy's statement to her that "on the road I want to grab you sometimes and just kiss the life outa you." As Linda is so thoroughly compliant with Willy's other desires, there is no reason to assume her to be otherwise in connection with sex. Similarly, Brian Parker, "Point of View in Arthur Miller's *Death of a Salesman," University of Toronto Quarterly* 35 (1966): 144–57, reprinted in *Twentieth Century Interpretations of* Death of a Salesman, ed. Helene Wickham Koon (Englewood Cliffs, N.J.: Prentice-Hall, 1983), pp. 41–55, discounts Linda's "traditional values and her downtrodden, loving loyalty" because they "blind audiences to the essential stupidity of Linda's behavior. Surely it is both stupid and immoral to encourage the man you love in self-deceit and lies" (Koon, p. 54). Yet, as is noted by Irving Jacobson, "Family Dreams in *Death of a Salesman," American Literature* 47 (1975): 247–58,

"given Loman's inability to accept disagreement from his sons or Charley, it is hard to suppose that he would tolerate a less acquiescent wife" (p. 257). Besides, rather than "encouraging" Willy's "lies," Linda instead balances delicately and skillfully between helping to maintain Willy's self-esteem and trying to keep him grounded in reality.

[20] In Arthur Miller, "The American Theater" [1955], in *Theater Essays*, ed. Martin, pp. 31–50, Miller tells the story of Mildred Dunnock's efforts to secure the role of Linda in the original 1949 production: "We needed a woman who looked as though she had lived in a house dress all her life, even somewhat coarse and certainly less than brilliant. Mildred Dunnock insisted she was that woman, but she was frail, delicate, not long ago a teacher in a girls' college, and a cultivated citizen who probably would not be out of place in a cabinet post. We told her this, in effect, and she understood, and left." She returned the next day, "had padded herself from neck to hem line to look a bit bigger, and for a moment none of us recognized her, and she read again. As soon as she spoke we started to laugh at her ruse; but we saw, too, that she *was* a little more worn now, and seemed less well-maintained, and while she was not quite ordinary, she reminded you of women who were. But we all agreed, when she was finished reading, that she was not right, and she left." But on every following day, "she was there again in another getup," and "each day she agreed with us that she was wrong; and to make a long story short when it came time to make the final selection it had to be Milly, and she turned out to be magnificent" (pp. 46–47). Thus it seems that Dunnock, better than Miller, understood Linda Loman to be a bright woman "disguising" herself to seem inferior to meet male expectations.

[21] Miller had originally written "shrimp," changed it to "walrus" to fit Lee J. Cobb in the original 1949 production, then changed it back to "shrimp" for Dustin Hoffman in the 1984 production.

[22] In "Introduction" to *Collected Plays*, Miller mentions having received "innumerable letters asking if I was aware that the fountain pen which Biff steals is a phallic symbol" (p. 28), and some critics continue to interpret the pen thusly, although none to my knowledge have discovered the other phallic symbols that I discuss, nor have they examined the castration theme further than do Schneider and Field, whom I cite below.

[23] According to Miller in "Introduction" to *Collected Plays*, one of the "simple images" out of which the play grew was that of "the son's hard, public eye upon you, no longer swept by your myth, no longer rousable from his separateness, no longer knowing you have lived for him and have wept for him" (p. 29).

[24] In Olga Carlisle and Rose Styron, "Arthur Miller: An Interview" [1966], in *Theater Essays*, ed. Martin, pp. 264–93, Miller calls the father-son relationship "a very primitive thing in my plays. That is, the father was really a figure who incorporated both power and some kind of a moral law which he had either broken himself or had fallen prey to. He figures as an immense shadow ... it had a mythical quality to me" (pp. 267–68).

[25] Benjamin Nelson, *Arthur Miller: Portrait of a Playwright* (New York: David McKay, 1970), unfairly burdens Linda with responsibility for the Loman men's dichotomizing of women into Madonna/whore categories, in order to blame her for their sexual misconduct: "In her well-meaning prudery and naïveté, and in her unswerving loyalty to Willy, she has unconsciously fostered adolescent sexual attitudes in all three of her men by creating an image of herself as the maternal counterpart of the infallible father. The more she is a paragon of virtue to them the less are they able to relate to her as adult males to a wife and mother. That view of her is pantingly adolescent and distorts all their relationships with women." Thus Happy's "image of Mom as goddess is partially responsible for his shoddy encounters with girls who are never fit to bring home to her, as well as for his father's cheap and pathetic adultery and Biff's traumatic reaction to it" (p. 113).

[26] Beverly Hume, "Linda Loman as 'the Woman' in Miller's *Death of a Salesman*," *Notes on Modern American Literature* 9 (1985): item 14, also sees connection between the two characters, but her interpretation finds in Linda an "intense materialism" that places her "in league with 'the Woman,'" who "is manipulating Willy only for money (or stockings)."

[27] Psychoanalyst Daniel E. Schneider, *The Psychoanalyst and the Artist* (New York: Farrar, Straus, 1950), pp. 246–55, suggests that the dinner was to be a "totem feast in which the sons recognize the father's authority and sexual rights" (p. 250).

[28] Eric Bentley, *What Is Theatre?* (New York: Atheneum, 1968), states that "one never knows what a Miller play is about: politics or sex. If *Death of a Salesman* is political, the key scene is the one with the tape recorder; if it is sexual, the key scene is the one in the Boston hotel" (p. 261). To me, the play is not about politics *or* sex but politics *of* sex, so even the scene with the tape recorder (actually a "wire recorder") is sexually political. Howard's presentation of the three females in his private life—daughter,

wife, and maid—recapitulates in miniature the treatment of women elsewhere in the play. Although Howard had bought the recorder for dictation, he tries it out on his family—testing Business World techniques in the Home. His daughter, the first guinea pig, whistles "Roll out the Barrel," then Howard whistles the same song, perhaps to demonstrate superiority over her. She is seven years old, and her chief value is in being "crazy for" her father. Howard's son, however, is the important one—five years old and reciting the state capitals, in alphabetical order. Father and son are the best performers, with the females only to express devotion, provide entertainment, or demonstrate supposed inadequacy to the male standard. The maid "kicked the plug out," but later Howard will depend on her to support the machine by recording radio programs for his convenience. Howard's wife is bullied into speaking into the machine, but she proves such an embarrassment that he interrupts her dissension by shutting off her voice. Willy's function throughout this episode is to admire but to be interrupted and silenced when the son displays his talents. Willy is thus put into the position of Woman, into the same role that he expects Linda to play. Furthermore, Willy even replays the actions of the wire-recorded women: like the daughter, Willy calls forth the admired father (Howard's father); like the wife, he has no interest in the recorder but is forced to interact with it; and like the maid who accidentally unplugs the machine, Willy (a "servant" of Howard's firm) accidentally turns it on, thereby becoming an embarrassment to be "shut off," again like the wife. Howard the "son" then begins the symbolic castration (completed by Biff) of Willy the "father" by asking him to turn in his samples, his two salesman's cases, representing his testicles.

[29] In "Introduction" to Collected Plays, Miller relates that "when asked what Willy was selling, what was in his bags, I could only reply, 'Himself'" (p. 28).

[30] Schneider, The Psychoanalyst and the Artist, labels as "castration-panic" Willy's flight to the bathroom after hearing of Biff's theft of Oliver's pen (p. 250).

[31] Cf. the hideous portrayal of Linda's self-assertion by Schneider, The Psychoanalyst and the Artist: "Her rage at being old and dried-up is implicit as she fights like a she-tiger against the sons who have cast off the father for their own sexual philandering" (p. 251).

[32] B. S. Field, Jr., "Death of a Salesman," Twentieth Century Literature 18 (1972): 19–24, reprinted in Twentieth Century Interpretations of Death of a Salesman, ed. Helene Wickham Koon (Englewood Cliffs, N.J.: Prentice-Hall, 1983), pp. 79–84, interprets Willy's hamartia to be his success in making his sons in his own image: "One may . . . say of Willy that 'he's got no balls.' And neither have his sons . . . They are morally and socially castrated. . . . he has made moral eunuchs of his own sons" (Koon, p. 84).

[33] As is noted by Chester E. Eisinger, "Focus on Arthur Miller's Death of a Salesman: The Wrong Dreams," in American Dreams, American Nightmares, ed. David Madden (Carbondale: Southern Illinois University Press; London and Amsterdam: Feffer & Simons, 1970), pp. 165–74, Biff "cannot and need not rely on a mere symbol of manhood. This conviction transcends the phallic value of the pen and sustains Biff in his honest self-knowledge at the end of the play" (p. 172).

[34] Note Parker's explanation in "Point of View": "After thirty-five years of marriage, Linda is apparently completely unable to comprehend her husband: her speech at the graveside . . . is not only pathetic, it is also an explanation of the loneliness of Willy Loman which threw him into other women's arms" (Koon, p. 54).

[35] Miller, in "Introduction" to Collected Plays, remembers that he "laughed when the line came, laughed with the artist-devil's laugh, for it had all come together in this line, she having been made by him though he did not know it or believe in it or receive it into himself" (p. 30).

[36] In Phillip Gelb, "Morality and Modern Drama" [interview, 1958], in Theater Essays, ed. Martin, pp. 195–214, Miller states that because he kills himself, Willy cannot be an "average American man," yet he "embodies in himself some of the most terrible conflicts running through the streets of America today. A Gallup Poll might indicate that they are not the majority conflicts; I think they are" (pp. 199–200).

[37] In "Introduction" to Collected Plays, Miller, recalling some of the widely varying evaluations of the play, says that "The letters from women made it clear that the central character of the play was Linda" (p. 28). But those women were not alone. Several critics have made a case for Biff as the play's tragic protagonist, and one (Schneider) has even done so for Happy. Recent criticism sometimes cites these readings, but it is much less often remembered that some early reviewers sketched in a similar possibility for Linda. Robert Garland, "Audience Spellbound by Prize Play of 1949," The New York Journal-American, 11 February 1949, p. 24, reprinted in Arthur Miller, ed. Gerald Weales (New York: Viking Press, 1967), pp. 199–201, saw Linda as the "the play's most poignant figure" whose "all-too-human single-mindedness holds Death of a Salesman together," and he found the "most tragic tragedy" to be her powerlessness to prevent Willy from being his "own worst tragedy" (Weales, p. 200). Similarly, William Beyer, "The State of the Theatre: The Season Opens," School and Society 70 (3 December

1949): 363–64, reprinted in *Arthur Miller*, ed. Weales, pp. 228–30, interpreted the play to be "essentially the mother's tragedy, not Willy Loman's. Willy's plight is sad, true, but he is unimportant and too petty, commonplace, and immature to arouse more than pity, and the sons are of a piece with their father.... We can only sympathize since they reflect human frailties all too common among men. Within her circumscribed sphere of living, however, the mother makes of her love a star which her idealism places on high, and when it is destroyed her heavens are wiped out. What the mother stands for is important, and when she goes down the descent is tragic" (Weales, p. 230).

CONTRIBUTORS

HAROLD BLOOM is Sterling Professor of the Humanities at Yale University and Henry W. and Albert A. Berg Professor of English at the New York University Graduate School. He is a 1985 MacArthur Foundation Award recipient, served as the Charles Eliot Norton Professor of Poetry at Harvard University (1987–88), and is the author of nineteen books, the most recent being *The Book of J* (1990). Currently he is editing the Chelsea House series Modern Critical Views and The Critical Cosmos, and other Chelsea House series in literary criticism.

RUBY COHN is Professor of Comparative Literature/French/Drama at the University of California–Davis. She has written *Modern Shakespeare Offshoots* (1976), *From Desire to Godot: Pocket Theater of Postwar Paris* (1987), and four works on Samuel Beckett.

DAN VOGEL is Professor of English at Yeshiva University/Stern College in New York City and is the author of a critical study, *Emma Lazarus* (1980), as well as *Indian Origins and the Book of Mormon* (1986) and *Religious Seekers and the Advent of Mormonism* (1988).

A. D. CHOUDHURI is a former Lecturer in English at the University of Calcutta, is the author of two studies on the plays of John Galsworthy, and has lectured on Indian literature at Oxford University.

ROBERT N. WILSON is Sociology Professor at the University of North Carolina at Chapel Hill. He is the author of *Man Made Plain: The Poet in Contemporary Society* (1958), *The Arts in Society* (1964), and *The Writer as Social Seer* (1979).

JEREMY HAWTHORN teaches at the University of Trondheim, Norway. Among his works are *Identity and Relationship: A Contribution to Marxist Theory of Literary Character* (1973), *Joseph Conrad: Language and Fictional Self-Consciousness* (1979), and *Unlocking the Text: Fundamental Issues in Literary Theory* (1987).

C. W. E. BIGSBY is Professor of American Studies at the University of East Anglia, Norwich, England. He is the editor of *A Critical Introduction to Twentieth-Century American Drama* (1981–85; 3 vols.) and has written books on David Mamet, Edward Albee, Joe Orton, and other modern dramatists.

LEAH HADOMI is Senior Lecturer of Comparative Literature at Haifa University, Israel. Her principal research interests and publications are in the area of comparative studies in drama and the postwar German novel and cinema.

KAY STANTON is Assistant Professor of English at California State University–Fullerton and has published articles on Shakespeare, Marlowe, and Milton.

BIBLIOGRAPHY

Aarnes, William. "Tragic Form and the Possibility of Meaning in *Death of a Salesman.*" *Furman Studies* 29 (1983): 57–80.

Austin, Gayle. "The Exchange of Women and Male Homosocial Desire in Arthur Miller's *Death of a Salesman* and Lillian Hellman's *Another Part of the Forest.*" In *Feminist Rereadings of Modern American Drama,* edited by June Schlueter. Rutherford, NJ: Fairleigh Dickinson University Press, 1989, pp. 59–66.

Bates, Barclay W. "The Lost Past in *Death of a Salesman.*" *Modern Drama* 11 (1968): 164–72.

Bertin, Michael. "Theater in New York: Ringing on a Smile and a Shoeshine: The Broadway *Salesman.*" *Theater* 16, No. 1 (Fall–Winter 1984): 75–79.

Bhatia, Santosh K. *Arthur Miller: Social Drama as Tragedy.* New Delhi: Arnold-Heinemann, 1985.

Bigsby, C. W. E. "Arthur Miller." In *Confrontation and Commitment: A Study of Contemporary American Drama.* Columbia: University of Missouri Press, 1968, pp. 26–49.

———, ed. *File on Miller,* London: Methuen, 1988.

Bloom, Harold, ed. *Arthur Miller.* New York: Chelsea House, 1987.

———, ed. *Arthur Miller's* Death of a Salesman. New York: Chelsea House, 1988.

Bonin, Jane F. "Work and Material Rewards." In *Major Themes in Prize-Winning American Drama.* Metuchen, NJ: Scarecrow Press, 1975, pp. 29–60.

Broussard, Louis. "Tennessee Williams and Arthur Miller." In *American Drama: Contemporary Allegory from Eugene O'Neill to Tennessee Williams.* Norman: University of Oklahoma Press, 1962, pp. 390–96.

Brucher, Richard T. "Willy Loman and *The Soul of a New Machine*: Technology and the Common Man." *Journal of American Studies* 17 (1983): 325–36.

Brustein, Robert. "Show and Tell: (*Death of a Salesman; Glengarry Glen Ross.*)" In *Who Needs Theatre?* New York: Atlantic Monthly Press, 1987, pp. 67–71.

———. "Arthur Miller's Mea Culpa." *New Republic,* February 8, 1964, pp. 26–30.

Cameron, Kenneth M., and Theodore J. C. Hoffman. "Arthur Miller: *Death of a Salesman.*" In *The Theatrical Response.* New York: Macmillan, 1969, pp. 170–78.

Carson, Neil. *Arthur Miller.* New York: St. Martin's Press, 1982.

Clurman, Harold. "Editor's Introduction." In *The Portable Arthur Miller.* New York: Viking Press, 1957, pp. i–xv.

Corrigan, Robert W., ed. *Arthur Miller: A Collection of Critical Essays.* Englewood Cliffs, NJ: Prentice-Hall, 1969.

Couchman, Gordon W. "Arthur Miller's Tragedy of Babbitt." *Educational Theatre Journal* 7 (1955): 206–11.

Dusenbury, Winifred L. "Personal Failure." In *The Theme of Loneliness in Modern American Drama.* Gainesville: University of Florida Press, 1960, pp. 8–37.

Evans, Richard I. *Psychology and Arthur Miller.* New York: Dutton, 1969.

Ferguson, Alfred R. "The Tragedy of the American Dream in *Death of a Salesman.*" *Thought* 53 (1978): 81–98.

Ferres, John H. *Arthur Miller: A Reference Guide.* Boston: G. K. Hall, 1979.

Field, B. S., Jr. "*Death of a Salesman.*" *Twentieth Century Literature* 18 (1972): 22–24.

Freedman, Morris. "The Jewishness of Arthur Miller: His Family Epic." In *American Drama in Social Context.* Carbondale: Southern Illinois University Press, 1971, pp. 43–58.

Gassner, John. "*Death of a Salesman:* First Impressions, 1949." In *The Theatre in Our Times: A Survey of the Men, Materials and Movements in the Modern Theatre.* New York: Crown, 1954, pp. 364–73.

———, ed. *A Treasury of the Theatre, Volume 3: Modern Drama from Oscar Wilde to Eugène Ionesco.* New York: Simon & Schuster, 1951, pp. 1060–62.

Greenfield, Thomas Allen. "*Death of a Salesman, All My Sons,* and *The Glass Menagerie.*" In *Work and the Work Ethic in American Drama 1920–1970.* Columbia: University of Missouri Press, 1982, pp. 101–29.

Hagopian, John V. "Arthur Miller: The Salesman's Two Cases." *Modern Drama* 6 (1963): 117–25.

Harshbarger, Karl. *The Burning Jungle: An Analysis of Arthur Miller's* Death of a Salesman. Washington. DC: University Press of America, 1978.

Hayashi, Tetsumaro. *An Index to Arthur Miller Criticism.* Metuchen, NJ: Scarecrow Press, 1967 (2nd. ed. 1976).

Hayman, Ronald. *Arthur Miller.* London: Heinemann, 1970.

Hynes, Joseph A. "Attention Must Be Paid . . ." *College English* 23 (1961–62): 574–78.

Jacobson, Irving. "Family Dreams in *Death of a Salesman.*" *American Literature* 47 (1975): 247–58.

Kernodle, George R. "The Death of the Little Man." *Carleton Drama Review* 1, No. 2 (1955–56): 47–60.

Koon, Helene Wickham. *Twentieth Century Interpretations of* Death of a Salesman. Englewood Cliffs, NJ: Prentice-Hall, 1983.

Lannon, William W. "The Rise and Rationale of Post World War II American Confessional Theatre." *Connecticut Review* 8, No. 2 (April 1975): 73–81.

Lawrence, Stephen A. "The Right Dream in Miller's *Death of a Salesman.*" *College English* 25 (1963–64): 547–49.

Leaska, Mitchell A. "20th Century Tragedy: British and American: Miller." In *The Voice of Tragedy.* New York: Robert Speller & Sons, 1963, pp. 273–78.

Lewis, Allan. "*Death of a Salesman.*" In *The Contemporary Theatre: The Significant Playwrights of Our Time.* New York: Crown, 1962, pp. 295–303.

Leyburn, Ellen Douglas. "Comedy and Tragedy Transposed." *Yale Review* 53 (1964): 555–57.

McAnany, Emile G., II. "The Tragic Commitment: Arthur Miller." *Modern Drama* 5 (1962): 11–20.

McCollom, William G. "The World of Tragedy." In *Tragedy.* New York: Macmillan, 1957, pp. 16–17.

Mander, John. "Arthur Miller's *Death of a Salesman.*" In *The Writer and Commitment.* London: Secker & Warburg, 1961, pp. 138–52.

Mason, Jeffrey D. "Paper Dolls: Melodrama and Sexual Politics in Arthur Miller's Early Plays." In *Feminist Rereadings of Modern American Drama,* edited by June Schlueter. Rutherford, NJ: Fairleigh Dickinson University Press, pp. 103–15.

Meserve, Walter J., ed. *The Merrill Studies in* Death of a Salesman. Columbus, OH: Merrill, 1972.

Miles, O. Thomas, "Three Authors in Search of a Character." *Personalist* 46 (1965): 65–72.

Morse, Donald E. "The 'Life Lie' in Three Plays by O'Neill, Williams, and Miller." In *Cross-Cultural Studies: American, Canadian and European Literature,* edited by Mirko Jurak. Ljubljana, Yugoslavia: University of Ljubljana, 1988, pp. 273–77.

Moss, Leonard. *Arthur Miller*. New York: Twayne, 1967.

Mottram, Eric. "Arthur Miller: The Development of a Political Dramatist in America." In *Stratford-upon-Avon Studies 10: American Theatre*, edited by John Russell Brown and Bernard Harris. London: Edward Arnold, 1967, pp. 127–62.

Murray, Edward. *Arthur Miller, Dramatist*. New York: Ungar, 1967.

Nelson, Benjamin. *Arthur Miller: Portrait of a Playwright*. London: Peter Owen, 1970.

Panikkar, N. Bhaskara. *Individual Morality and Social Happiness in Arthur Miller*. Atlantic Highlands, NJ: Humanities Press, 1982.

Porter, Thomas E. "Acres of Diamonds: *Death of a Salesman*." In *Myth and Modern American Drama*. Detroit: Wayne State University Press, 1969, pp. 127–52.

Ross, George. "*Death of a Salesman*." *Commentary* 11, No. 2 (February 1951): 184–86.

Scanlan, Tom. "Reactions I: Family and Society in Arthur Miller." *Family, Drama, and American Dreams*. Westport, CT: Greenwood Press, 1978, pp. 126–55.

Schlueter, June, and Jane K. Flanagan. *Arthur Miller*. New York: Ungar, 1987.

Schneider, Daniel E., M.D. "Play of Dreams." *Theatre Arts* 33, No. 9 (October 1949): 18–21.

Schroeder, Patricia R. "*Death of a Salesman*: A Mobile Concurrency of Past and Present." In *The Presence of the Past in Modern American Drama*. Rutherford, NJ: Fairleigh Dickinson University Press, 1989, pp. 89–93.

Seivers, W. David. "Fathers and Sons." In *Freud on Broadway: A History of Psychoanalysis and the American Drama*. New York: Cooper Square, 1955, pp. 388–99.

Sharpe, Robert Boies. "Modern Trends in Tragedy." In *Irony in the Drama: An Essay on Impersonation, Shock, and Catharsis*. Chapel Hill: University of North Carolina Press, 1959, pp. 180–203.

Trowbridge, Clinton W. "Arthur Miller: Between Pathos and Tragedy." *Modern Drama* 10 (1967): 221–32.

Welland, Dennis. *Miller: The Playwright*. London: Eyre Methuen, 1979 (3rd ed. 1985).

Worsley, T. C. "American Tragedy." *New Statesman*, August 23, 1958, p. 220.

ACKNOWLEDGMENTS

"Tragic Perspectives: A Sequence of Queries" by John Gassner from *Tulane Drama Review* 2, No. 3 (May 1958), © 1958 by Tulane University. Reprinted by permission of Caroline Levine for Mrs. John Gassner.

"Strength and Weakness in Arthur Miller" by Tom F. Driver from *Tulane Drama Review* 4, No. 4 (May 1960), © 1960 by The Tulane Drama Review. Reprinted by permission of the author.

"Arthur Miller: The Strange Encounter" by Henry Popkin from *Sewanee Review* 68, No. 1 (Winter 1960), © 1960 by The Sewanee Review. Reprinted by permission of The Sewanee Review.

"Arthur Miller and the Common Man's Language" by Leonard Moss from *Modern Drama* 7, No. 1 (Summer 1964), © 1964 by A. C. Edwards. Reprinted by permission of *Modern Drama*.

Tragedy and Fear: Why Modern Tragic Drama Fails by John von Szeliski, © 1962, 1971 by The University of North Carolina Press. Reprinted by permission.

"Death of a Salesman" by Stanley Kauffmann from *Persons of the Drama* by Stanley Kauffmann, © 1975, 1976 by Stanley Kauffmann. Reprinted by permission of Brandt & Brandt Literary Agents, Inc.

"Arthur Miller: Eden and After" by Arthur Ganz from *Realms of the Self: Variations on a Theme in Modern Drama* by Arthur Ganz, © 1980 by New York University. Reprinted by permission of New York University Press.

"Consumer Man in Crisis: Arthur Miller's *Death of a Salesman*" from *American Literature and Social Change: William Dean Howells to Arthur Miller,* © 1983 by Michael Spindler. Reprinted by permission of Macmillan Publishers Ltd. and Indiana University Press.

Salesman in Beijing by Arthur Miller, © 1983, 1984 by Arthur Miller. Reprinted by permission of International Creative Management and Viking Penguin Inc.

Modern Drama and the Death of God by George E. Wellwarth, © 1986 by The Board of Regents of the University of Wisconsin System. Reprinted by permission of the University of Wisconsin Press.

Dramatic Encounters: The Jewish Presence in Twentieth-Century American Drama, Poetry, and Humor and the Black-Jewish Literary Relationship by Louis Harap, © 1987 by Louis Harap. Reprinted by permission of Greenwood Publishing Group Inc.

"Jung's 'Anima' in Arthur Miller's Plays" by Priscilla S. McKinney from *Studies in American Drama, 1945–Present* 3 (1988), © 1988 by *Studies in American Drama, 1945–Present.* Reprinted by permission of *Studies in American Drama, 1945–Present* and Patricia S. McKinney.

"Introduction" by Arthur Miller from *Collected Plays* by Arthur Miller, © 1957 by Arthur Miller. Reprinted by permission of International Creative Management and Viking Penguin Inc.

"The Articulate Victims of Arthur Miller" by Ruby Cohn from *Dialogue in American Drama* by Ruby Cohn, © 1971 by Indiana University Press. Reprinted by permission.

"Willy Tyrannos" by Dan Vogel from *The Three Masks of American Tragedy* by Dan Vogel, © 1974 by Louisiana State University Press. Reprinted by permission.

"Death of a Salesman: A Salesman's Illusion" by A. D. Choudhuri from *The Face of Illusion in American Drama* by A. D. Choudhuri, © 1979 by A. D. Choudhuri. Reprinted by permission of Macmillan India Inc.

"The Salesman and Society" (originally titled "Arthur Miller: The Salesman and Society") by Robert N. Wilson from *The Writer as Social Seer* by Robert N. Wilson, © 1979 by The University of North Carolina Press. Reprinted by permission.

"Sales and Solidarity" (originally titled "Sales and Solidarity: Arthur Miller's *Death of a Salesman*") by Jeremy Hawthorn from *Multiple Personality and the Disintegration of Literary Character: From Oliver Goldsmith to Sylvia Plath* by Jeremy Hawthorn, © 1983 by Jeremy Hawthorn. Reprinted by permission of Edward Arnold (Publishers) Ltd. and St. Martin's Press Inc.

"Arthur Miller" by C. W. E. Bigsby from *A Critical Introduction to Twentieth-Century American Drama, Volume 2: Tennessee Williams, Arthur Miller, Edward Albee* by C. W. E. Bigsby, © 1984 by C. W. E. Bigsby. Reprinted by permission of Cambridge University Press.

"Dramatic Rhythm in *Death of a Salesman*" (originally titled "Fantasy and Reality: Dramatic Rhythm in *Death of a Salesman*") by Leah Hadomi from *Modern Drama* 31, No. 2 (June 1988), © 1988 by the University of Toronto. Reprinted by permission of *Modern Drama.*

"Women and the American Dream of *Death of a Salesman*" by Kay Stanton from *Feminist Rereadings of Modern American Drama,* edited by June Schlueter, © 1989 by Associated University Presses, Inc. Reprinted by permission.

INDEX

the rich, 81, 83, 85; as Everyman, 4, 58–60, 101; and exhaustion, 1, 17, 23, 36; as failed father, 142; and failure in the business world, 9, 44, 62, 69, 78–79, 81–88, 96, 145, 147; his failure to receive love, 4, 135; his false values, 9, 25, 78, 84; and familial love, 1, 4, 69, 76; and "fantasy offspring," 7; and femininity, 145, 149; and fragmentation, 91, 94, 97; his funeral, 5, 13, 24, 72–73, 150; and Jay Gatsby (*The Great Gatsby*), 88; and gold, 146; and Clyde Griffiths (*An American Tragedy*), 26; and guilt, 102; and Happy, 64, 81; and Hickey (*The Iceman Cometh*), 56; his home, 56, 61–62, 135; and Howard, 129; and illusions, 69, 70, 72, 77, 104–5, 109–10; incapacity for introspection, 70; as internalized exile, 3–4; and the jungle, 23–24, 28, 86, 96, 133; "keeping up with the Joneses," 44; and King Lear (*King Lear*), 1; his language, 13, 50–51, 54, 56; and Linda, 30–31, 52–53, 55–56, 63, 70–71, 129–56; and male-coupling, 149; and marital infidelity, 31; and masculinity, 138, 146; and materialism, 16–18, 69; and mental illness, 12, 20–21, 91, 120; and Miller, 56; and mystery of his wares, 10, 81; and his neighbors, 24; as nonhero, 16; his obsolescence, 97; and Oedipus, 1, 7, 58–60, 80; and Bill Oliver, 124; and the outdoors, 129; and paranoia, 18; and the past, 51, 62; as pathetic, 9–10, 48, 58, 72–73, 155–57n.37; and pathos, 4, 19, 58; and peripety, 60; and the phallus, 145–47, 149; and pride, 61, 78; as representation of a sick society, 12; as salesman, 11, 44, 81, 69, 76; and security, 61; and self-awareness, 7, 13, 31, 41–42; and self-contradictions, 14, 52, 61; and self-deception, 27, 31; as self-destructive 19, 72; and his sexuality, 31, 80, 118, 142; and Dave Singleman, 53, 82–83, 85,

87, 115, 131–32; and Solange (*The Maids*), 53; and spiritual exhaustion, 1, 17; and success, 13, 16, 22, 51, 64, 79, 82–88; his suicide, 6, 15, 20, 22, 26, 31, 52, 56, 64, 85, 104, 145–48, 150–51; as tragic figure, 2, 7, 9, 17, 30, 48, 59–60, 64, 73–74, 88–89; and U.S. history, 11; and values, 19, 45, 84; as victim, 6, 8, 15, 18, 24, 26, 28, 41; as wage earner, 67; and The Woman, 22, 31, 138, 142; and World War II, 21; as wrongdoer, 18; and his youth, 108
Loman men, the, 61, 73, 79; and the phallus, 149; and self-esteem, 135–37; and sports, 79, 138–40
Lomans, the, 18, 78, 130; as the "Everyfamily," 11; their home, 56, 61–62, 135–36; as Jews, 11, 73; their origins, 11; and pathos, 13; and sports, 138–39; and the Tyrones (*A Long Day's Journey into Night*), 89
London Merchant, The (Barnwell), 14
Long Day's Journey into Night, A (O'Neill), 80, 88

McBird (Garson), 50
McCarthy, Mary: on Willy's Jewishness, 30, 50, 100
McCollom, William, 6
Maids, The (Genet), 53
Mann, Thomas: on *Salesman*, 88
Meredith, George, 80
Merton, Robert K., 82–84, 86–87; on success, 82–83
Mielziner, Jo, 51, 102
Miller, Arthur: and American democracy, 66, 68–69; on Aristotle, 39; and his characters as victims, 15; and confusion, 2, 9–10, 20–21, 23, 54; and his critics, 39, 41, 46; on destiny, 47; as determinist, 26, 77; and Expressionist theatre, 10–11, 51, 71; on failure, 44; and Greek tragedy, 1, 28, 67–68, 70; and his heroes, 25, 39–40; on Hippocrates, 39; on history, 39–40; and Henrik Ibsen, 1, 51, 71; on immortality, 37; and Jewish content